Studying Human Resource Management

2nd edition

Edited by Stephen Taylor and Carol Woodhams

The Chartered Institute of Personnel and Development is the leading publisher of books and reports for personnel and training professionals, students, and all those concerned with the effective management and development of people at work. For details of all our titles, please contact the publishing department:

tel: 020 8612 6204

email: publishing@cipd.co.uk

The catalogue of all CIPD titles can be viewed on the CIPD website:

www.cipd.co.uk/bookstore

An e-book version is also available for purchase from:

www.ebooks.cipd.co.uk

Studying Human Resource Management

2nd edition

Edited by Stephen Taylor and Carol Woodhams

Chartered Institute of Personnel and Development

Published by the Chartered Institute of Personnel and Development
151 The Broadway, London SW19 1JQ

This edition first published 2016

Designed and typeset by Exeter Premedia Services, India

Printed in Great Britain by Ashford Colour Press Ltd., Gosport, Hampshire.

British Library Cataloguing in Publication Data

A catalogue of this publication is available from the British Library

ISBN 9781843984153
eBook ISBN 9781843984405

The views expressed in this publication are the authors' own and may not necessarily reflect those of the CIPD.

The CIPD has made every effort to trace and acknowledge copyright holders. If any source has been overlooked, CIPD Enterprises would be pleased to redress this in future editions.

Chartered Institute of Personnel and Development

151 The Broadway, London SW19 1JQ
Tel: 020 8612 6200
Email: cipd@cipd.co.uk
Website: www.cipd.co.uk
Incorporated by Royal Charter.
Registered Charity No. 1079797

Contents

List of figures and tables

Contributor biographies

Stephen Taylor is a Senior Lecturer in Human Resource Management at the University of Exeter Business School and also a Chief Examiner for the Chartered Institute of Personnel and Development (CIPD). He previously taught at Manchester Business School, at Manchester Metropolitan University Business School and worked in a variety of HR management roles in the hotel industry and in the NHS. He teaches HRM and general management subjects as well as employment law at postgraduate and undergraduate level. He has authored and co-authored several books on HRM and employment law.

Professor Carol Woodhams is an Associate Professor of Human Resource Management at the University of Exeter Business School. She has held a number of positions within CIPD including National Examiner for Designing and Delivering Training, External Moderator for the Advanced Qualification and Editor of the flexible learning materials at Intermediate and Advanced levels. She previously taught at Plymouth University and Manchester Metropolitan University. Her specialist teaching subjects are employee resourcing and equality and diversity. Her research topics include studies of gender and disability discrimination in the UK and China. Prior to her academic career she held posts in management in the hospitality sector.

The late **Dr Ted Johns** served as a Chief Examiner at the Chartered Institute of Personnel and Development and its predecessor bodies for over thirty years, taking a leading role in a wide range of its educational initiatives and activities. He wrote and co-wrote many books on a range of subjects including customer care, organisational change and ethical leadership. He was a founder director and later Chairman of the Institute of Customer Service, having previously worked in higher education and management consultancy. Ted was also a noted conference and seminar speaker.

Dr Graham Perkins is a Lecturer in Human Resource Management at the University of Exeter Business School. Alongside interests in the areas of learning and development, knowledge management and reward management, Graham conducts research into how small-medium enterprises encourage creativity. Graham is also involved with the marking of CIPD examinations, and has several years' of operational HR experience with a variety of organisations.

Dr. Krystal Wilkinson is a recent PhD graduate, with a specific focus on work-life balance and qualitative research methodologies. She is a Senior Lecturer in HRM at Manchester Metropolitan University and has been a National examination marker for the CIPD for several years. Prior to commencing her doctoral studies, she worked in operational HR in a range of sectors including construction, retail & hospitality.

Walkthrough of textbook features and online resources

KEY LEARNING OUTCOMES

By the end of this chapter, you should be able to:

- appreciate the requirements necessary to gain the CIPD's intermediate-level qualifications
- define the term 'human resource management' and explain how it has evolved in recent years
- distinguish between 'nuts and bolts' HR activities and those which have a more strategic character
- understand the importance of using robust third-party evidence when making HR decisions and justifying arguments
- access significant research findings in the HR field
- explain the key ways in which thinking about HR is influenced by different frames of reference and sets of assumptions.

KEY LEARNING OUTCOMES

At the beginning of each chapter a bulleted set of key learning outcomes summarises what you expect to learn from the chapter, helping you to track your progress.

CASE STUDY 5.1

IDENTIFYING AN AREA OF RESEARCH

It was a Sunday morning and Ben was stuck behind his computer struggling to think of a relevant idea that could form the basis of his Master's dissertation. He was studying part-time whilst working in his position as an HR Officer for a leading accountancy organisation. He knew that he needed a substantial, original topic, but could not find a spark of inspiration.

had not yet been solved. While doing this, Ben recognised that his HR team was struggling significantly with its graduate recruitment, the number of unfilled vacancies having risen for three consecutive years.

CASE STUDIES

A range of case studies from different countries illustrate how key ideas and theories are operating in practice around the globe, with accompanying questions or activities.

? **REFLECTIVE ACTIVITY 1.3**

1 Think about an organisation you, your friends or relatives have worked for. Would you say that the approach to management was characterised more by a stockholder or by a stakeholder perspective?

2 Why might it be in the long-term financial interests of an organisation to move towards a stakeholder perspective and away from a stockholder perspective?

3 In what circumstances might the reverse be the case?

REFLECTIVE ACTIVITY

In each chapter, a number of questions and activities will get you to reflect on what you have just read and encourage you to explore important concepts and issues in greater depth.

FURTHER READING

CIPD (2010) *Next generation HR: time for change – towards a next generation for HR*. London: CIPD. This is the outcome of the CIPD's future-focused research that examines the future of the role. It positions HR leaders as building sustainability and equity by being 'insight-driven provocateurs' who are assured and confident in influencing.

PURCELL, J., KINNIE, N., HUTCHINSON, S., RAYTON, B. and SWART, J. (2003) *Understanding the people and performance link: unlocking the black box*. London: CIPD The CIPD's seminal study that examines the nature and contribution of people management to organisation performance.

TYSON, S. (2006) *Essentials of human resource management*. 5th ed. Oxford: Butterworth-Heinemann. Chapters 3 and 4. Reviews the development of the profession, the goals of specialist HR professionals and how the function assists in the achievement of organisation goals. Also explores in more depth the debates aired in this chapter.

FURTHER READING

Further reading boxes contain suggestions for further reading and useful websites, encouraging you to delve further into areas of particular interest.

ONLINE RESOURCES FOR TUTORS

- PowerPoint slides – design your programme around these ready-made lectures.
- Lecturer's guide – including guidance on the activities and questions in the text.
- Additional case studies – these can be used as a classroom activity, for personal reflection and individual learning, or as the basis for assignments.
- Multiple choice questions – a series of questions for each chapter to test your understanding of the text.

ONLINE RESOURCES FOR STUDENTS

Please visit our new student website: http://books-taylorwoodhams.cipd.co.uk

- Videos – access a range of videos including:
  - Why HR?
  - What does an ethical approach to HRM involve in practice?
  - HRD: The most significant and current developments
- Podcasts – access a range of our podcasts including:
  - Reasons for continued inequality between men and women at work
  - How best to promote creativity in organisations
  - Rising individualism and its implications
- Annotated web-links – access a wealth of useful information sources in order to develop your understanding of employment law issues.
- Multiple choice questions – a series of questions for each chapter to test your understanding of the text.
- Glossary of key terms.

CHAPTER 1

Studying HRM

STEPHEN TAYLOR AND CAROL WOODHAMS

CHAPTER CONTENTS

- Introduction
- Studying HRM at Levels 5 and 6
- What is HRM?
- Evidence-based HRM
- Core HRM debates

KEY LEARNING OUTCOMES

By the end of this chapter, you should be able to:

- appreciate the requirements necessary to gain the CIPD's intermediate-level qualifications
- define the term 'human resource management' and explain how it has evolved in recent years
- distinguish between 'nuts and bolts' HR activities and those which have a more strategic character
- understand the importance of using robust third-party evidence when making HR decisions and justifying arguments
- access significant research findings in the HR field
- explain the key ways in which thinking about HR is influenced by different frames of reference and sets of assumptions.

1.1 INTRODUCTION

This is one of three textbooks that the Chartered Institute of Personnel and Development (CIPD) publish for students who are studying towards achieving its intermediate-level (Level 5) qualifications in human resource management (HRM) and human resource development (HRD). Whether you have enrolled on a discrete programme provided by a college or are looking to gain your CIPD award as part of an undergraduate business degree, you will find that these books provide you with a sound introduction to your studies.

This first book covers the learning outcomes for the four core units that everyone aiming to achieve the intermediate diploma must successfully complete. We have also edited a companion text called *Human Resource Management: People and Organisations* which covers the learning outcomes that make up the optional units, at least four of which you will be studying in order to complete your qualification. The CIPD is also publishing a further book for people who are focusing their studies on human resource development, edited by Jim Stewart and Pat Rogers. This is entitled *Studying Learning and Development: Context, Practice and Measurement* and it is complemented by thirteen separate e-books covering different HRD electives.

Our aim in this chapter is to introduce you to the study of HRM at undergraduate level, defined by the **Quality Assurance Agency for Higher Education** (QAA) as being at Levels 5 and 6. We start by explaining exactly what level 5 and level 6 study involves and what you will need to do in order to achieve it. After this we discuss the meaning of the term 'human resource management' before going on to explain how effective HR managers base their decisions and their thinking on solid evidence. Finally, we introduce you to a range of tensions and differences of perspective which underlie the study and practice of HRM and which you will find helpful to understand as you embark on your programme of study.

1.2 STUDYING HRM AT LEVELS 5 AND 6

The UK's QAA for Higher Education has the role of setting definitive, generic standards which all awarding bodies and institutions of higher education must observe when developing courses, as well as teaching and assessing their students. This is therefore a good place to start understanding what you will be expected to achieve on your programme. The CIPD's intermediate-level awards are set at level 5, but if you are studying them as part of a bachelor's honours degree programme you will be required to meet the level 6 expectations. The level 5 standards and the level 6 standards are set out below.

DESCRIPTOR FOR A HIGHER EDUCATION QUALIFICATION AT LEVEL 5: FOUNDATION DEGREE

The descriptor provided for this level of the FHEQ is for any **foundation degree**, which should meet the descriptor in full. This qualification descriptor can also be used as a reference point for other level 5 qualifications, including diplomas of higher education, higher national diplomas, and so on.

Foundation degrees are awarded to students who have demonstrated:

- knowledge and critical understanding of the well-established principles of their area(s) of study, and of the way in which those principles have developed
- the ability to apply underlying concepts and principles outside the context in which they were first studied, including, where appropriate, the application of those principles in an employment context
- knowledge of the main methods of enquiry in the subject(s) relevant to the named award and ability to evaluate critically the appropriateness of different approaches to solving problems in the field of study
- an understanding of the limits of their knowledge and how this influences analyses and interpretations based on that knowledge
- knowledge and critical understanding of the well-established principles of their area(s) of study, and of the way in which those principles have developed
- the ability to apply underlying concepts and principles outside the context in which they were first studied, including, where appropriate, the application of those principles in an employment context
- knowledge of the main methods of enquiry in the subject(s) relevant to the named award and ability to evaluate critically the appropriateness of different approaches to solving problems in the field of study

- an understanding of the limits of their knowledge and how this influences analyses and interpretations based on that knowledge.

Typically, holders of the qualification will be able to:

- use a range of established techniques to initiate and undertake critical analysis of information, and to propose solutions to problems arising from that analysis
- effectively communicate information, arguments and analysis in a variety of forms to specialist and non-specialist audiences, and deploy key techniques of the discipline effectively
- undertake further training, develop existing skills and acquire new competences that will enable them to assume significant responsibility within organisations.

And holders will have:

- the qualities and transferable skills necessary for employment, requiring the exercise of personal responsibility and decision-making.

DESCRIPTOR FOR A HIGHER EDUCATION QUALIFICATION AT LEVEL 6: BACHELOR'S DEGREE WITH HONOURS

The descriptor provided for this level of the FHEQ is for any **bachelor's degree with honours**, which should meet the descriptor in full. This qualification descriptor can also be used as a reference point for other level 6 qualifications, including bachelor's degrees, graduate diplomas, and so on.

Bachelor's degrees with honours are awarded to students who have demonstrated:

- a systematic understanding of key aspects of their field of study, including acquisition of coherent and detailed knowledge, at least some of which is at, or informed by, the forefront of defined aspects of a discipline
- an ability to deploy accurately established techniques of analysis and enquiry within a discipline
- conceptual understanding that enables the student:

  - to devise and sustain arguments, and/or to solve problems, using ideas and techniques, some of which are at the forefront of a discipline
  - to describe and comment upon particular aspects of current research, or equivalent advanced scholarship, in the discipline

- an appreciation of the uncertainty, ambiguity and limits of knowledge
- the ability to manage their own learning and to make use of scholarly reviews and primary sources (for example, refereed research articles and/or original materials appropriate to the discipline).

Typically, holders of the qualification will be able to:

- apply the methods and techniques that they have learned to review, consolidate, extend and apply their knowledge and understanding, and to initiate and carry out projects
- critically evaluate arguments, assumptions, abstract concepts and data (that may be incomplete), to make judgements, and to frame appropriate questions to achieve a solution – or identify a range of solutions – to a problem

- communicate information, ideas, problems and solutions to both specialist and non-specialist audiences.

And holders will have the qualities and transferable skills necessary for employment requiring:

- the exercise of initiative and personal responsibility
- decision-making in complex and unpredictable contexts
- the learning ability needed to undertake appropriate further training of a professional or equivalent nature.

You can see from this that a great deal of emphasis is placed at both levels on being able to demonstrate knowledge and understanding of core, well-established principles across the student's field of study. However, the standards go beyond this, requiring students also to demonstrate the following:

- an ability to analyse these principles critically
- an ability to apply the principles in the workplace
- a capacity to evaluate the evidence on which the principles are founded, including academic research
- an appreciation of the limits to our knowledge in any area of study
- an ability to communicate the principles to a variety of audiences
- the capacity to undertake further professional development independently in the future
- skills associated with effective decision-making, problem-solving and exercising personal initiative in their field of study.

1.2.1 WHAT DOES ALL OF THIS MEAN AS FAR AS STUDYING HRM IS CONCERNED?

First of all, it means that you will need to study how HR managers apply the principles of their management discipline across a wide range of settings. If you have studied HRM previously, it is likely that you were encouraged to focus your attention primarily on your own organisation, perhaps evaluating what it did and discussing what improvements it might make. You now need to widen your perspective very considerably. A key point about studying HRM at this level is the way that it requires you to gain a good understanding of the variety of different approaches that are used to manage people in different organisations, industries and also in different countries.

Secondly, it means that you must be able not just to advocate an approach to use or to take a decision in the field of HRM, but also to justify your approach or decision with good, robust, evidence-based arguments. The same is true of practical problem-solving. So you need to become familiar with the most important and influential contemporary research studies that have been published in the field of HRM. It also requires you to develop a good understanding of the business environment in which HRM is carried out and of ways in which this is changing and evolving.

Thirdly, it means that you need to develop a good understanding of the major contemporary, professional debates that exist in HRM, and to be in a position to engage in these debates yourself. This means thinking beyond some of the rather simplistic prescriptions of 'good practice HRM' that are often advanced and to develop a more sophisticated appreciation of the complex and sometimes messy realities of practical people management in a workplace.

Finally, you need to be able to communicate your ideas, together with the evidence that underpins them, effectively to a variety of potential audiences. This presents a range of challenges. Communicating to a specialist audience with a significant understanding of HRM is straightforward insofar as a lot of prior understanding and familiarity with terms can be assumed, but sophisticated arguments must be developed, backed up by credible evidence, if you are to be persuasive. By contrast, a non-specialist audience that does not have extensive understanding of HRM often requires as much (if not more) convincing, but will only be persuaded if you can communicate the more basic ideas and arguments effectively.

1.2.2 STRUCTURING YOUR STUDIES

A key to successful study at all levels and across all subjects is the ability to organise yourself and to plan your course effectively. Studying HRM is no exception. Your tutors will help you to do this by guiding you through a structured course of study that they have designed, step by step. At each point readings will be recommended, learning exercises provided and key points underlined.

However, there are also additional things you can do to help structure your studies effectively. These involve making use of two key documents that have been published by the CIPD and also, more generally, exploring the wealth of resources that are available to you on the CIPD's extensive website (www.cipd.co.uk).

The first of the key documents is the CIPD's guide to its intermediate-level qualifications. Hard copies are widely available, but you can also download the contents from the qualifications area of the Institute's website. Here you will find for each unit of study (core or optional) a summary of the main learning outcomes that you need to work towards being able to demonstrate, together with short summaries setting out what each encompasses in practice. The document also sets out the CIPD's 'rules of combination', which allows you to see which core units and which optional units can be combined to make up a programme of study.

The second key document you will find useful to refer to when structuring your studies is the **CIPD's HR profession map**. This can also be found in a prominent position on the Institute's website in the section called 'CIPD and the HR profession'. The map is an extensive tool which can be used for many purposes. It sets out the following in a user-friendly format:

- eight behaviours that HR professionals need to develop in order to carry out their roles effectively in the contemporary business world
- ten areas of professional practice which help define the typical boundaries around generalist and specialist career paths in both HRM and HRD
- four bands and transitions which provide broad guidelines for career development across the HR field, from 'delivering fundamentals' (band 1) to 'Leadership colleague, client confidante and coach'.

You will read more about the CIPD's HR profession map in Chapter 6, 'Developing the knowledge and skill of the HR professional'.

1.3 WHAT IS HRM?

The term **human resource management** was not used in organisations until relatively recently. Until 20 years ago it was usual for people who were employed in management roles with particular responsibility for employment policy and practice and the management of an organisation's employment relationships to be called personnel managers or sometimes personnel administration managers. Since the 1990s the term 'human resource management' has replaced 'personnel management' in most organisations, but other titles are also used, particularly at senior management level. 'Directors of People', for example and 'Directors of Workforce and Organisational Development' are now not uncommon.

The origins of the HR profession can be found in the larger workplaces of the late nineteenth and early twentieth centuries. In the main these were factories, railway companies, government departments and local government offices employing large numbers of people to carry out relatively routine tasks under the direction of small management teams. Being stable and hierarchical, these organisations tended to employ people for long periods of time, developing and promoting them internally when the opportunity arose. They put a high priority on maximising the efficiency of their operations, constantly looking for ways of encouraging people to carry out their jobs more quickly and productively. In the UK retaining people was also a major management objective as was the maintenance of good industrial relations, this being a period in which trade unions and the recently founded Labour Party were building their political strength. It was in such organisations that personnel administrators were first employed and on their experience that the first books and articles about this body of work were written (for example Carpenter 1905, Gantt 1910 and Hoxie 1916). The first textbook written for budding personnel professionals by Ordway Tead and Henry Metcalfe was published in the USA in 1920.

After this as trade unions became stronger, as governments began to legislate about health, safety and welfare, as the number of people employed in more skilled work grew and as municipally provided services proliferated, a personnel management profession firmly established itself as a presence in larger organisations in all the industrialised countries. For much of the twentieth century the majority of the work was concerned with promoting employee welfare and managing the relationship with trade unions. However, because most UK-based organisations of any size were members of employers' associations and adhered to nationally negotiated terms and conditions of employment, there was little scope for the development of people management strategies which differentiated the approach used by one organisation from that of another. The way people were managed across whole industries was thus very similar, pay rates being the same as well as all the other major terms and conditions of employment (Gospel 2014).

The term human resource management was first coined in the early 1960s in the USA. For a number of years before this, academics and policy-makers had been using the term 'human resources' alongside 'natural resources' when talking about a nation's economic assets (see Ginzberg 1958), but the word 'management' was only added later. An academic journal entitled *Human Resource Management* was launched in 1961 at Michigan University, but it was not until the 1980s that the term became widely used all over the world in the context of employment in organisations.

At first HRM signified a new way of managing people that was clearly distinct from traditional personnel management: more strategic, less reactive and more firmly focused on achieving organisational objectives. In the UK the steady collapse of national, industry-level collective bargaining from the 1980s onwards, provided huge opportunities for HR managers to develop distinct approaches that met the specific needs of their organisations and the people they employed. Freed from the requirement to follow industry standards and able to design their own policies and practices, they began to experiment with new approaches and to develop distinct human resource strategies. As the business environment became more competitive and unstable, flexible working practices became more common as did performance management systems aimed at maximising competitiveness. In the early years of the twenty-first century, as labour markets tightened and skills shortages became chronic in many industries, HR managers were obliged to focus more on recruiting and retaining people, focusing more on talent management and the development of distinct employer brands.

Before long, at least for most people, HRM started to be used simply to describe a body of management activities rather than any particular approach to carrying them out. During the 1990s in particular, people who had previously been called personnel directors, personnel managers, personnel officers, personnel advisers and personnel assistants re-labelled themselves as human resource professionals.

At the same time organisations tended to rebrand training activities under the banner of human resource development. 'Industrial relations' became 'employment relations', while 'pay and benefits' tended to be renamed 'reward management'.

HRM has thus now come to be the most commonly used label for a group of activities that are all, one way or another, related to the management of an organisation's relationship with the people who work for it. These people may be employees working under contracts of employment, but they are also increasingly self-employed persons, casual staff, agency workers and employees of partner organisations. Interestingly, the term 'HRM' is now sometimes being replaced in job titles by other terms. In some larger organisations the function is now headed up by a 'Director of People' or a 'Director of Workforce and Organisational Development'. Time will tell whether or not this becomes more common or whether 'human resources' remains the dominant term.

On one level, therefore, professional HR managers are concerned with the nuts and bolts of day-to-day people management. Alongside line managers they design jobs and organisational structures, recruit and select new staff, issue contracts, lead induction processes, ensure that everyone is paid correctly and on time, run training courses, develop succession plans, reward good performance, seek to improve poor performance, negotiate and consult with staff representatives, develop management careers, discourage absence, administer retirements and resignations, and, as and when necessary, ensure that dismissals are carried out legally.

Increasingly, however, HRM is becoming a strategic activity. HR managers are not just concerned with achieving the nuts and bolts tasks efficiently; they are also both integral to the delivery of an organisation's longer-term strategic objectives and leading figures in the development of business strategies.

Central to this side of their work is active involvement in the management of both structural and cultural change. They help ensure that the crucial people management side of change is given proper attention alongside its legal, financial and technical aspects. HR managers help to plan change management episodes and to communicate the need for them, as well as being centrally involved in their implementation and subsequent evaluation.

In order that an organisation's strategic objectives can be achieved, supportive and deliverable HR strategies need to be developed, communicated and implemented. Remuneration arrangements have to be designed so that they reward behaviours which increase the chances that the organisation will meet its objectives and diminish the chances that it won't. The same goes for resourcing, development and employee relations strategies, all of which also need to reinforce one another.

Another aspect of strategic HR activity is the management of an organisation's reputation as an employer. Here we increasingly see the use of marketing language (for example, employer branding, segmentation, employee value propositions) being used as organisations seek to position themselves strategically in the labour market. Central to this development is a keen understanding that recruiting and retaining effective performers is a highly competitive business, and that there is a need to differentiate what we offer potential recruits from that which our chief competitors offer. Maintaining a reputation as an ethical employer is also widely understood to be increasing in importance.

Reputation-building is a long-term project which managers can influence, but cannot control. The same is true of other strategic HRM initiatives, such as organisation development (OD), the development of effective knowledge management systems, the promotion of employee well-being and other activities that one way or another involve building up an organisation's human capital.

Developing an actively and positively engaged workforce which demonstrates initiative and discretionary effort is another crucial HR activity that can neither be achieved overnight nor introduced by management diktat.

Importantly, all of this – both the nuts and bolts activities and those which are more strategic in character – has to be carried out against the backdrop of an increasingly volatile, unpredictable, competitive, highly regulated and complex global business environment. Effective HR managers thus have to keep more than half an eye on the future, always seeking to ensure that their organisations are better placed than others to meet coming challenges. More often than not, this means thinking about multiple, alternative, possible future scenarios and planning for as many as possible. A premium thus has to be placed on developing organisational agility, along with a capacity for flexible working and for the swift and productive implementation of change.

1.4 EVIDENCE-BASED HRM

A key part of studying HRM seriously as part of a degree-level qualification involves getting into the habit, wherever you can, of justifying your views on the subject using robust and credible evidence. This approach is called **evidence-based HRM**. This will not only help you to secure your qualification, but it should also mean that you carry your 'habit' over into the workplace. In the future you will take decisions, develop policies and, when debating with colleagues, take up positions which are informed by robust evidence.

You may think it strange that this point has to be made at all. Surely all successful managers base their decisions on robust and credible evidence? Of course many do, or at least take account of it. But decisions, policies and debating positions are also often informed by hunches, limited anecdotal evidence, singular personal experience, widely believed myths of various kinds and sometimes by raw prejudice. Even quite senior managers with successful careers behind them commonly dismiss published research on human resource management matters as being overly theoretical and largely irrelevant to their line of business. More often they are simply disinclined to take account of it because they prefer to manage by instinct, or take on board from the research only the points which match their own pre-existing beliefs.

Pfeffer and Sutton (2006, pp1–12) coined the phrase '**the knowing–doing gap**' to describe this phenomenon. All over the world, including in major public sector organisations and international corporations, they found examples of managers implementing policies that 'often clashed with, and at times were the opposite of what we know about organisations and people'. Instead of basing thinking and decision-making on evidence, there is a preference for 'casual benchmarking', 'doing what seems to have worked in the past' and 'following deeply held unexamined ideologies'. The result, at best, is sub-optimal performance in the field of HRM and, at worst, business failure and wholly avoidable job losses.

In other fields of professional endeavour this casual approach to evidence would never be tolerated. Imagine how we would react if a doctor was to prescribe treatments which were not wholly informed by robust scientific research or if an engineer built a bridge using hunches and myths when drawing up the designs.

Government policy also has to be informed by robust research as well as by the results of consultation exercises, and is only implemented after regulatory impact assessments have been carried out, not to mention extensive scrutiny by Parliament and the media. Yet for some reason the same philosophy has yet to permeate fully into the realm of management decision-making.

A major aim of the CIPD is to actively encourage evidence-based management in the HR field. It does this partly by undertaking and sponsoring major research projects and then disseminating the results as widely as possible, and partly by promoting good practice through its professional education activities.

1.4.1 MAKING USE OF ROBUST EVIDENCE

When studying at undergraduate level you are not going to be expected to gain an in-depth understanding of contemporary research that has been published in your field of study. You are, however, going to be expected to justify any arguments that you make in assignments and when answering exam questions, and to do so reasonably convincingly. While you may well sometimes want to justify a point of view with an ethical argument or with reference to your own experience, you will also need to tap into published research when it is available. Moreover, especially when debating contentious professional issues, you will need to evaluate pieces of published research that reach different conclusions about the same issue.

Academic research

Academic writers publish the findings from their research projects in books, but more commonly in learned journals. These are excellent sources of research data because, in order to get published, any article is first subjected to peer review. That means that it must first be scrutinised anonymously by reviewers who are specialists in the field. They typically suggest that amendments must be made before publication is possible. As a result, before you read an account of any research findings, the article concerned will have been rewritten, resubmitted to the journal and re-reviewed, often extensively and on a number of occasions. You will find a list of recommended journals providing credible evidence in Chapter 6.

It is important, however, not to restrict yourself to findings that are published in UK-based HR or HR-related journals. Most of the most important recent research has been published in international HRM journals, in those which have a more general management focus and, sometimes, in journals that are not management-focused at all. This is particularly true of developments in the wider business environment which are of general significance, but which happen also to be important from a practical HRM perspective.

?   REFLECTIVE ACTIVITY 1.1

An example of an academic journal article that has had considerable influence on thinking among HR professionals in the UK was published in 2007 in *The Review of Economics and Statistics*, an economics journal published by the Massachusetts Institute for Science and Technology. The authors were Maarten Goos and Alan Manning and their article was called 'Lousy and lovely jobs: the rising polarization of work in Britain'. This took forward research that they originally published a few years earlier and an analysis that they subsequently applied across the EU (see Goos and Manning 2003; Goos et al 2009; Goos et al 2014).

In their article Goos and Manning demonstrate, using detailed statistical analysis, that over three decades in the UK there has been strong growth both in the number of jobs which are highly skilled in nature and in the number of lower-paid, low-skilled jobs in the service sector. By contrast, the proportion of jobs that fall between these two stools – skilled manual work and clerical jobs, for example – has been in long-term decline. They conclude that the major cause of this trend has been the development of technologies which can carry out the jobs in 'the disappearing middle' more cost-effectively than people can.

Their article was published in an American journal whose readership consists mainly of economists, while the conclusions are aimed primarily at government policy-makers. The findings are, however, hugely relevant to HRM, not least because they strongly suggest that further polarisation of our labour market is likely in the future. This means that organisations are likely to struggle to recruit higher-skilled people in the coming decades, with labour markets tightening as demand for the relatively few appropriately qualified people increases. By contrast, recruitment for people to do less skilled work will become less problematic. Finding people to do these jobs will get easier, but in many cases people seeking and holding these jobs will be overqualified.

Questions

1   How would you go about accessing copies of Goos and Manning's articles on the polarisation of labour markets?

2   Based on your reading here, consider the following: what is the significance of their findings for managers who are charged with undertaking long-term human resource planning (HRP) activities for their organisations?

Indeed, one of the things that makes studying HRM interesting is the way that in doing so we draw on research findings that come from a wide variety of fields.

The following are the main examples:

- occupational psychology
- sociology of work
- behavioural and labour market economics
- employment law
- business ethics
- business history
- human geography.

In recent years **HR specialists** have also increasingly drawn on research findings from other disciplines. The chief example is neuroscience, where the use of functional magnetic resonance imaging technologies is allowing scientists vastly to increase our understanding of when, how and why our brains respond to external stimuli, including when we are at work. While much of the research is still in its infancy, important new insights on, for example, the power of praise from a senior manager to stimulate positive emotions and behaviours, are being established. Another promising field of research is predictive business analytics which involves designing IT systems which are able to analyse vast amounts of data, both quantitatively and qualitatively, in order to provide very high quality information about the likely impact of different types of business decisions. Multiple linear regression analysis allows researchers to search for patterns in data sets that show how one measure is related to another, the aim being to establish unexpected and (on the face of it) unexplained correlations from which otherwise non-existent insights can be gleaned and considered. At present, in HRM, these approaches are mainly being used in the field of talent management, the aim being to maximise the efficiency and effectiveness of hiring practices, induction and initial training, and later HRD interventions, and also to minimise unwanted employee turnover.

People who specialise in each of these disciplines have a tendency to come at their subjects with different sets of assumptions, diverse perspectives and, in some cases, widely divergent views on the appropriate approaches to use when carrying out research. While this makes tracking down and evaluating research of relevance to practical HRM fascinating, it also complicates matters (see Coyle-Shapiro et al 2004). Sometimes, for example, research will have great potential relevance for practical HRM, but this will not be apparent from the conclusions reached by the author, whose focus is elsewhere.

Edited books provide good summaries of recent academic research, setting out the key findings and debating different interpretations.

Finally, of course, textbooks written for students, such as this one, aim to provide good introductions to and overviews of key findings from the academic research. Following up the references that the authors of textbooks cite is often the best starting point when seeking out robust research on key contemporary HR issues.

Other sources of robust research

Academic research published in peer-reviewed journals is generally the most authoritative. But it is sometimes written in an inaccessible style and often assumes a great deal of prior knowledge on the part of its readers. The focus can also be overly theoretical for students who are just starting their studies at level 5 or level 6. Moreover, it is the case that some areas of HRM activity which have a great deal of practical significance for organisations have not attracted much interest from academic researchers. The field of recruitment and selection provides a good example. If you are researching methods of selection (interviews, personality tests, aptitude tests, assessment centres, and so on), their relative utility and their capacity to predict future job performance, you will find hundreds of peer-reviewed articles of a very high quality reporting research findings from all over the world. Employee selection is a very well-researched field. By contrast, the process of recruitment (that is, actively encouraging applications from would-be employees), despite being just as significant practically, has never been the focus of much academic research internationally, and almost none at all of any serious value in the UK. You will also search in vain for any robust academic research on company car schemes, for example, or on the practical impact of much recent UK employment law.

Fortunately these gaps are filled pretty effectively by other sources of published research. You will, for example, find a great deal of highly relevant HR-related research published on the CIPD's website. The Institute has a substantial Public Policy and Research (PPR) division, which both carries out its own research projects and sponsors research from leading teams of academics and consultants.

Indeed, some of the most significant and influential UK-based research has been carried out under the auspices of the CIPD. Examples are the well-known '**black box studies**' carried out by John Purcell and his colleagues (see Purcell et al 2003) and much of the most important recent research on the state of the psychological contract in the UK pioneered by David Guest and his colleagues (see Guest and Conway 2001).

Government departments, as well as international institutions, also commission and publish excellent research which has considerable practical relevance for HRM. A great deal is freely available to download from websites, while the number of publications made available increases each year. Some of the best examples are the following:

- **Workplace Employment Relations Survey (WERS)**: a huge nationwide study that is carried out every few years into many aspects of employment practice in UK workplaces, including the very smallest. Summaries of the findings are published on the Department for Business, Innovation and Skills (DBIS) website.
- **Leitch Review**: a comprehensive government-sponsored investigation into the state of skills in the UK, carried out between 2004 and 2006, which has informed government policy since. The final report is published on the HM Treasury website along with much of the research which informed its key findings.
- **Macleod Report on Employee Engagement**: published by the BIS in 2009, it has been hugely influential (see Macleod and Clarke 2009).

- The Skills at Work in Britain Survey (2012) and the OECD's Skills Outlook (2013) which report on the UK's relative and ongoing record on education and skills.
- The **Office for National Statistics** (ONS) publishes a vast amount of data on employment matters on its website. This includes regularly collected statistics alongside articles and larger research reports on particular topic areas. And you will find other examples listed in Chapter 6.

Finally, you will in addition find that some commercially produced research is also relevant and useful to you. Companies such as Incomes Data Services (IDS) and Industrial Relations Services (IRS) are both well-established and very well-respected publishers of HR-related research whose publications are widely available both in libraries and, at a fee, online. Major consultancies such as PricewaterhouseCoopers, Towers Perrin and Hay also undertake important research which is published online.

1.5 CORE HRM DEBATES

Aside from the need to develop a capacity for evidence-based thinking about HRM, in order to succeed in your level 5 or level 6 study of HRM, you also need to grasp the idea that HRM is a heavily contested field. That is to say that different people have very different ideas about it and, in particular, approach its study with different perspectives and different sets of assumptions. In short, there are competing schools of thought about HRM which tend to give rise to considerable tensions between people. In fact, it is often the case that neither side in a debate is either wholly right or wholly wrong. Both hold positions which are readily defended and entirely credible.

From a student's point of view the key is not to take up one position or another, but simply to appreciate the different perspectives and to be aware of how they necessarily infuse what you read on the subject of HRM. In this final section of the chapter we are going to introduce you to some of the major rival sets of perspectives. Some are of greatest relevance to HR practitioners looking to improve the effectiveness of their function's activities; others tend more to preoccupy the thinking of researchers.

1.5.1 BEST PRACTICE VS BEST FIT

Underlying many contemporary debates about the contribution made by HR to the achievement of organisational objectives is the ever-present division between **best practice thinking** and **best-fit thinking**.

This division at root concerns the extent to which it is ever really possible to identify a clear 'best way' of carrying out HR activities which is universally applicable. Adherents of a best practice perspective argue that there are certain HR practices and approaches to their operation which will invariably help an organisation in achieving competitive advantage. There is therefore a clear link between HR activity and business performance, but the effect will only be maximised if the 'right' HR policies are pursued.

While there are differences of opinion on questions of detail, all strongly suggest that the same basic bundle of human resource practices tends to enhance business performance in all organisations, irrespective of the particular product market strategy being pursued.

The main elements of the **best practice bundle** include the use of the more advanced selection methods, a serious commitment to employee involvement, substantial investment in training and development, the use of individualised reward systems and harmonised terms and conditions of employment as between different groups of employees.

The alternative **best fit** school also identifies a link between human resource management practice and the achievement of competitive advantage. Here, however, there is no belief in the existence of universal solutions. Instead, all is contingent on the particular circumstances of each organisation.

What is needed is HR policies and practices which 'fit' and are thus appropriate to the situation of individual employers. What is appropriate (or best) for one will not necessarily be right for another. Key variables include the size of the establishment, the dominant product market strategy being pursued and the nature of the labour markets in which the organisation competes.

?   REFLECTIVE ACTIVITY 1.2

Some fields of HRM practice are dominated by best practice thinking, while others broadly accept best fit assumptions.

A good example of the former is employee selection. Academics and consultants who undertake research in this field overwhelmingly share a best practice perspective on their work. They often disagree about exactly which method of selection is best and about how much better than its rivals it is, but they agree that there is 'out there', somewhere, a method which is more effective than all the others. The idea that some approaches to employee selection are most appropriate in one setting while others are best in other settings is only very rarely articulated in their work.

By contrast, research in the field of reward management has long been dominated by best-fit thinking. Whether or not there is a single, universal approach to the management of pay and benefits which trumps all the others never seems to be considered. The idea of even asking such a question does not seem to occur to those who research in this field. Instead the aim is always to establish what set of reward practices, used in combination, is most appropriate in different types of settings.

Questions

1   Why do you think that the frame of reference used by researchers focusing on employee selection and reward management varies so much?

2   Do you tend towards 'best fit' or 'best practice' when thinking about HRM practices? Why do you think that is the case?

1.5.2 TAYLORISM VS HUMANISM

Two distinct traditions to the management of people in organisations, based on totally opposing principles, can be identified.

The first is known as the **scientific management**, or **Taylorist**, approach (the two terms are used interchangeably), after Frederick W. Taylor, who pioneered these principles when designing jobs in the first factories to make use of large-scale production lines. The second is often referred to as the humanist approach, pioneered by managers who saw that a fundamental flaw in Taylorist principles was their tendency to dehumanise work.

The scientific management approach is systematic and very logical. It involves examining in great detail all the individual tasks that need to be carried out by a team of workers in order to achieve an objective.

The time it takes to accomplish each task is calculated and jobs are then designed so as to maximise the efficiency of the operation. In short, an analyst works out on paper how many people need to be employed, carrying out which tasks and using which machinery. Waiting time and duplication of effort is minimised to reduce costs.

Principles of scientific management, or Taylorism, allow tasks to be designed so as to minimise the number of more-skilled people the organisation requires. This is done by packaging all the specialised tasks to form one kind of job, which is then graded more highly than others made up of less specialised, lower-skilled tasks. The workforce is thus deployed with machine-like efficiency. Each plays a carefully defined role in a bigger process that is overseen, supervised, controlled and maintained by managers.

While originally developed for use in engineering and car assembly plants, the principles of Taylorism live on and are still widely deployed. For example, call centres are very much organised along Taylorist principles, each employee having a tightly defined role and being responsible for hitting targets of number of calls made or answered in each hour of work. As a result, it is planned that costs are kept as low as possible given the expected throughput of work.

The public sector also makes heavy use of Taylorist principles in designing and redesigning jobs so as to maximise efficiency. In recent years many skill mix reviews have been carried out in hospitals, schools and in the police, the aim being to allocate duties between staff by seeking to ensure that highly qualified (and highly paid) staff spend 100% of their time carrying out duties that only they can perform. Lower-skilled activities are then packaged together into jobs carried out by support workers.

The major criticism made of scientific management is that it is dehumanising and, therefore, ultimately bad for business. The adoption of Taylorist principles leads to the creation of jobs which are tedious, repetitive and unpleasant to perform. The result is a disengaged workforce and, hence, absence, high staff turnover and the development of adversarial industrial relations. It also often creates resentment among people forced into workplace straightjackets, which leads to low motivation, low commitment and low performance.

Moreover, because of this, more supervisors are needed than would be the case if people are positively motivated by the content of their jobs. Taylorism can thus be criticised for being a relatively inefficient approach over the long term.

An alternative **humanist** approach evolved in the middle of the twentieth century that draws on notions of intrinsic motivation and involves designing jobs and managing work in ways which engage and even excite people.

The alternative principles start with the idea that employees achieve higher levels of motivation, satisfaction and performance if the jobs they do are made more interesting and challenging. The key is to maximise the enjoyment, satisfaction and well-being that job-holders derive from their work. While it must be accepted that many jobs are never going to be highly enjoyable, it can be argued that managers should nonetheless try to design them and manage people in such a way as to maximise the satisfaction that job-holders derive from their work.

This then in turn leads to:

- an organisation which is able to attract and retain good performers
- reduced levels of absence, stress and burnout
- a high-trust industrial relations environment
- highly motivated and engaged staff
- discretionary effort.

Humanism is associated with HR practices that seek to enrich jobs, to reward hard work, to manage performance positively and to involve people in the management of their areas of work. In recent years there has been a particular focus placed on teamworking, on partnership approaches to management, on employee well-being and on the development of emotionally intelligent leaders. A key tool used in this approach to management is the staff survey. This enables organisations to measure levels of work satisfaction, to identify areas of under-performance and to track progress over time.

1.5.3 PLURALIST VS UNITARIST

This difference in perspective is particularly associated with the management of employee relations in organisations and infuses much of what is written about employee relations. The implications are profound because those who come at issues with unitarist perspectives invariably advocate different managerial approaches than those whose outlook is pluralist in nature. Put simply, a **unitarist** assumes that, for the most part, employers and employees share the same fundamental, long-term objectives as far as their relationship with one another is concerned. Both, for example, have an economic interest in the financial success of their organisation: the employer in order to maximise profit and the employee in order to maximise job security and career opportunity. It follows that any conflict between staff and management is solvable and short term in nature. Once the 'correct' policies and practices are put in place, a good relationship can be restored and maintained. Harmonious relations between employer and employee is the norm, conflict is abnormal.

None of these assumptions are held by **pluralists**. Pluralists believe that not only do employers and employees have different interests; they have multiple different interests. What employees seek (high wages, limitations on hours, control over their work, maximisation of health and safety, generous benefits, job security, and so on) are an inevitable source of conflict. This is because employers are looking for something rather different from the employment relationship (flexibility, low labour costs, a high degree of management control, improved productivity, and so on). The result, inevitably, is tension between 'two sides of industry'. A situation in which, for example, trade unions maintain a low-trust relationship with management is seen by people with a pluralist perspective as being entirely normal and expected. Pluralists see HRM as a process by which two parties with divergent interests continually negotiate the terms of their relationship.

1.5.4 BUREAUCRATIC VS PRAGMATIC

In some organisations HRM is characterised by the presence of **bureaucracy**. The HR function tends to direct people management activities through the issuing of written policies and by requiring line managers to complete documentation to demonstrate that they are putting policies into action.

Such approaches have the advantage of ensuring that people are treated equally and that 'the rule of law' effectively applies across an organisation. This helps to reduce perceptions of unfairness, which is a major source of demotivation in organisations. At its worst, however, it means that process replaces thought in the way that people are managed. For example, completing performance appraisal documentation can become more important than actually managing individual performance effectively.

The alternative approach, known as **pragmatism**, is to cut back as far as possible on rules, form-filling and written policies. Managers are able to treat good performers more favourably than poor performers and are free to manage their teams by 'gut instinct'. The result can be considerable diversity of practice across an organisation. This may work well for some, but also tends to lead to inequity.

1.5.5 CENTRALISED VS DECENTRALISED

The way the HR function is organised always seems to be a problem in organisations, with changes occurring regularly as senior managers search in vain for the ideal situation.

The traditional approach is **centralised**, with an HR director to whom all other HR staff report directly or indirectly. Some aspects of HR work are carried out by officers who carry responsibility for the people in particular departments, while others (typically payroll, recruitment and training) are managed centrally by specialists on behalf of the whole organisation.

By contrast, the **decentralised** approach locates most HR staff in departments, reporting to local managers and making the effective management of their teams the priority.

In recent years the so-called **three-legged stool model** associated with Dave Ulrich (1997) has become fashionable. This involves the creation of three distinct types of HR specialist. Much administrative work is carried out in call-centre-type, centralised teams who provide 'shared services' across the whole organisation. The second group are specialists in areas of HR work who provide advice as and when necessary to managers. They typically cover employment law, training and development and all strategic HR issues. The final, third group are labelled 'business partners'. They tend to be generalists who work alongside line managers and are concerned primarily with the management of case work and dealing with individual employee issues in departments. The three-legged stool model thus seeks to blend centralisation with decentralisation so as to maximise both efficiency and effectiveness.

1.5.6 INTERNALLY FOCUSED VS EXTERNALLY FOCUSED

This division in approach relates primarily to the relationship an organisation has with its labour markets – a crucial aspect of effective HRM. Externally focused approaches involve looking outside the organisation when new people are required, hiring people who have gained their experience and skills in other organisations. This approach requires that pay rates are set at or above the going market rate and that the organisation spends plenty of money advertising jobs and promoting its image in the labour market as a desirable employer to work for. The benefits derive from the wide field of talent the organisation has to choose from when recruiting staff and the diversity of professional experience that tends to infuse senior management teams.

By contrast, the internally focused approach involves developing internal labour markets. People tend to be hired early in their careers, often as school-leavers or graduate recruits, and brought into organisations with a strong commitment to HRD. They are then developed internally and promoted up the organisation when they are ready for new challenges and responsibilities. It is relatively rare in such organisations for senior people to be recruited from outside the organisation. Pay rates are primarily set with reference to internal fairness and the need to maximise effort among staff who are invited to compete for promotion up an organisational hierarchy.

The approach has the advantage of being highly motivating to existing staff, but inevitably it also means that the range of talent that the organisation has to choose from when filling senior posts is both limited and lacking in diversity.

1.5.7 STAKEHOLDER VS STOCKHOLDER ORIENTATIONS

This is another fundamental difference of perspective that can be observed in different organisations. An organisation that is heavily stockholder-oriented is one which is managed almost entirely in the interests of its owners. Shareholder value is the only really significant management target, and this increasingly means 'short-term shareholder value'. In other words, the organisation's sole purpose (in its own managers' eyes) is to gain for its owners a quicker and more substantial financial return on their investment than their competitors are able to achieve. As far as employees are concerned, this perspective tends to be associated with job insecurity, the intensification of work and an approach to management that is sometimes described as 'asinine'. This means that people are treated in an unsophisticated manner, being motivated via the use of financial incentives on the one hand and tight discipline on the other. If you work really hard and deliver the stockholders' objectives, you are well rewarded. If you don't, you are likely to be dismissed rapidly without sentiment.

The alternative stakeholder orientation is far more pleasant from an employee perspective, but can mean that the organisation is less competitive and financially successful – at least in the short term. Stakeholder thinking recognises that a number of groups of people have a legitimate stake in an organisation's long-term success and that there is therefore a shared interest between owners, managers, staff, suppliers, customers and the wider community. All will pull together and work collaboratively in the organisation's interests if they are all treated fairly. As far as employees are concerned, this stakeholder perspective means that managers are interested in their long-term development, in retaining their skills in the organisation and in providing them with the opportunity to thrive. Not only will they benefit, but the organisation will too.

? REFLECTIVE ACTIVITY 1.3

1 Think about an organisation you, your friends or relatives have worked for. Would you say that the approach to management was characterised more by a stockholder or by a stakeholder perspective?

2 Why might it be in the long-term financial interests of an organisation to move towards a stakeholder perspective and away from a stockholder perspective?

3 In what circumstances might the reverse be the case?

Our aim in this chapter has been to introduce you to the area of human resource management at level 5. We have reviewed what constitutes a level 5 approach to the area of study and how this is integrated with the CIPD's framework of professional development. One of the requirements of HR professionalism is that we are well prepared to offer the best advice and on the basis of the most solid evidence available. This necessitates having the skills, knowledge and sufficient curiosity to keep up to date with developments in the field, critically evaluating their application in practice. To this end we introduced the discipline of human resource management, exploring as we did so its development and some of its key debates. We trust that we have given you sufficient understanding of the field that you are able to embark on the rest of your programme of study from a solid base.

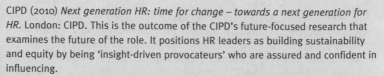

FURTHER READING

CIPD (2010) *Next generation HR: time for change – towards a next generation for HR*. London: CIPD. This is the outcome of the CIPD's future-focused research that examines the future of the role. It positions HR leaders as building sustainability and equity by being 'insight-driven provocateurs' who are assured and confident in influencing.

PURCELL, J., KINNIE, N., HUTCHINSON, S., RAYTON, B. and SWART, J. (2003) *Understanding the people and performance link: unlocking the black box*. London: CIPD. The CIPD's seminal study that examines the nature and contribution of people management to organisation performance.

TYSON, S. (2006) *Essentials of human resource management*. 5th ed. Oxford: Butterworth-Heinemann. Chapters 3 and 4. Reviews the development of the profession, the goals of specialist HR professionals and how the function assists in the achievement of organisation goals. Also explores in more depth the debates aired in this chapter.

REFERENCES

CARPENTER, C. U. (1905) The working of a labor department in industrial establishments. *The Engineering Magazine*. 25. pp1–9.

COYLE-SHAPIRO, J., TAYLOR, S., SHORE, L. and TETRICK, L. (2004) Commonalities and conflicts between different perspectives of the employment relationship: towards a unified perspective. In: COYLE-SHAPIRO, J., TAYLOR, S., SHORE, L. and TETRICK, L. (eds). *The employment relationship: examining psychological and contextual perspectives*. Oxford: Oxford University Press. pp119–32.

FAYOL, H. (1949) *General and industrial management* [translated from the French edition (Dunod) by Constance Storrs]. London: Pitman.

GANTT, H. L. (1910) *Work, wages and profits*. New York: The Engineering Magazine Company.

GINZBERG, E. (1958) *Human resources: the wealth of a nation*. New York: Simon & Schuster.

GOOS, M. and MANNING, A. (2003) McJobs and MacJobs: the growing polarisation of jobs in the UK. In: DICKENS, R., GREGG, P. and WADSWORTH, J. (eds). *The labour market under New Labour*. Basingstoke: Palgrave. pp70–85.

GOOS, M. and MANNING, A. (2007) Lousy and lovely jobs: the rising polarization of work in Britain. *The Review of Economics and Statistics*. Vol 89, No 1. pp118–33.

GOOS, M., MANNING, A. and SALOMONS, A. (2009) Job polarisation in Europe. *The American Economic Review*. Vol 99, No 2. pp58–63.

GOOS, M., MANNING, A. and SALOMANS, A. (2014) Explaining job polarization: routine-biased technological change and offshoring. *The American Economic Review*. Vol 104, No 2. pp2509–26.

GOSPEL, H. (2014) The evolution of human resource management in the UK. In: KAUFMAN, B. (ed.). *The development of human resource management across nations.* Cheltenham: Edward Elgar. pp186–210.

GUEST, D. E. and CONWAY, N. (2001) *Public and private sector perceptions on the psychological contract.* London: CIPD.

HOXIE, R. F. (1916) *Scientific management and labor.* New York and London: D. Appleton and Company.

MACLEOD, D. and CLARKE, N. (2009) *Engaging for success: enhancing performance through employee engagement. A report to government.* London: Department for Business, Innovation and Skills.

MAYO, E. (1933) *Human problems of an industrialised society.* New York: Harpers.

PFEFFER, J. and SUTTON, R. I. (2006) *Hard facts: dangerous half-truths and total nonsense: profiting from evidence-based management.* Boston, MA: Harvard Business School Press.

PURCELL, J., KINNIE, N., HUTCHINSON, S., RAYTON, B. and SWART, J. (2003) *Understanding the people and performance link: unlocking the black box.* London: CIPD.

TEAD, O. and METCALFE, H. C. (1920) *Personnel administration: its principles and practice.* New York: McGraw-Hill.

ULRICH, D. (1997) *Human resource champions: the next agenda for adding value and delivering results.* Boston, MA: Harvard Business Press.

WEBER, M. (1925, reissued 1964) *A theory of social and economic organization.* New York: Free Press.

CHAPTER 2

Managing and Co-ordinating the HR Function

KRYSTAL WILKINSON AND STEPHEN TAYLOR

CHAPTER CONTENTS

- Introduction
- Purpose and key objectives of the HR function
- How HR objectives are delivered in different organisations
- How the HR function can be evaluated
- The HR contribution to change management
- Ethical HRM
- HR and organisational performance

KEY LEARNING OUTCOMES

By the end of this chapter, you should be able to:

- explain the purpose and key objectives of the HR function in contemporary organisations, and how the focus of the function has evolved over time
- understand the various ways in which the HR function can be structured, and the common choices in different types of organisation
- explain the importance of considering cultural and institutional variance when dealing with HR across national borders
- understand how the HR function can be evaluated in terms of value added and contribution to sustained organisational performance
- understand the contribution of HR to effective change management
- explain the role of ethics and professionalism in HR management and development
- understand the relationship between HR activities and broader organisational performance.

2.1 INTRODUCTION

The purpose of this chapter is to introduce you to human resources (HR) activity and to the role of the HR function in organisations in general terms. It covers the aims and objectives of the function and the ways that these are evolving; different ways of delivering HR objectives; emerging developments in the management of the employment relationship; and methods that can be used to demonstrate how the function adds value to its organisation. The chapter also covers the role and requirements of contemporary HR professionals – in terms of the key contribution they can make to organisational change programmes, and the importance of professionalism and **ethics** in all activities. You will also be alerted to published research which links HR activity with positive outcomes at an organisational level, in terms of increased performance and reputation.

2.2 PURPOSE AND KEY OBJECTIVES OF THE HR FUNCTION

The purpose of the HR function is to support the delivery of the organisation's strategy and objectives through the effective management of people and performance. As such, an organisation's HR strategy and all activities should be clearly aligned with the strategy and activities of the business.

The CIPD website foregrounds the centrality of the function and the professionals working within it to their organisation's success:

> Today HR is at the centre of business performance. HR professionals have an important role to play in driving decisions that enable their organisations to thrive in both the short and the longer term. Where in the past the function delivered the fundamentals that underpinned the employee lifecycle (such as recruitment, induction and salary administration), supporting organisation performance is now the theme running through HR's work.

> Recognising that HR is a business discipline – and encouraging managers to view business as a 'people' discipline – is crucial. This partnership approach is vital in order for HR professionals to be able to deliver maximum benefit to their organisations.

> To ensure that HR professionals can deliver to this wider agenda, we're seeing greater specialism. We're also seeing an increasing globalisation of the profession, and an increasing number of CIPD members with overseas responsibilities.

In the rest of this section we explore some of these trends in more detail, including key objectives and areas of focus for HR professionals; how objectives and areas of focus have evolved over time, and where the future is seen to lie; the relationship with line management; and key issues in international HRM.

2.2.1 KEY OBJECTIVES AND HOW THEY HAVE EVOLVED

The core purpose and activities of the HR function evolve in response to developments in the business environment, but do not tend to change radically from one decade to another. In 2007 the CIPD carried out a survey of 787 HR professionals in the UK asking what they considered to be the major objectives of their functions. The top four were as follows:

- to recruit and retain key staff (cited by 70% of respondents)
- to develop employee competencies (62% of respondents)
- to improve the management of people performance (61%)
- to maximise employee involvement and engagement (59%).

The same broad priorities always top the lists whenever questions of this kind are asked in surveys, confirming that at its heart HRM is about attracting and retaining people with the required skills and experience and then seeking to develop them, maximise their performance, involve and engage them in the work of the organisation.

When labour markets are tight, as happens when unemployment levels in a region are low and employers have difficulties sourcing staff with the skills that they require, recruitment, retention and developmental activities naturally tend to dominate the HR agenda in organisations. By contrast, when labour markets are loose and employers find that they can recruit the people they need fairly easily, attention tends to shift to performance management and to initiatives aimed at cutting costs.

Over time objectives that were perhaps seen as being lower in terms of their priority sometimes move up the HR agenda. In recent years this is true of employee well-being activities, the need to comply with growing regulatory requirements and helping to build and maintain an organisation's public reputation. Linked to all of these is a further objective, namely the requirement to act ethically in managing employment relationships and to be seen to be doing so. Moreover, of course, the HR function is well-placed in fulfilling its recruitment and performance management roles to help encourage greater ethicality in organisations generally. It is therefore likely that the coming decade will see increased interest in and a greater level of commitment to HR ethics. A recent CIPD research report summed this up nicely in its call for a move away from 'best practice thinking' towards more 'good practice thinking' (CIPD 2015).

At UK government level there is another significant emerging priority which all organisations are likely to have to grapple with to a greater extent in the future. This is the UK economy's poor record on productivity, at least when contrasted to those of other comparable countries. The statistics suggest that others emerged from the recession of 2008–10 in fitter, leaner and potentially more competitive shape than the UK. The UK's record on economic growth and employment creation is excellent, but when it comes to productivity and efficiency there is a lot more work required (HM Treasury 2015). The result, over time, will be added pressure from government agencies as well as international markets radically to improve workforce skills levels, to innovate faster and more effectively and to make better use of new technologies in the workplace. Ministers will also be enlisting the support of employing organisations when seeking to reduce welfare dependence and raise levels of pay across the economy. In all these areas the HR function is likely to be at the forefront of organisational responses.

The birth of the function: personnel management

The evolution of people management as a distinct profession can be seen to date back to the Industrial Revolution, and particularly to the establishment of big manufacturing operations in the late nineteenth and early twentieth centuries. First companies and then local and national government office operations became large enough to set up dedicated employment or personnel departments to look after the wages and welfare of workers. Key activities were: employee record-keeping; adherence to policies regarding recruitment, training and wage administration; welfare-oriented initiatives such as providing medical care or housing; attempts to increase productivity via wage increases and training; dealing with trade unions; and basic report-card performance appraisal.

The move to human resource management

Towards the end of the twentieth century, increasing attention was being given in the industrial world to the notion that non-monetary factors could have a bigger influence on worker productivity and motivation than wages. There was a new importance assigned to behaviour, and so people management was required to develop its passive and administrative approach into something more dynamic – human resource management – where people are seen as a valuable resource to be developed rather than as mere cogs in the company machine. The main concerns became recruitment and development that was directed towards increasing worker commitment and loyalty; efforts to provide employees with a challenging work environment and a range of benefits; behaviourally driven training and development activities; more sophisticated performance appraisal; and an emphasis on leadership.

The move to strategic human resource management (SHRM)

The evolution of the field took a further turn at the end of the century when new power was given to the function. Due to increased free market competition at a global level and the growth of technology and knowledge-based industries, the importance of people to company success was elevated. The workforce, having previously been promoted from 'cogs' to 'resources', were now to be viewed as 'assets' – a valuable source of competitive advantage. This marked the elevation of the HR function to a strategic player in the organisation, responsible for aligning individual and team goals with organisation objectives, facilitating a participative culture, and even directly shaping organisation strategies. Activities of the SHRM department include the following:

- linking HR practices to organisation strategy
- fostering a healthy psychological contract in a context of short-term employment rather than job security
- the linking of compensation to contribution
- training and development linked to encouraging innovation
- knowledge management and talent development planning
- employee participation
- motivation through enriching the work experience
- performance and talent management as opposed to appraisal
- cross-cultural issues
- measuring the value added by HR activities.

The evolution of the HR function is unlikely to have finished, and speculation is already being made about future developments in focus. In the CIPD's 2010 *Next Generation HR* report – which was based on a substantial research project into the changing nature of the HR function – two key objectives were highlighted as priorities for HR moving forwards:

1 Future-proofing the organisation. The report notes a new focus on building 'future-fit cultures', which go beyond being healthy (engaged employees), to become agile and changeable – a culture for always staying one step ahead of the game. Key concepts here are trust and transparency, and treating employees in the same way that we treat customers. The report goes on to talk about the need for HR to become organisation guardians and commentators: managing brand risk; designing processes that support progressive ways of doing business; and being prepared to challenge behaviour (even of the most senior leaders) when it breaches what the organisation stands for.

2 Being insight-driven. The report states that 'the best HR functions understand exactly how their organisation in their market facing their specific challenges can respond in a way unique to it'. It goes on to clarify that 'organisation insight' requires an understanding of both context (market, stage of evolution) and culture (what really make things happen here – in terms of people and politics).

2.3 HOW HR OBJECTIVES ARE DELIVERED IN DIFFERENT ORGANISATIONS

The HR function can be organised in several different ways: in small to medium-sized organisations, there can be one individual (HR sole practitioner) who works closely with operational managers to manage and deliver the people agenda. In larger organisations, there are likely to be a team, or teams, of HR professionals.

In this section we will consider generalist and specialist HR roles; the role of line managers in HR delivery; different delivery options such as shared-service centres, HR outsourcing and the use of consultants; and the Ulrich model for HR provision. We will also consider how HR tends to be delivered in different organisational and national contexts.

2.3.1 GENERALIST AND SPECIALIST ROLES

HR generalists have knowledge of, and involvement in, all areas of the HR function. Sole practitioners will always tend to be generalists as they need to be able to deal with every part of the HR remit on their own. However, sometimes a whole HR team will be made up of generalists – each member may have main areas of responsibility, but they are all capable of handling activities in all areas. Such a structure can be very useful when there are peaks in demand (large recruitment drives) or when the business operates on a 24/7 basis (so that training sessions and employee relations meetings that are out of hours, for example, can be spread around the team). The workload is likely to consist of a variety of tasks – working with managers to determine people needs; taking part in activities; developing policies, procedures and information systems.

Recruitment, resourcing and talent planning specialists are responsible for managing the people in the organisation in order to meet the changing needs of the business – focusing on the company's short-term and long-term objectives. They need to understand and plan around changing demographics, supply and demand, staff turnover and scarce skills. They then need to be able to identify, attract and select the sort of individuals who can create a competitive advantage for the organisation. Finally, they have an important role in developing processes to identify talent across the organisation and integrating them with succession planning and other HR activities such as performance management.

Learning and talent development specialists are responsible for ensuring that the company has employees who possess the skills that it needs now and who are developing the skills that it will need in the future. They do this by producing a learning and development strategy that is in alignment with the overall organisation strategy, and then utilising a broad range of appropriate provisions in order to deliver the strategy – often including structured development programmes, off-the-job training events, on-the-job training provisions, coaching and mentoring schemes, and online provisions. They are also required to evaluate the effectiveness of all provisions.

Organisation development specialists are responsible for ensuring the health of the business itself in the long term. It is widely acknowledged that 'change-ready' and agile businesses are best placed to cope with the challenges of a fast-changing external environment, and OD specialists have a key role in building this capability – working on the organisation's culture, improving the capability of employees, or altering the focus of an organisation (towards quality or customer service, for example).

Employee engagement specialists are responsible for issues such as internal communications, employee relations and the employer brand. It is about what motivates employees to turn up to work each day, and then what makes them go the extra mile. Specialists will design a range of quantitative and qualitative mechanisms to gain information, analyse the results and develop action plans for improving engagement. They will also be responsible for managing procedures to deal with any conflict in the organisation.

Performance and reward specialists are responsible for monitoring the contribution that individuals and teams are making to the business; taking action to improve performance when it is lagging; and ensuring that positive employee skills, behaviours, attitudes and contributions are effectively rewarded – in the forms of salary, allowances, benefits and more intrinsic ways (autonomy, recognition, and so on). Specialists must ensure that reward is managed in a way that is fair, market-based and cost-effective.

2.3.2 THE ROLE OF LINE MANAGERS

As you are aware, the whole purpose of the HR function is the effective management of people and performance issues in the business. The HR team, however, are not the only people who have an involvement in this. Each and every individual employee will have their own line manager (or several people to whom they report) who is responsible for allocating work and monitoring performance. As the line managers have day-to-day contact with employees, they are also likely to be the first point of call when an employee has any questions or concerns about any aspect of the employment experience, or has a personal issue that may have an impact on their work.

It is essential, therefore, that the HR department and line managers work together to manage people issues effectively and consistently. HR managers need to make sure that key HR information, policies and procedures are communicated to line managers; that line managers receive regular training on the implementation of policies and procedures; and that line managers are aware of the importance of seeking HR advice when they are unsure of how to proceed or are faced with complex issues. There is also another reason for HR partnership with line management. If many of the operational people activities can be devolved to the line, more HR time can be devoted to strategic issues, which should in turn elevate the status of the HR function within the organisation.

In CIPD surveys, the extent to which the allocation of HR-related tasks is divided between the HR function and line management is reported to vary substantially between organisations. There are, however, some general trends. It seems that the responsibility for pay and benefits, employee relations, training and development, and implementing redundancies tends to be retained by the HR team; while responsibilities for work organisation and for recruitment and selection lie mainly with line managers.

2.3.3 SHARED SERVICES, OUTSOURCING AND HR CONSULTANCY

Some organisations opt for a **shared service centre** for their HR provision. Such centres are also used for other support functions (such as finance, IT) and are seen as a way to provide a corporate service across a large organisation or, sometimes, across several partner organisations (such as a group of NHS trusts or local councils).

There are two distinctive features of HR shared service centres: they offer a common service provision of routine HR administration and sometimes more complex HR activities; and they are service-focused, enabling the customers of the shared service to specify the level and nature of the service.

The benefits that can be gained from a move to shared service include the following:

- reducing costs and avoiding duplication of effort
- benefiting from economies of scale (when securing training provisions, benefits provisions, and so on)
- improving the quality of service to customers – the use of more efficient processes can deliver greater consistency, and more timely and accurate information and advice to the customers of the service (individual employees or line managers)
- shared knowledge
- as a possible profit centre (if services are sold to third-party organisations)
- as a precursor to outsourcing.

Outsourcing

The practice of HR **outsourcing** refers to purchasing a service from an external source rather than performing it in-house. In factories and hospitals, for example, support services such as catering and cleaning are often outsourced – because this proves cheaper than employing people directly and the quality is often better (the company that provides the service being experts in the field).

In recent years, the practice has been more evident in office functions, with companies deciding to outsource entire support functions (HR, finance and IT being common targets) to expert providers, or to outsource parts of a function – such as payroll, basic training or recruitment – so that those employed by the company can focus on strategic issues and work which requires specific company know-how.

Consultancy

Some organisations may choose to hire specialist HR consultants to provide advice on certain issues or develop specific strategies or policies (but not usually implement them). A consultant would work for a consultancy firm or be self-employed, and would be contacted by an organisation to enter the business, perform a specific task and then leave. As consultants engage with multiple and changing clients, they can bring deeper levels of expertise than a company could hope to have in-house, and each client only has to purchase as much service as they need.

For each individual assignment, a contract should be drawn up between the client and the consultant. Cope (2003, pp78–9) suggests the following general model:

- background (client area, situation under consideration, business context)
- outcome (goals and objectives, measurement)
- engagement plan (timeframe, methodology, resource allocation, key milestones, initial known data requirements)
- responsibilities (client, consultant, stakeholders)
- boundaries and scope (areas for inclusion and exclusion, potential risk)
- specifics (payment, terms and conditions)
- confidentiality (termination process, liability, disclosure policy)
- review process
- closure (process and review dates).

If outsourcing or HR consultants are used, it is extremely important to ensure that regular evaluation occurs to ensure that the services received are as agreed and that they are effective.

2.3.4 THE ULRICH MODEL

US business academic David Ulrich proposed a pioneering new model for HR service delivery, which has since become known as the 'three-legged stool' model for HR. It is based on three different types of HR professionals in an organisation, each working in distinct ways:

- *HR business partners*: senior HR professionals working closely with business leaders or line managers, usually embedded in the business unit, influencing and steering strategy and strategy implementation
- *centres of excellence*: small teams of HR specialists – developing and delivering innovative HR solutions in areas such as reward, learning, engagement and talent management
- *shared service centre*: a large unit that handles the routine 'transactional' services across the business.

Despite the intense interest surrounding the Ulrich model and business partnering, there is little empirical evidence to illustrate how many companies actually structure their HR function in this way. In the CIPD's 2010 *HR Outlook* survey, 30% of survey respondents from large organisations described their structure as being akin to that recommended by Ulrich, although far fewer did so in medium and small organisations.

2.3.5 APPROACH TO THE FUNCTION IN DIFFERENT CONTEXTS

It should be noted that different types of organisation are likely to organise their HR function in different ways, and that the function will have different primary objectives in different contexts. We will not spend too long on this issue as there is undoubtedly a lot of variation in approach within each type of organisation, but it is important to be aware of key traits and differences. You will also find more discussion of some of these issues in Chapter 3.

- *Large private sector companies*: as the company is privately owned, the key objective for all functional departments will be revenue generation (making money for the shareholders) and proving that the function adds value. The function itself is likely to be large, and may be made up of mainly generalists, mainly specialists, or something akin to the Ulrich model.
- *Public sector*: as the company is a public body, the key objectives will be linked to enhancing the service provision to the public. Revenue generation is likely to be less of an issue, but maximising efficiency to save public money will be a key objective. The HR team are likely to have more constraints on how they design and deliver certain activities due to government stipulations and expectations surrounding best practice in issues of equality of opportunity and diversity, and so on. The function itself is likely to be structured in a similar way as in large private sector companies.
- *Voluntary sector*: as the company is likely to be limited in terms of funds, the focus on all functions will be to operate in a cost-effective way, but to try to attract new investment and volunteer staff. HR activities will be based on trying to attract individuals with a certain value stance and make them feel valued and appreciated in the company (as financial rewards are likely to be minimal or non-existent). The size of the HR function will depend on the size of the organisation.
- *Small and medium-sized enterprises (SMEs)*: as the size of the workforce and resources of the company are likely to be small, the HR function is likely to consist of a sole practitioner working in partnership with operational management, or there might not be any direct HR presence at all – with basic people management issues being conducted by an office manager or operations manager, and HR consultants being brought in only when there are specific issues to deal with or new policies/practices are required.
- *Networked organisations*: this refers to organisations working in collaboration to develop products or deliver services. HR may well be delivered through a shared service centre that covers all of the organisations in the network, or each organisation may have its own HR people who are required to work collaboratively with their counterparts throughout the network.
- *Multinational organisations (MNCs)*: as most MNCs are privately owned, one key objective for all functions will be revenue generation, but an additional objective will be ensuring the smooth running and effective operation of the company across national borders. We will consider this issue further in the next section.

You may wish to consider such organisation type variations – in terms of HR priorities, available resources and team structure – when you are thinking about personal job transitions and how you want your HR career to progress. Different contexts come with different experiences and opportunities, and not every type of organisation is likely to be equally appealing.

2.3.6 CULTURAL AND INSTITUTIONAL VARIATIONS ACROSS NATIONAL BORDERS

When considering HR in the global context, there are a number of different issues to bear in mind:

- Different countries have different cultures, which can affect employee expectations and behaviours in work.
- Different countries have different employment legislation frameworks. UK immigration legislation is also a key issue.

- Different countries have different tax arrangements, and different provisions for things such as medical cover.
- Different countries have different labour markets – as a result of economic factors (whether the markets are tight/loose) and welfare provisions (whether parents, etc, are better off in work or at home).
- Different countries have different standards of living – which affects pay expectations.
- Different countries have different education systems – which affects the age at which individuals enter the labour markets and the skill sets they have.

Cultural variations across national borders are especially important to be aware of, as they will have an impact on all aspects of HR activities. One of the most famous authors on national culture variations is Hofstede (1991), who initially developed four main factors of culture differentiation:

- *Power distance*: this refers to the extent to which people believe that power should be distributed equally or unequally. In work terms, it relates to the centralisation of authority within an organisation. Countries with a 'high power distance' (such as the Philippines, Singapore, France and Greece) tend to have hierarchical organisations in which it is accepted that the more senior employees have more power. Countries with a 'low power distance' (such as the UK, Sweden and New Zealand) tend to have flatter organisation structures and a less autocratic style of management.
- *Uncertainty avoidance*: this refers to the extent to which people feel uncomfortable with ambiguous situations. Countries such as France, with a 'high uncertainty avoidance', tend to have lots of rules and regulations in organisations and employees are not expected to take risks.
- *Individualism/collectivism*: this refers to the extent to which people operate on an individual basis or as part of a group. In a 'high individualism' culture, such as the USA, people tend to look out for themselves, preferring individual objectives, individual performance assessment and reward based on individual performance. In 'low individualist' or 'high collectivist' cultures, such as Japan, people prefer to work in teams, have team-based assessment and have collectively negotiated reward.
- *Masculinity/femininity*: this refers to the extent to which people demonstrate what are seen to be masculine or feminine traits. The former include aggressiveness and assertiveness, the latter caring and emotional intelligence. Cultural and institutional variations across national borders will be relevant not only when an HR professional wants to work in a different country themselves, but also when they work in any company that is international, or where employees may be posted for overseas assignments.

When it comes to developing an HR strategy in an international company, one of the key decisions to be made will be the extent to which national variations in the above factors are taken into consideration. There are several options:

- *Ethnocentric*: the home-country strategy and practices are rolled out across the company; key decisions are made by the home-country headquarters; and employees from the home country tend to fill important jobs.
- *Polycentric*: strategy and practices are adapted to each national context; local managers usually head up each subsidiary and decide how things should be done.
- *Geocentric or global*: the most effective policies and procedures from around the business are implemented and the most effective individuals selected for key roles and to make key decisions. For example, the vacuum cleaner company Electrolux has recruited and developed a group of international managers from a range of different countries. They now have a mobile base of managers that can be deployed in different locations as the need arises, and who can learn from each placement and spread that knowledge as they move on.

The decision over which approach to follow for the HR strategy may well be linked to the approach adopted at the organisational level, but this is not always the case. Furthermore, even where a company decides to operate a specific approach at both the company and departmental level, certain processes may well need to be adapted somewhat to ensure things such as legal compliance and effectiveness (with the ethnocentric approach) or the development of a unified company identity (with the polycentric approach).

2.4 HOW THE HR FUNCTION CAN BE EVALUATED

In order for the HR function to demonstrate that it adds value, it must have in place robust systems for the evaluation of its activities – both at an individual level and cumulatively.

2.4.1 COMMON METHODS AND METRICS

Traditionally, HR evaluation has focused on the efficiency and effectiveness of the range of practices operated by the function. Efficiency concerns establishing that each activity is as cost-effective as possible in terms of time and money; effectiveness concerns establishing that the activity is meeting its objectives. A range of techniques are available for evaluating individual HR activities on these grounds and also for assessing the cumulative effect.

The most commonly used evaluation tools include the following:

- *HR statistics*: this refers to things such as recruitment spend; number of job applications; number of new recruits; absence figures; turnover levels; disciplinary and grievance statistics; training and development spend; training hours per employee; and so on. While they may not tell the company much if gathered in isolation, they can be very useful in terms of **benchmarking** – either internal (comparing current performance with previous years, or comparing different departments to target problem areas) or external (comparing the company with others in the industry and/or local area).
- *Key performance indicators (KPIs)*: this refers to identifying the aspects of HR performance that are the most critical for the achievement of business objectives, often including a target for each activity, and then assessing the performance against this target. The ideal for KPIs is that they are specific, measurable, achievable, performance-relevant and timebound (have a deadline).
- *Balanced scorecard*: this is a document that lists an agreed set of performance measures in a series of tables, along with a 'high-level strategy map' showing how these measures relate to each other and the firm's strategic objectives.

The scorecard's measures are grouped under four 'perspectives': customer; financial; internal business process; and learning and growth. All departments would have their own scorecard, with the specific measures under each of the perspectives tailored to their own specific functional activities. This enhances the sense that all departments are working to the same objectives and enables cross-company comparisons.

2.4.2 MEETING THE NEEDS OF THE CUSTOMERS

As well as assessing the efficiency and effectiveness of HR activities, another way in which the function can be evaluated concerns the extent to which the HR department are seen to be meeting the needs of their customers. In order to do this, the function first needs to consider who their customers are.

This can be done by conducting a stakeholder analysis – where you identify all of the parties that require some sort of service from the department and then you consider what the specific requirements are of each.

2.4.3 EVALUATING EMERGING HR GOALS AND PURPOSES

As mentioned above, in the context of the evolution of people management, key areas of focus for the profession moving forward are seen to be future-proofing the organisation and ensuring that HR is 'insight-driven'. This refers to a new emerging purpose for the function – going beyond the traditional people–performance remit and focusing instead on contributing to overall long-term organisational performance. In one *People Management* feature, 'A new way of seeing HR: insight-led HR', some pioneering HR leaders were seen to display new capabilities, including the ability to 'read' the health of the organisation as a whole and operate considerably 'off piste' if required.

This also means new requirements for evaluation. HR professionals need to look beyond people–performance metrics to assess their own abilities and consider whether they personally possess the 'three savvies' that are required for being 'insight-driven':

- *contextual savvy*: being alert to the external factors and macro trends that affect the organisation now and in the future
- *organisational savvy*: having a sophisticated understanding of the people and cultural aspects of the organisation – how to get things done with these unique individuals in our very particular context
- *business savvy*: having a true understanding of how the organisation makes money and what most matters when looking at its current and future commercial health.

This requires self-evaluation and perceptiveness to the responses given by key organisational stakeholders. For example, are HR included at board level, are they involved in key organisation strategy-making, are they respected? As summarised by Jackie Orme, former CIPD chief executive:

> We need to change the unspoken currency of success in HR. Too often we get stuck in a cycle of measuring ourselves on the volume of activities and initiatives, and on the multiple demands we are responding to. We feel this is what is necessary to demonstrate value and be recognised accordingly.

> We need to unlock our curiosity and realise that having a unique viewpoint and a clear sense of what matters in light of this has to be a much bigger part of our definition of success.

? REFLECTIVE ACTIVITY 2.1

Who are the different 'customers' of the HR department in your own organisation or one you are familiar with? What do they require from the HR function?

2.5 THE HR CONTRIBUTION TO CHANGE MANAGEMENT

Change is a key, and unavoidable, issue in the modern organisational world. All sorts of things cause organisational change – the challenges of growth, especially global markets;

challenges of economic downturns and tougher trading conditions; changes in strategy; technological changes; competitive pressures, including mergers and acquisitions; customer pressure and shifting markets; new legislation and government initiatives. Research indicates that organisations are undergoing major change approximately once every three years, while smaller changes are occurring almost continually (CIPD 2011). As the old saying goes, the only constant in life is change.

Effective change management is hugely important, as despite the extent of change faced by modern business, evidence suggests that a considerable number of organisation change initiatives fail. CIPD research suggests that less than 60% of reorganisations meet their stated objectives.

If a change management is to be successful, the HR function usually has a vital part to play. This is because effective change management concerns more than just the controllable (business processes that can be designed and implemented) – it also concerns the uncontrollable (people, and the meanings that people attach to such processes).

2.5.1 THE HR CONTRIBUTION TO THE CONTROLLABLE

HR professionals can contribute to the development of change programmes in the following ways:

- involvement at the initial stage in the project team
- advising project leaders in skills available within the organisation – identifying any skills gaps, training needs, new posts, new working practices, and so on
- balancing out the narrow/short-term goals with broader strategic needs
- assessing the impact of change in one area/department/site on another part of the organisation
- balancing the interests of different stakeholder groups
- understanding stakeholder concerns to anticipate problems
- understanding the appropriate medium of communication to reach each group
- evaluating and reporting on the impact of change initiatives on human resources – this can include absence levels; turnover figures; number of grievances raised; internal moves; training spend; employee feedback (satisfaction survey scores); and so on.

2.5.2 THE HR CONTRIBUTION TO THE UNCONTROLLABLE

Individuals and their reactions to proposed changes are 'uncontrollable' because everyone is different. Each employee will have their own personality (more or less comfortable with change); their own history (experience of changes in the past); and their own unique position in terms of the change under consideration (it might or might not affect them, and if it does, this might be positive or negative).

The HR function can help to deal with the somewhat uncontrollable human element of change by being aware of the more typical reactions and being aware of the interpersonal activities they can instigate to facilitate the change initiative. It has been established that most people pass through a typical cycle of emotions as they deal with change and its consequences – a sort of emotional roller-coaster. This is illustrated in Figure 2.1.

Here are some thoughts that might be expressed by someone passing through the change cycle in relation to something they see as bad news:

- What? Oh no!
- It can't be true!
- You cannot be serious!
- Can we sort this out some other way?
- That's it – after 20 years of service they want me to . . .
- Am I going to be part of this?

?   REFLECTIVE ACTIVITY 2.2

Try to think of a major change that you have experienced in the past. Can you relate your feelings at the time to the change cycle?

Research has also found that certain types of organisation change will be more emotive than others. The findings of one survey on organisational change (Guest and Conway 2001) suggest that, contrary to popular opinion, employees generally have a positive view of change and will often see it as helping them do their jobs better. Changes in job design, new technology and products thus tend to be welcomed by employees. The types of change that were perceived more negatively, and therefore require more careful handling, were the following: those that might affect job security, prospects or careers; changes to reward, pay or appraisal; changes to information, communication, involvement and relationships; and changes to policies affecting how, when and where work is done.

Figure 2.1 Approaches to change

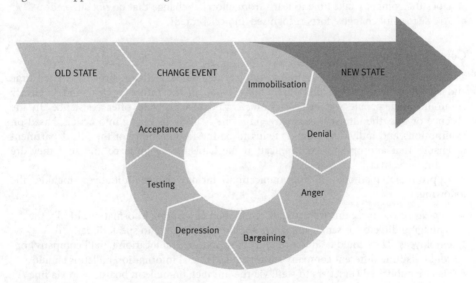

Unfortunately, these are just the sort of changes that you are likely to be involved in. So what is HR's role in dealing with the uncontrollable? While there can be no magic formula to ensure that everyone will react positively, there are some general elements that will improve the likelihood of employee buy-in. These include: an organisational culture that embraces change; appropriate communication; ensuring employee participation in any change; HRD interventions; and the management of expectations and conflict. We will now explore some of these issues in more depth, focusing on HR's role in each.

Change-ready culture

Different organisations have different 'cultures' when it comes to receptiveness to change. The HR team can gain an understanding of the culture of the organisation by holding informal employee focus groups, including questions on change initiatives in staff satisfaction surveys, or holding interviews with a range of company stakeholders.

You can also think about how changes have been carried out and conducted in the past. If you can answer yes to the following questions, adapted from the Positive Employee Practices Institute, then the culture is likely to be more receptive to new change initiatives:

- Does the company take time to thoroughly plan for each change?
- Do the people affected by a change get to take part in the planning and implementation?
- Are the goals, purposes and potential benefits of change efforts clearly communicated to everyone in the organisation?
- When changes are announced, is there open dialogue about the disruptions they may create and the difficulties that may need to be addressed in order to make the changes successful?
- When people have problems implementing changes, do they communicate freely about them and ask for help?
- When people express negative feelings about change, are they listened to and are their concerns addressed?
- When difficulties or disruptions arise, are people quick to address and fix them?
- Has the company experienced recent successes in implementing major changes?
- Does the company take time to learn from efforts at change that do not succeed?
- Are successful change efforts recognised and celebrated?

Communication

The importance of internal communication throughout any change process is cited time and again in management literature. If the vision of the future is clear and is clearly communicated, people will be less confused and less likely to offer resistance. In the absence of this, the informal company grapevine is likely to spring into action, based on assumptions and individual fears. It tends to be the responsibility of the HR department to ensure that appropriate communication mechanisms are in place and that they are operating effectively.

Appropriate methods of communication during change initiatives include the following:

- *Top-down channels*: this is for the dissemination of accurate information. Ideally the managing director or senior managers should take the time to speak directly to employees. They could hold a formal meeting in a central location (small company) or could visit the different company sites. Regular official information bulletins should also be publicised (in letters to staff; via the intranet; on bulletin boards; and via line managers in team meetings).
- *Bottom-up channels*: this is to allow employee participation and idea generation. There could be collective consultation, change workshops, and so on.
- *Two-way discussion*: there should be one-to-one meetings between employees and their line managers and/or the HR department to discuss the personal implications of change initiatives and any concerns that individuals may have.

The skills and attributes that the HR department needs to exercise include the following:

- *Stakeholder awareness and the ability to influence at all levels*: HR professionals need to be aware not only of the employees during change initiatives, they may also need to persuade senior management of the importance of commitment to communication activities, and/or coach line managers in effective communication.

- *Honesty*: 'users, management and other stakeholders will demand honest, consistent and up-to-date information whether the news is good, bad or unremarkable' (CIPD 2005).
- *Thoroughness and patience*: it is important that communication provides all of the information that stakeholders need, including the following:
  - the need for, the nature and the scope of the change
  - who will be affected
  - training, retraining and/or redeployment implications
  - implications for quality of work/life
  - implications for staffing and work patterns
  - the proposed rate and timing of implementation
  - the expected benefits and adverse effects of the change.

This can take some time, and the same message may need to be delivered several times.

- *The ability to listen*: providing information is only half of the process; the key is to ensure that communication is two-way and that employees have the opportunity to ask questions and express their opinions/concerns.
- *Empathy and concern for stakeholder reactions* to change and the ability to ensure stakeholder understanding.
- *Monitoring of the effectiveness of communication channels*.

HRD interventions

Training and development initiatives can help with change management in a number of areas, including:

- *enhancing employee responsiveness to change*: employees can be instructed on the importance of being aware of what is happening externally (the business environment) and how to be more responsive to the views and experiences of suppliers and customers; they can also be given development opportunities where they are expected to be creative and innovative
- *enhancing the ability of employees to adapt to change*: by addressing any skills gaps that arise as a result of a change initiative
- *coaching and mentoring activities* for those finding it difficult to cope with change.

2.5.3 PUBLICISING SUCCESS

One crucial activity throughout any organisational change programme, and in the aftermath, is the widespread publicising of success stories. This includes not only the overall impact of the programme (that is, company performance), but also individual success stories – examples of employees whose actions or attitudes have had a significant positive impact on the success of the change; and also employees who have gained from it. This will help 'bed in' the change, support a change-ready culture and put employees in a more positive frame of mind in the event of future change initiatives.

2.6 ETHICAL HRM

The *Oxford English Reference Dictionary* defines the terms as follows:

- Ethics is 'the rules of conduct recognised as appropriate to a particular profession or area of life'.
- Professionalism is 'the qualities or typical features of a profession or of professionals, especially competence, skill, etc'.

Here we are going to focus on thinking about ethics in HR practice. In Chapter 3 you will find a discussion on professionalism in HRM.

2.6.1 THE BUSINESS CASE FOR AN ETHICAL APPROACH TO HR MANAGEMENT

Kew and Stredwick (2010, p351) make reference to a definition of ethics that has three core elements: fairness; deciding what is right and wrong; and the practices and rules which underpin responsible conduct between individuals and groups.

It is absolutely vital that the HR function takes an ethical approach in all its actions. Ethical behaviour is a core element of the required standards of an HR professional. There is also a clear business case for ethical HR management, covering several areas:

- Ethical behaviour is essential in the development and maintenance of positive relationships with the workforce. The workforce needs to trust the HR function and this is only possible if the function acts fairly and decently at all times.
- Ethical standards are a key determinant of the employer brand and reputation. Ethics is a hot topic in society in general and individuals are increasingly considering ethical factors when they are deciding which companies they are willing to work for. It is certainly clear that individuals are unlikely to want to work for a company with a reputation of unethical treatment towards its employees.
- Role-modelling – if the department is going to champion ethical behaviour in the workforce as a whole, it must practise what it preaches.

Furthermore, there is even evidence to suggest that ethical practice can improve overall business performance. Kew and Stredwick (2010, pp381–2) cite a study carried out by the Institute of Business Ethics in 2003, which compared a number of FTSE-350 companies that met certain ethical criteria (including having a long-standing code of ethics and scoring highly on certain league tables) with a control sample. It was found that the ethical companies scored more highly on three different measures of financial performance.

Taylor (2011, p254) notes the irony in HR taking a leading role in ethical issues, however – after having spent years and years trying to distance itself from its 'pink and fluffy' welfare roots to gain credibility as a strategic player:

It is a paradox, given the centrality of ethics to so much HR activity that our function has generally sought, at least in recent years, to distance itself from perceptions that it plays a significant ethical role... Since the 1980s the emphasis has been on shedding our image as a management function concerned with employee welfare or even one which seeks to represent the interests of employees... Instead a very deliberate attempt has been made to craft a vision of HRM as being 100% business-focused, delivering key strategic objectives on behalf of the organisation and adding financial value.

In the future it is likely that there will be some reversal of this established trend... HR managers will have to rediscover an interest in ethics, actively promote ethical behaviour across the organisation and take care that they apply ethical approaches towards the management of people themselves.

2.6.2 CODES OF ETHICS

As well as having a personal responsibility for ethical decision-making and acting as role-models for others, the HR team often has a leading role to play in the promotion of ethical behaviour for all. One of the ways they can do this is via the development and publicising of a corporate code of ethics. This is a form of code of conduct that can be defined as 'written, distinct, formal document(s), which consists of moral standards which help guide employee or corporate behaviour' (Schwartz 2001, p248).

Such codes can be of three different types: educational (aimed at increasing moral awareness and behaviour within the company); regulatory (detailing rules for behaviour providing help on the resolution of moral conflicts); or aspirational (laying down general values and communicating ideals to individuals).

Good codes of ethics recognise the importance of relationships with all major stakeholders (both internal and external). The specific content will vary from company to company, but they tend to have an introduction to the purpose of the document, followed by sections detailing the expected behaviour of all employees in relation to a range of specific topics.

2.6.3 THE HR ROLE IN PROMOTING KEY PHILOSOPHIES

Just as the HR function was seen to have a responsibility for both demonstrating and promoting ethical decision-making and good communication in relation to change management, there are several other issues that HR has primary responsibility for championing and promoting throughout the workplace. These include the following:

- *Equality of opportunity*: HR professionals should ensure:
  - that all policies, procedures and activities guarantee fairness to all (fair access, fair treatment, and so on)
  - that decisions about things such as recruitment, promotion, training and redundancy are made in relation to job requirements (and other fair and objective criteria) and are in no way discriminatory
  - that channels are available for employees to raise their concerns if they feel they have been treated unfairly
  - that equal opportunity training is delivered to all employees, especially those in management positions.

- *Diversity*: HR professionals should:
  - monitor levels of diversity in the workplace and take action to promote the interests of under-represented groups (via targeted recruitment campaigns, targeted training and development activities, and so on)
  - provide training for all management staff on the importance of diversity at work, including the business case.

- *Dignity at work*: HR professionals should ensure:
  - that there is a clear policy relating to dignity at work – that the policy is clearly communicated to all employees at the time of induction
  - that training is provided for all employees on the importance of respect and dignity at work
  - that channels are available for employees to raise their concerns if they feel they have been the victim of bullying or harassment at work
  - that full investigations take place in relation to allegations of bullying or harassment and that appropriate action is taken if allegations are proven.

- *Work–life balance*: HR professionals should:
  - ensure that the company is meeting legal expectations in the field of work–life balance; this includes monitoring compliance with the Working Time Directive and clearly communicating employee rights
  - champion the importance of work–life balance to senior management and try to secure funding for work–life balance provisions
  - consider the usefulness (versus costs) of different work–life balance provisions

○ develop suitable work–life balance policies and provisions
○ communicate the importance of work–life balance to all line management staff and provide training in the various policies and provisions available
○ be prepared to coach on personal work–life balance with some management staff. If senior staff work extremely long hours, they might be communicating an expectation of this to junior employees, the result of which can be a long-hours culture. Managers should be encouraged to change – both for their own well-being and for that of those they manage
○ communicate work–life balance provisions to all employees
○ monitor the take-up of work–life balance provisions and evaluate their effectiveness.

● *Health and well-being*: HR professionals should:

○ champion the importance of employee health and well-being to senior management and try to secure funding for provisions
○ develop a policy around health and well-being at work
○ ensure that all line management staff receive training on monitoring the health and well-being of their staff, and on providing the first level of support if team members have problems (with things such as stress, for example)
○ consider the usefulness (versus costs) of different health and well-being provisions
○ communicate the selected health and well-being provisions to all managers and employees.

2.6.4 THE SIGNIFICANCE OF LEGAL COMPLIANCE

It is essential that HR practitioners comply with employment legislation. At times, it is possible that the requests of senior management (based on operational concerns) may contradict the stipulations of employment law, which can put HR professionals in a difficult position. For example, management may try to dismiss an employee on the grounds of capability, when the real reason is that they don't like the individual or they want to avoid having to pay a redundancy settlement. In such situations, it is essential that professional integrity and legal obligations are adhered to. The HR professional should argue the business case for compliance and ensure that senior managers are aware that lawful remedies are more beneficial to the company in the long run (avoiding tribunal costs, ensuring that the reputation of the company is not damaged).

Having said this, it is important to be aware that legal compliance simply stipulates the minimum standards in terms of ethical behaviour towards employees. Some would argue that 'the rules of the ethics game' are set by legislators in the EU, Parliament and the courts – meaning that organisations and individuals do not have to ask themselves any further questions about the ethics of their actions if they are within the bounds of the law.

We would argue that this position could only really be sanctioned if the law were more robust – covering all issues and protecting all individuals. In the case of employment law, for example, there are several weak points, and employee protection from unfair treatment by their employers is only achieved in a patchy way – people can be disadvantaged due to their contract type, their length of service, their age (National Minimum Wage), the norms of their industry (Working Time Regulations exclusions), and so on.

Legal compliance is thus about meeting the minimum standards set by external bodies, whereas truly ethical business requires a proactive, internally driven approach that seeks to continually work towards fairness for all.

2.7 HR AND ORGANISATIONAL PERFORMANCE

Over the last 15 years or so, there has been a lot of research interest in the HR–performance link – that is, the relationship between HR policies and practices and the overall performance of the organisation. Furthermore, the findings of much research have been positive – that organisations with certain combinations of HR policies and practices do indeed perform well.

It is important to be aware, however, that there are serious gaps in our understanding. For a start, the direction of causation is unclear – is it that a certain combination of HR practices are improving organisational performance, or is it simply that high-performing companies tend to invest in HR more and implement a range of policies?

Another issue to consider is the wide range of perspectives on which specific combinations of policies and practices are seen to constitute the 'magic HR formula' for organisational success. Dominant theories include 'best practice', 'best fit' or contingency theory, and the resource-based view.

The 'best practice' approach suggests that there is a set of HR practices that will create high performance in an organisation no matter what the context. The main underlying principle is that HR practices should be aimed at improving the commitment of workers – thus alternative names have been developed for this approach over time, including 'high-commitment' work systems or 'high-involvement' HRM. The idea is that a committed and involved employee is more likely to give 'discretionary effort' – going above and beyond the basic requirements of their role because they like their job and care about the success of the company.

Kew and Stredwick (2010, pp413–16) highlight the following ten 'best practices' as being linked to high levels of employee commitment:

- flexibility/teamworking: cultivating employees who are willing to undertake a range of tasks, irrespective of job title, in order to meet customer requirements. This is further emphasised through teamworking
- employee involvement
- employee voice
- performance-related reward: this includes other aspects of the total reward package and is not restricted to pay alone
- employee ownership: giving employees the chance to own shares in the company – so that employee and owner interests are aligned
- sophisticated selection
- internal promotion: showing employees that there are opportunities for advancement, provided they possess the ability and commitment
- employment security: showing that employees really are seen as the company's most important resource
- commitment to learning
- harmonisation: developing a culture that aims to remove unnecessary status differences.

Key research in the 'best practice HRM' field has been conducted by John Purcell and his colleagues at the Work and Employment Research Centre at the University of Bath. Central to the 'Bath Model of People and Performance' is ability, motivation and opportunity (AMO). The assertion is that for employees, individually and collectively, to engage in the sort of discretionary behaviour that is beneficial to the firm, the three conditions of AMO must apply:

- There must be enough employees with the necessary *ability* (skills, experience, knowledge) to do current, and perhaps future, jobs.
- There must be adequate *motivation* for them to apply their abilities. These motivation factors may be financial but will almost certainly include social rewards and recognition of employee contribution.

- There must be an *opportunity* for employees to engage in discretionary behaviour. This should be within the individual's specific job; as a member of a team or work area; and as a 'citizen' of the whole organisation.

The **'best fit' approach**, also known as the contingency model, argues that there is no one model of HR strategy which will suit all circumstances and that organisations should seek the specific mix of HR practices that are appropriate to their specific context. This does not mean that there will not be common practices amongst companies – just as a company will tend to pursue one of a limited number of competitive strategies, they will tend to find that one of a limited number of HR policy configurations will be suitable.

The **resource-based view** turns traditional approaches on their head. Rather than seeking to identify an optimum set of HR practices and policies and use them to source and shape employees, the approach starts with the current 'human capital resources' (experience, skills, judgement and intelligence of managers and employees) of the company, and then develops policies and procedures around them – to make the most of what you already have. The belief here is that competitive advantage can be gained not only by acquiring resources, but also by developing, combining and effectively deploying existing resources in a way that adds unique value and is difficult for other companies to imitate.

 RESTRUCTURING HR

CASE STUDY 2.1

You are the newly appointed HR director for a national hotel chain that currently employs an HR team of 24 people – one stand-alone HR generalist in each of the chain's hotels. This HR structure has been in place for many years. The chain started in 1980 with only four properties in the north-west, and while each hotel had its own HR manager, they would contact each other frequently and write all policies and procedures together. In the last 30 years, the chain has expanded rapidly, via the acquisition of small independent hotels throughout the UK. Each time a hotel was taken over, the existing workforce were all offered continued employment, and where no HR provision was in place, a generalist HR manager was appointed from the local area. You have been appointed because the managing director is concerned that there is no consistency to the HR provision in the company: each hotel seems to operate different HR practices and procedures; the HR managers appear to have different levels of ability in different areas of the function; and there

is virtually no lateral communication between members of the HR team. The managing director has informed you that the next board meeting will take place in three months, at which he would like you to make a presentation outlining suggestions for the function moving forward.

Questions

1 What would you need to do before writing the proposal?

2 You finally decide to suggest a model that includes a shared service centre and regional business partners with different specialisms (recruitment; development; reward; and employee relations). What would you need to include in the proposal to the board?

3 What are the advantages and disadvantages of such a transition?

FURTHER READING

CIPD (2012) *Information pages* [online]. Information pages are available on the website which provide factsheets, podcasts and survey reports on each of the following topics:

HR function: www.cipd.co.uk/hr-topics/hr-function.aspx

Change management: www.cipd.co.uk/hr-topics/change-management.aspx

Business partnering: www.cipd.co.uk/hr-topics/business-partnering.aspx

HR trends: www.cipd.co.uk/hr-topics/hr-trends.aspx

CIPD *HR Outlook* survey report series: quarterly reports based on the findings of large-scale surveys of UK HR practitioners – providing detailed commentary on the HR profession and emerging trends in HR activity.

REFERENCES

CIPD (2005) *Managing change: the role of the psychological contract*. London: Chartered Institute of Personnel and Development.

CIPD (2007) *The changing HR function*. Survey report. London: Chartered Institute of Personnel and Development.

CIPD (2010) *Next generation HR*. London: Chartered Institute of Personnel and Development.

CIPD (2011) *Change management*. Factsheet. London: Chartered Institute of Personnel and Development.

CIPD (2015) *From best to good practice. HR: developing principles for the profession*. London: Chartered Institute of Personnel and Development.

COPE, N. (2003) *The seven Cs of consulting*. 2nd ed. London: Prentice Hall.

GUEST, D. E. and CONWAY, N. (2001) *Public and private sector perceptions on the psychological contract*. London: CIPD.

HM TREASURY (2015) *Fixing the foundations: creating a more prosperous nation*. London: HMSO.

HOFSTEDE, G. (1991) *Cultures and organisations: software of the mind*. London: McGraw-Hill.

KEW, J. and STREDWICK, J. (2010) *Human resource management in a business context*. London: Chartered Institute of Personnel and Development.

SCHWARTZ, M. (2001) The nature of the relationship between corporate codes of ethics and behavior. *Journal of Business Ethics*. Vol 32, No 3. pp247–62.

TAYLOR, S. (2011) *Contemporary issues in HRM*. London: Chartered Institute of Personnel and Development.

CHAPTER 3

Business Issues and the Contexts of Human Resources

STEPHEN TAYLOR AND KRYSTAL WILKINSON

CHAPTER CONTENTS

- HRM in the different sectors
- Developments in the external environment
- Forming organisational and HR strategies

KEY LEARNING OUTCOMES

By the end of this chapter, you should be able to:

- understand key contemporary business issues affecting the HR function within private, public and third sector organisations
- understand the main external contextual factors impacting on organisations and the HR function
- understand the role of HR in the managing of contemporary business issues and external contexts
- understand how organisational and HR strategies are shaped and developed
- know how to identify and respond to short-term changes in the business and external contexts.

3.1 HRM IN THE DIFFERENT SECTORS

While there are some areas of HR practice that are carried out in a similar way across all types of organisation and plenty that HR managers operating in different sectors can learn from one another, it is important to recognise that there are also always going to be significant differences. Business objectives vary considerably, as do current business agendas and strategies. Different organisations also face a huge variety of diverse commercial and regulatory pressures. Some are in the position of being able to plan ten or twenty years ahead with considerable confidence that their plans will come to fruition. Others, due primarily to the volatility of their environments, cannot realistically plan in a detailed way more than a year or two ahead. There is an obvious knock-on effect for HRM, which has to take on a character that is appropriate for the particular context in which it is obliged to operate. Gaining an understanding of how organisations differ in terms of their objectives and the particular contexts in which they operate is therefore fundamental to the effective study of HRM.

A good place to start is by looking at the broad sectors that organisations form a part of. In fact, almost all belong to one of the three major economic sectors: the private sector, the public sector and the voluntary (or third) sector. There are, however, some organisations which cross the boundaries, being, for example, **private–public partnerships**.

3.1.1 THE PRIVATE SECTOR

The private sector is made up of businesses which are owned by private individuals or families, by other organisations or by large numbers of individual and institutional shareholders, including, sometimes, employee shareholders. Most are commercial in nature and aim to make profits for their owners. However, there are also not-for-profit organisations that operate as social enterprises.

Regulation

Legally, private sector organisations take one of three distinct forms: sole traders, partnerships or companies. In terms of their ownership, sole traders are one-man or one-woman organisations, but this does not mean that they can't employ people as well. They are not required to register with any authorities and are regulated fairly lightly. The downside of being a sole trader is that as an owner you are the business, so you are personally liable to an unlimited extent for all debts and can become bankrupt if your business gets into a great deal of debt.

This means that a failure by a customer to pay you can have serious personal financial consequences – like the loss of your house.

Partnerships are firms owned and run by two or more people who have entered a joint partnership. As far as the law is concerned they are not companies, even though many call themselves companies or have '& Co.' in their titles. Legally they are 'unincorporated associations'. As with sole trading arrangements, regulation is light. There is no requirement to register and no requirement to produce audited accounts. Individual partners are agents of the firm and can enter into contracts on its behalf with other parties. When a partnership becomes insolvent, all partners are 'jointly and severally' liable to an unlimited level for the payment of debts. Professional services firms (accountants, solicitors, stockbrokers, and so on) are able to have as many partners as they like, but other types of business are generally restricted to a maximum of 20 partners.

Since 2001 it has been possible for traditional partnerships to become limited-liability partnerships. In practice, this means that they take on the rights and responsibilities of limited companies and are governed by company law, even though technically they remain partnerships rather than companies.

Companies, like partnerships, must have at least two members (that is, shareholders), but there is no limit on how many they can have. They are subject to a great deal more regulation than partnerships and sole trading organisations, but they also have important privileges. Of these, by far the most important is 'limited liability'. Essentially this means that the company is itself a legal personality separate from the people who own and run it. They may leave or die or become personally bankrupt, but the company continues trading indefinitely.

This means that a company can borrow money and can be taken to court as an entity separate from those who control it. It also means that if the company becomes insolvent, it can be liquidated without its owners being legally responsible for any of the debts. Liability is limited to the value of the shares owned (that is, to the extent that any individual or institution has invested in the company). Importantly, this is true even if a company is essentially controlled by a single person (that is, if there are 1,000 shares and 999 are owned by the chairman/managing director).

UK companies must register as in 'England and Wales' or in Wales or in Scotland or in Northern Ireland. All formal records and documents of companies registered in 'England and Wales' or in Wales are handled at Companies House in Cardiff to which companies must complete an annual return. They must also present their annual reports and accounts to Companies House, where they are publicly available for inspection. They must hold annual general meetings at which directors present reports to members (that is, shareholders). The letters 'Ltd' in a company name indicate a privately owned concern, 'PLC' indicates a company whose shares are traded on the open market. If it wishes, a private company can apply to be listed on the Stock Exchange, in which case it can issue shares and raise capital by selling them on the open market. It then becomes a publicly limited company (PLC). The larger PLCs are not controlled by any one individual or family, or even by a group of partners. Instead, their shares are traded and can be bought and sold by anyone. In practice, the big majority of the shares in such companies are owned by institutional shareholders such as pension funds, investment funds and insurance companies.

In Scotland, the equivalent of Companies House in Cardiff is located in Edinburgh. Registration and administration of companies in Scotland is under the jurisdiction of Scots law.

The Northern Ireland administrative equivalent is in Belfast but is effectively a satellite office of Companies House in Cardiff.

HRM in the private sector

PLCs almost always employ teams of HR specialists to carry out much of their people management work. A substantial HR division or department will exist, headed by a senior director who will often report directly to the chief executive.

Companies vary in terms of how powerful their HR directors and HR functions are, but the trend is towards the functions assuming a higher profile. In recent years HR in large PLCs has become increasingly strategic in its orientation, focused on longer-term decision-making and proactively supporting the achievement of key business objectives. Administrative HR work has tended to be delegated to line mangers, outsourced or centralised in shared-service arrangements. The same trends can be observed in larger partnerships, but here they tend to be less well advanced. The bigger law firms, for example, have started to set up discrete HR functions in recent years. But HR managers report to senior partners and often struggle to develop cutting-edge HR strategies of the kind we associate with publicly limited companies.

Smaller private companies, partnerships and sole trading organisations do not in the main have sizeable HR functions. They may employ an HR specialist or two to carry out basic HR tasks (recruitment, payroll, training, and so on), but they do not generally have sufficient numbers of employees to justify the presence of a sophisticated, strategically focused HR department. Such organisations invariably rely on outside help when managing HRM matters. Many nowadays pay for advice from employment law consultancies and outsource their payroll function. They often make extensive use of recruitment consultants and buy in required training as and when they need it. HR managers in smaller organisations thus tend to be generalists, taking responsibility for the full range of standard HR activities we described in Chapter 1 and, often, many other management tasks too.

In most smaller firms there remains a preference for informality in the way that managers deal with staff (Edwards and Ram 2010). Features of HR practice that are almost standard in larger companies – such as performance appraisal, clear disciplinary procedures, standardised induction programmes, pay spines, pension schemes and written policies on employment matters – are often absent or undeveloped in smaller firms. There are advantages and disadvantages arising from informality. On the positive side, it allows the retention of a family atmosphere which is conducive to effective teamworking and high levels of job satisfaction. Flexible working is also the norm in an informal employment setting, as is open communication between managers and employees. On the negative side, informality can easily lead to perceptions of unfairness and undue favouritism arising. The absence of clear policies which are generally applied means that 'one rule' does not apply to all. The result is demotivation and reduced job satisfaction.

Larger private sector companies, particularly those operating in the **knowledge economy**, have pioneered most of the new approaches to the management of people that have proved influential in recent years. These have tended to focus on delayering management hierarchies and empowering employees, the aim being to benefit from positive engagement, a willingness to share ideas and the extra effort that can result when a sustained and genuine attempt is made to involve and inspire people.

Another major recent trend in the private sector has been a reduced role for trade unions and for **collective bargaining** as the major means of determining pay and conditions. Trade unions remain a significant presence in transport, mining, energy production, construction and in car manufacturing, but across most of the private sector their role is nowadays, at best, marginal. The most recent **Workplace Employment Relations Survey (WERS)** (conducted in 2011) reported that only 6% of private sector workplaces use collective bargaining to determine rates of pay, while 49% of UK workplaces employing more than 25 people have no union members at all, which means a good majority of private sector organisations (Van Wanrooy et al 2013). This trend has allowed the HR function to revolutionise itself in many organisations. Whereas 40 years ago most large companies participated in national-level collective bargaining exercises which set the same terms and conditions for all employees across an industry, it is now more common for pay determination to be individualised. Pay rises are conditional on effective personal performance, other conditions of employment being set by managers without the need for union negotiations. As a result, companies have been able to develop their own distinct HR strategies and to develop 'employee value propositions' (EVPs) which are deliberately distinct from those of their major competitors. The result is considerable competition between employers to attract and retain the best performers. Moreover, as unions have withered away, HR managers have had to find new ways of establishing what employees are really thinking about their employer. We have thus seen much more use of staff survey tools and of upward and downward communication exercises of various kinds.

3.1.2 THE PUBLIC SECTOR

The major types of public sector organisation are:

- central government departments
- local and regional government organisations
- public service providers
- QUANGOs (quasi-autonomous non-governmental organisations)
- publicly owned corporations.

These are largely if not wholly funded by the taxpayer. They are also subject to a degree of public accountability, being managed either directly or indirectly by elected officials such as ministers, or the majority group on a local council.

In the case of public corporations and some **QUANGOs**, ministers have no direct day-to-day responsibility for their management. Around 20% of the UK's workforce is employed in public sector organisations.

There used to be large numbers of public corporations in the UK, but they have almost all now been privatised and have thus become PLCs. However, public corporations remain a major feature of the commercial landscape in many countries. In the UK there are currently three major public corporations: the BBC, the Royal Mail and Network Rail. A fourth, the Bank of England, is technically a publicly owned corporation. In practice, however, despite the extent of its independence, it has become an integral part of government.

In recent years governments have sought to encourage public service providers to organise themselves according to commercial principles, not only having to meet government targets, but also having to compete for business with other organisations in 'internal markets' and sometimes 'external markets' too.

Public sector organisations tend to have large HR functions which carry considerable managerial clout. HR directors are prominent and influential members of most senior executive boards, enabling them to insist that good HR practice is followed, particularly in respect of legal compliance. HR divisions carry out a wide range of tasks, specialists often being employed to work alongside generalists and to head up recruitment, employment relations, reward management and HRD departments. In recent years, as in larger private sector organisations, moves have been made to make HR more business-focused, more strategic in its activities and less cautious in its approach. But older styles still survive and thrive in many places. As a result, HR practice in the public sector is often criticised by other functions for being a touch old-fashioned, overly bureaucratic in its approach and limited in terms of the value that it adds.

In recent years the major pressures faced by HR managers working in the public sector have derived from the recent recession and the subsequent need to reduce public spending in order to reduce the government's financial deficit.

This has led to recruitment freezes, extensive reorganisations and to many thousands of redundancies. The HR function is not generally classed by ministers as providing any kind of 'front-line service' and so has been a major target for savings itself. In the process a lot of 'fat' has had to be cut, which has resulted in less bureaucracy, more use of outsourcing arrangements and slimmer HR departments.

There are a number of features which differentiate HRM in public sector organisations from that which prevails across most of the private sector. First, as Bach (2010, p563) points out, employment decisions are 'subject to levels of public accountability and transparency that arise from the government's role as a custodian of public funds'. This inevitably means that a reasonably high standard of management practice has to be observed. People have to be treated with respect and fairness. This tends to be achieved by having in place quite detailed written policies that have to be followed by everyone without exception.

There is thus less room for spontaneity in people management than is the case in the private sector and much less opportunity for 'maverick' managers to develop innovative approaches that differ from the norm. HR managers in the public sector tend to be keener than their private sector counterparts to avoid employment tribunal proceedings and are not in a position simply to pay people off with lump sums in order to ensure that cases are not lodged. The result is a tendency towards bureaucracy and much less freedom of manoeuvre for line managers in terms of how they go about leading their teams.

Another distinguishing feature of HRM in the public sector is the continued presence of trade unions. Membership levels vary greatly, but there has not been anything like the decline that has characterised the experience of private companies and PLCs in recent years and the 2011 Workplace Employment Relations Survey found that 57% of public sector employees are members of a trade union (Van Wanrooy et al 2013). Despite attempts by successive governments to introduce performance-related pay and **decentralised bargaining** arrangements, national pay scales still survive across many of the public services. The amount each person is paid thus owes much more to how their job is graded than it does to their individual performance in that job. This means that managers have fewer levers to use in order to motivate their staff and hence exercise less control. If someone is not suitable for promotion, little can be done to motivate them extrinsically. Pay scales are also transparent, everyone effectively knowing what all their colleagues at all levels are paid in relation to them. Trade unions also have the right to be consulted on employment-related matters and can be intransigent in their dealings with managers. Low-trust employment relations climates thus often prevail, which tends to make HR managers rather more cautious in their approach than is the case in many private sector organisations.

3.1.3 THE THIRD SECTOR

This comprises organisations that do not fit either into the public sector or private sector categories. They are either:

- co-operatives
- campaigning organisations or pressure groups
- charities
- controlled by boards of trustees and are subject to the law of trust
  or
- are chartered bodies such as universities and professional bodies.

These organisations are run on a not-for-profit basis and are neither subject to direct government control nor to company law. In some countries the terms 'community sector' and 'civic sector' are more commonly used to describe the third sector.

HR varies vastly across the third sector organisations. In some it is well resourced and operates very much as it does in a large PLC or public sector organisation. Resources, however, are often a problem, particularly in charities and in smaller campaigning organisations. Here HR tends to have quite a peripheral role, is not represented on the senior management team and carries out what are essentially basic, administrative activities. HR practices therefore tend to lack sophistication and there is little opportunity for HR managers to add significant strategic value.

Developing a more sophisticated, commercially minded approach to HR has thus tended to preoccupy senior HR people working in the third sector in recent years.

Kelliher and Parry (2011), drawing on analysis of the data on voluntary organisations collected for the 2004 Workplace Employment Relations Survey, conclude that there have been major attempts in recent years to professionalise HRM in the sector and that these have had considerable success. In particular they found evidence of increased use of formal performance management mechanisms, employee welfare programmes, written policies of various kinds and employee involvement initiatives. Interestingly they conclude that the model the voluntary bodies tend to imitate is closer to that of the public sector than to the private sector's commercially oriented alternative. This, they think, is because government, and particularly local government, exercises a growing and profound influence over the third sector. Voluntary organisations are increasingly involved in contracting for services that are either wholly or partially publicly funded. They do not secure these contracts unless they are able to satisfy public bodies that they operate the same high standards of HRM practice. James (2011) agrees with this analysis, but argues that reductions in available resources in more recent years are forcing voluntary sector organisations to downgrade HRM standards again, reducing pay and conditions in order to secure public contracts.

? REFLECTIVE ACTIVITY 3.1

The 2015 CIPD survey on absence management reported that the average number of days of absence in the UK is 8.3 per employee, a figure that has come down somewhat in recent years. There remain, however, big differences between organisations. In smaller private sector companies, rates of 3 or 4 days a year are achieved, while in the bigger public sector organisations it is common for average absence figures to be in excess of 10 days per employee over the course of a year.

1   What factors do you think might explain why overall absence levels in the UK have fallen in the last four or five years?

2   Why do you think that absence rates in public sector organisations are typically so much higher than those in private sector companies?

3.2 DEVELOPMENTS IN THE EXTERNAL ENVIRONMENT

Just as HR practice tends to vary from sector to sector, it also necessarily has to change in response to major developments in the external business environment. As these affect some organisations more than others and in different ways, the impact on HR is also varied.

The external environment is huge in its scope and complex. It covers developments in the worlds of politics, economics and technology at national, international and local level. It also encompasses major trends in social attitudes and behaviour, population and in government regulation. In one short chapter it is not possible to deal with all of these issues. So we have to be selective and focus on those trends which are having, in combination, the biggest impact on contemporary HR practice. Two which stand out can loosely be defined as relating to 'developments in product markets' and 'developments in labour markets'.

3.2.1 KEY CONTEMPORARY DEVELOPMENTS IN PRODUCT MARKETS

In recent years we have seen very profound changes occurring in the operation of markets for goods and services. The net result has been a very substantial increase in the extent to which pretty well all organisations in countries such as the UK are obliged to compete with others. In some industries, such as financial services and technology, competition has become particularly intense.

Some economists now describe the position in some industries as being 'hypercompetitive' in that no single organisation, however large, is able to hold on to a position of competitive advantage for long (McNamara et al 2003).

Measuring competitive intensity in any precise, objective way is impossible because the characteristics of each industry vary so much. But all the proxy indices which are typically used, such as reductions in the length of time leading firms are able to maintain dominance of a market, increases in the extent of churn in 'industry membership' and increases in the incidence of financial instability in an industry, have all been accelerating in recent years. Moreover, interview-based studies which draw on the reflections of people who have spent their careers in particular industries also suggest much increased competition and, more importantly, the likelihood of greater competitive intensity in the future. Some industries have been much more affected than others, but everywhere, including in the public services, competition between providers has been increasing and accelerating in terms of its intensity over the past three or four decades.

The major causes of increased competitive intensity have been widely studied. Here are three that are particularly important, none of which shows any signs of moving in a different direction – globalisation, technology and government policy.

Globalisation

Since the end of the Second World War we have seen a steady growth in the extent to which goods and services are traded internationally and to which national economies have integrated across the world. Dicken (2015) explains that during the second half of the twentieth century, while total world output (that is, the value of goods and services produced and consumed) increased sixfold, the volume of world trade increased twentyfold. Moreover, the trend has accelerated considerably in the past two decades, with the rise of China as a major exporter, industrial development in agricultural economies throughout Asia, Africa and South America, and the reintegration of the Eastern European countries into the world economy.

The impact on competitive intensity has been huge and very rapid. Companies that previously dominated national markets have found themselves within a few short years simply to be small fry in much bigger international markets.

Some UK-based companies have responded by cutting costs dramatically and by outsourcing much of their work to overseas countries where labour costs are lower. Others have abandoned low-cost, lower value-added activities altogether, focusing instead on hi-tech, cutting-edge industrial activities. A third group have either gone under altogether or have survived by merging, being taken over or forming strategic alliances with overseas competitors.

Every major sector has been affected, most profoundly. In the UK some formerly dominant industries are now mere shadows of their former selves, if they exist at all. Shipbuilding, mining and textile manufacturing are all examples.

Labour costs in the UK are simply too high to withstand competition from the developing world. Other traditional industries have survived, but only by embracing new technology and integrating themselves internationally. The car and steel industries are good examples, as is food production. These industries now employ far fewer people than they used to, but are much more productive. Moreover, those who remain employed in them work for overseas-based corporations such as Toyota, Tata and Kraft.

In the UK **globalisation** has brought with it massive industrial restructuring, which is still very much in the process of transforming the industrial landscape. No longer able to earn our living in the world as a manufacturing powerhouse (as was the case for most of our recent history), like other highly developed economies, we have had to develop our service sector very quickly in order to compete effectively. Despite its recent difficulties, the UK's financial services sector remains pre-eminent in Europe, London being one of the world's three great financial centres. It is three and a half times bigger than Frankfurt and four and a half times bigger than Paris in terms of the amount of business it transacts. In terms of international business (as opposed to domestic business), London is by far the major financial centre in the world. The UK financial services sector is thus a major exporter – earning the country about £20 billion a year in foreign currency. It accounts for between 5% and 10% of national GDP. Alongside financial services we have seen rapid growth in business services (consultancy, accountancy, and so on), cultural industries (film, TV, theatre, publishing, computer gaming), in higher education and tourism – all of which are major UK exporters operating very competitively in global markets. At the same time we have seen substantial growth in retailing, hotels and restaurants, leisure services of all kinds (gyms, hairdressers, and so on) and media-related industries of all kinds.

Technology

The advent of new technology is both a major cause of increased globalisation and a driver of increased competitive intensity in its own right. The rapid growth in international trade we discussed above was largely made possible by developments in transportation and in ICTs (information and communication technologies). Put crudely, these twin developments now mean that a consumer in the UK can purchase a product manufactured anywhere in the world with terrific ease and can have that product shipped to their home or office within a few weeks. The World Wide Web, broadband technology and the advent in more recent years of tablets and smartphones in particular have created a situation in which anyone with the resources to do so can buy any goods or services from anyone else across the planet. They can also now communicate face to face very cheaply indeed using Skype and will soon be able to do so with pretty well anyone thanks to the development of simultaneous translation technologies. Modern container ships circumnavigate the world in eight weeks or so, connecting production lines in China with European and American shopping malls in less than a month. The volume of goods shipped across the world by air (in a few hours) has also grown hugely in the last 20 years as costs have plummeted. The competitive landscape thus continues to be utterly transformed by technology.

Technology drives competition in other ways too – mainly by increasing productivity levels all the time. Organisations which fail to adopt new technologies soon enough find that their cost bases are simply too high to allow them to compete effectively. So there is a big premium now placed on research and development (R&D), organisations being obliged to stay ahead of the technological game just in order to survive. Technologies rapidly become obsolete, rendering companies that rely too heavily on them unproductive and uncompetitive vis-à-vis others.

It is not just a question of productivity, though. Sudden breakthroughs in technology can destroy whole industries, transform them and create new ones very rapidly. At the present time we are witnessing the rapid development of industries in the **biotechnology** sector, for example, creating new medical procedures which are increasing average life expectancy across the world, developing new sources of energy (for example solar panels, biofuels) and increasing agricultural production through genetic modification of seeds and of livestock.

The impact on the competitive environment of all of these developments and of others in **nanotechnology** looks as if it will be as great over the next 50 years as it has been in the last 50. The impact may in fact be considerably greater, particularly in the world of work where many current jobs are likely to be replaced by machines.

Government action

The third major driver of increased competitive intensity in recent decades has been government. As with technology, governments have acted in order to promote globalisation in order to boost international economic development.

It has often been a rocky road, steps backwards occurring alongside steps forward. But the overall trend internationally over the past 20 or 30 years has unquestionably been towards the active promotion of global economic exchange. This has been achieved by a mixture of regulation and deregulation. Of particular importance has been the relaxation and, in many countries, the total abolition of foreign exchange controls. It seems strange now to reflect that 40 years ago people were heavily restricted in the amount of currency they could legally take out of the UK to spend overseas (£60 in the 1960s). Overseas trade was vastly limited as a result, as was tourism. The position has now utterly changed. The USA abandoned restrictions altogether, followed by the UK in 1979. Since then the same has occurred in most countries: 150 now have no meaningful controls. They still remain in major economies such as China and India, but in both cases it is now a question of when it would be most prudent to remove them rather than if.

At the same time, through the auspices of the **World Trade Organization (WTO)**, governments have negotiated major reductions in import tariffs, while customs unions such as the European Union have developed, allowing free movement of capital, goods, services and people across national boundaries. In each case the result has been to foster much greater international competition.

Some industries that were until recently very heavily regulated are now subject to hardly any regulation, transforming their competitive environment. Nowhere is this more true than in the airline industry, which used to be subject to heavy government control. Until the 1990s government officials used to allocate routes to airlines across Europe, a practice that continued until 2008 as far as transatlantic routes were concerned. National flag-carrying airlines (British Airways, Lufthansa, Air France, and so on) were owned and operated by governments and took all the most profitable routes, leaving only the less profitable 'pickings' for a small independent sector to mop up. Open skies policies are now proliferating across the world. Government has withdrawn, permitting airlines to compete with one another to fly routes that are agreed with the airports without ministerial interference. The volume of air traffic has increased massively as a result, the competitive structure of the industry being transformed with the rise of low-cost carriers such as easyJet and Ryanair, which are now as big as many of the national carriers.

Another major deregulatory step of great significance has been the move towards **privatisation** of state-run industries. The UK pioneered this approach in the 1980s when the Thatcher Government privatised most state-run corporations, including British Telecom, British Steel, British Airways, British Gas, the train and bus companies, the electricity and water generators, the mines, the car manufacturers, the airports and a host of smaller concerns. Wherever possible, privatisation was accompanied by the breaking up of corporations into separate parts that were thenceforth obliged to compete with one another in free markets.

Subsequent governments continued to privatise where they could, also seeking to engineer commercial discipline in the public services. Internal markets were created in the health and education sectors, competitive tendering being introduced in many areas so that private concerns (companies and charities) competed with one another for contracts to provide public services. All over the world governments have been taking a similar approach in recent years, privatising state assets, creating markets and generally pursuing an agenda of 'competition and choice'.

It is important to remember, though, that regulation has played an important part in this process alongside deregulation. Globalisation has been promoted in large part by establishing standardised approaches through international conventions. Hence we now see the same standard size of containers shipped around the world and lifted onto the back of lorries and trains for distribution.

Customs documentation and biometric passports have now been standardised internationally, along with accountancy conventions. Copyright is increasingly well protected by international law, as are patents and property rights. Within the European Union extensive regulation is seen as a necessary prerequisite for free trade between member states. It ensures 'a level playing field' (that is, fair competition) and means, for example, that extensive employment law has been passed and can be enforced at the European level.

3.2.2 COMPETITIVE INTENSITY AND HRM

Increased competitive intensity and, particularly, increased global competition have necessitated a transformation of management thinking in organisations – a revolution that we are still very much in the middle of. HRM has had to change in response and continues to do so. The impact has been greatest in industrial sectors, which have felt the full force of technological change and globalisation, but there are few parts of the public sector that have been untouched. Even the armed services, the prison service and the police are now obliged to contract out parts of their operations. In addition, of course, they like all the rest of the public sector have to become a great deal more productive in order to help meet the government's deficit reduction plans.

So what does all of this mean for HRM practice? A number of major points can be made. First, and most significantly, increased competitive intensity brings with it uncertainty and unpredictability. This means that organisations cannot plan ahead with any great certainty beyond three or four years, in some cases less. Whereas in the past it made sense to develop strategic plans that focused ten or twenty years ahead, this is less and less possible. The volatility of markets has rendered this sort of approach much less plausible.

The knock-on effect on HRM is profound because uncertainty in product markets has necessarily meant that organisations are less able than they once were to offer long-term, stable employment to anyone. Even where this is possible, contracts need to be written in such a way as to allow for considerable flexibility.

We may still remain employed with the same organisations for many years, but increasingly our roles change regularly as a result of internal reorganisations and we are obliged to retrain and embrace new approaches regularly. In short, organisations have had to become a great deal more agile. They regularly have to morph as a result of exercises in downsizing, upsizing, outsourcing, offshoring and mergers and acquisitions. Companies become part of a big international group, then get reorganised and sold on. Management buyouts occur, while contracts are won and lost, resulting in parts of an organisation growing while others are shrinking.

As far as HRM is concerned, a key implication is a need to be actively and much more frequently involved in change management than used to be the case. All the research on the effective management of organisational change (cultural and structural) demonstrates clearly that success or failure depends in large extent on how effectively the 'people aspects' are managed. This requires active involvement by HR people, including at the most senior levels, in the planning and communication of change. This has required HR people to acquire more political skills, because change is very often a deeply political process. There are winners and there are losers, there are perceived winners and losers and there are people who, while not hugely affected personally, are allies of perceived winners and losers.

Change also therefore tends to breed conflict. Managing these matters is very difficult. It involves sensitivity in terms of management style, combined with a hard-headed appreciation of commercial realities. Moreover, there is a need to have in place policies and practices which allow an organisation to become increasingly agile and able to respond more rapidly than its competitors can to changed circumstances in the business environment. This tends to mean less bureaucracy and much more flexibility. Administrative convenience is less and less possible to use as a reason for not changing rapidly when it is necessary to do so. HR also needs actively to build a culture which embraces change and expects it. Central here is the development of a generation of leaders who are emotionally intelligent, politically savvy, flexible, good at communication of all kinds and very well informed about wider developments in the business environment.

Flexibility has also become central to HRM practice. People are increasingly employed on non-standard or atypical contracts. We employ many more people on a short-term basis, for example, to avoid a need to make people redundant during periods of change. We also employ more people on a part-time basis but without fixed hours, so that they can be deployed flexibly as required. There is more sub-contracting, more employment of self-employed professionals, much more employment of agency workers and more use of annual hours and zero hours (that is, casual contracts). This marks a very significant change in HRM, which has traditionally focused on employing people on traditional, permanent, full-time contracts with an intention of forging a long-term relationship with them. Atypical contracting makes people management much harder to achieve effectively simply because there is no expectation of a long-term, stable relationship. Promising pay rises and future promotions as a means of exercising management control becomes less plausible, as does securing employee commitment generally. How can we say to people 'We want you to work really hard and demonstrate great commitment to us' if at the same time we as managers are less and less able to show commitment to our staff?

Secondly, increased competitive intensity inevitably leads to greater work intensity. It is only possible to compete effectively internationally if we match and beat the levels of productivity that our competitors are able to achieve. This means that we are continually obliged to look for ways of 'achieving more with less' and, in short, extracting greater effort from our people at minimal cost. Technology plays a big part here, but it is also increasingly a matter simply of finding ways of encouraging people to work harder without paying them more.

This can be done using harsh management techniques, such as threatening people with the sack if they do not increase their work rates. HRM, however, is increasingly associated with the development of more sophisticated approaches to the management of performance which try to intensify work in a more positive manner, extracting greater effort from staff in ways which benefit them as well as the organisation. You will be reading about all of these later in this book as well as in other books in the series, so it is only necessary to summarise here. Major examples are the evolution of 'high commitment working practices', performance-related and profit-related pay, accelerated management development programmes, employer branding, employability initiatives, employee involvement exercises, strengths-based management thinking and, most important of all, HR practices which serve actively to engage staff in their work and with their organisations.

Thirdly, it is important to appreciate that increased competitive intensity is also having a profound effect on the way the HR function organises itself and approaches its objectives. Like all management functions, HR has to organise its own activities so as to be as efficient as possible. In recent years this has led to the adoption in many organisations of innovative approaches which involve HR professionals specialising rather than taking a traditional generalist role.

Business partners work closely with line managers on day-to-day case work, while others manage HR administration out of shared-service centres. They are then supported by expert trainers, reward specialists, employment lawyers and recruiters, many of whom are employed as sub-contractors. Another major change that the HR function itself is having to get used to is the need continually and effectively to justify its own existence. This can no longer be taken for granted in a highly competitive business environment. The function is thus increasingly obliged not just to add value, but also to demonstrate that it does so – and in raw financial terms too.

3.2.3 KEY CONTEMPORARY DEVELOPMENTS IN LABOUR MARKETS

The term 'labour market' refers to the market for staff and their skills that employers compete in so as to ensure that they can employ the best people in the jobs they have available. Like all markets, labour markets operate according to the rules of supply and demand. Ultimately this means that employers who can offer the best terms and conditions, the best chance of long-term job security, the best career development opportunities – or all three – give themselves the best opportunity of recruiting and retaining the strongest performers. And it is not just employers that compete in labour markets; would-be employees do too, as do existing employees vying with one another for promotion.

There are many contemporary developments in labour markets which are having an impact on HR practice. We only have space here briefly to summarise some of the most striking and significant of these: increasing cultural diversity, increasing regulation and increasing inequality in UK labour markets.

Cultural diversity

In recent years we have seen a substantial increase in the level of international migration. According to the United Nations, in 2013 there were 232 million people living long term in a country other than the one they were born in. Of these, the vast majority are part of a group labelled 'economic migrants', meaning that their major motivation in moving across an international border was the wish to earn more money or to develop their careers.

?   REFLECTIVE ACTIVITY 3.2

Think about a major HR activity such as recruitment, management development or reward management.

In respect of one or all of these, how can HR managers go about evaluating their contribution to organisation success and then demonstrating this in financial terms?

Numbers of international migrants have been growing for most of the past 50 years, but there has been a substantial acceleration in the past decade. Back in 1970 the UN estimated that just 81.5 million people fell into this category.

Large numbers of people both leave the UK and enter it each year, but since the early 1990s we have seen rising net inward migration. In the year to September 2014, government statistics record that an estimated 624,000 people entered the UK to stay for a period of a year or more.

This compares with 327,000 people leaving. This means that net inward migration into the UK is currently running at around 300,000 a year, a figure that has been creeping upwards in recent years despite government ministers stating that their aim is to achieve substantial reductions.

The result has been a fast period of growth in the UK's overall population (now over 64 million) and far greater levels of cultural diversity. Moreover, because people entering the UK tend on average to be rather younger than those who leave, the impact on the diversity of our labour markets is greater still, particularly in the major urban areas, where immigrants from overseas tend to prefer to settle.

The implications of this trend for HRM have been profound and are likely to become more prominent in the future. Put simply, we are now obliged to manage and make effective teams of staff from all over the world who have a variety of different cultural backgrounds. Furthermore, the globalisation of business activity means that UK-born employees are far more likely than they were in the past to be working in international corporations and reporting to senior management teams that are themselves culturally diverse.

Over many years extensive research has been carried out into cultural variations between workplaces across the world (for example, Hofstede 1980, 1991, Trompenaars 1993, House et al 2004). While there are disagreements between the authors about the detailed conclusions, all find evidence of substantial differences between countries across a range of measures. In other words, it makes complete sense and is entirely accurate to talk about a defined 'UK business culture'. This is similar to those found in other 'Anglo-Saxon' countries such as the USA, Canada and Australia, and also quite similar to the workplace culture in the Netherlands, but is nonetheless quite distinct in key respects. Moreover, it is much more different from the prevailing cultures found in Southern Europe, in the Scandinavian countries, in Eastern Europe and across Asia and Africa.

International migrants, and particularly those who work as **expatriates** on behalf of their companies in relatively senior roles overseas, often find it difficult to acclimatise to their new workplace cultures and to work effectively in them.

Multicultural teams therefore need careful and sensitive management if they are to operate successfully. As Richard Sennett (2012) rightly argues, effective co-operation with people who are different from ourselves is a skill that has to be learned. Goodwill alone is not enough. We cannot simply assume that everyone will fit in naturally and work well with one another. There is a major training and development role here, the significance of induction and socialisation programmes being particularly important. Everyone's expectations need to be managed and people have to become a great deal more culturally aware in order to help ensure that international diversity becomes the very real strength that it can become rather than a cause of sub-optimal performance.

Regulation

A second labour market trend of great significance has been the considerable increase we have seen over recent years in the amount of regulation that employers are obliged to take account of when employing people.

A generation ago the UK was highly unusual internationally in having very little employment law. The long-held consensus here was that the state was best staying out of the way as far as the employment relationship was concerned. Strong trade unions and national/industry-level collective agreements helped to protect social justice at work, ensuring that people were not overworked, underpaid or dismissed for no good reason. The situation has now wholly changed, giving the UK one of the most regulated labour markets in the world. Change started to occur in the 1960s with the introduction of regulations that required employers to make severance payments to their staff when making them redundant. The 1970s then saw the introduction of equal pay law, sex and race discrimination law, unfair dismissal law, comprehensive health and safety legislation and the right to take paid maternity leave. More recently we have seen the extension of many of these rights as well as many additions to them in the form (to name just a few) of disability discrimination law, age discrimination law, the National Minimum Wage, working time rights, a variety of trade union legislation and new rights for agency workers, fixed-term employees and part-timers. There are now more than 80 separate types of claim that can be heard in the employment tribunal and many others that are employment-related but which remain the preserve of the county court and the High Court.

The number of cases that come before employment tribunals has fallen very considerably since a claimants' fee was introduced in 2013 making people less inclined to pursue cases. From an employer's point of view this has undoubtedly reduced the extent of the risk that a management decision may be challenged in court and hence turn out to be very costly. It has not, however, by any means eliminated that risk and, as a result, there remains a need to keep on top of developments in employment law and to comply with its requirements.

As long ago as 2002, before much recent legislation was passed, a CIPD survey found that two-thirds of HR specialists were spending in excess of 20% of their time 'dealing with employment law issues', while a further quarter reported apparently spending 40% of their working time on such matters (CIPD 2002). In a further CIPD survey carried out five years later, 'securing compliance with employment regulations' was one of the top five objectives for 40% of HR professionals, while 90% saw employment regulation as likely to become more important for their organisations in the future (CIPD 2007).

Many organisations nowadays have simply decided, as a matter of policy, not to fight employment tribunal claims. They do this not because they don't think they can win them, but simply because the costs and sheer hassle that are involved with mounting a defence nearly always outweigh the costs of settling cases out of court by a substantial margin. But there are still costs, so even in such organisations HR people need to be continually aware of how their actions and those of line managers may have potential legal consequences, even if there is no intention whatever of acting outside the law. This is particularly true when hiring and firing staff, but as the increasing case load in areas such as working time, unlawful deduction from wages and whistleblowing testifies, the need for legal vigilance extends across almost all HR activities. Risks continually have to be assessed, and in order that this can be done in a timely and effective manner, HR officers now need as a matter of necessity to possess a good working knowledge of employment legislation. They also need to have access to advice in the form of lawyers, consultants and/or reference materials.

Labour market inequality

A third key development is one that shows every sign of growing in importance in the future. This is the tendency for the UK labour market to take on 'an hourglass' character over time (see Nolan 2001, Goos and Manning 2003). That is to say that we are seeing the emergence of a divergence between conditions in markets for higher-level skills (that is, professional, managerial, graduate jobs) and markets for lower-skilled jobs that are suited to people who do not have higher-level qualifications.

Mainly as a result of globalisation and the industrial restructuring that has had to follow in its wake, the vast majority of new jobs and of new job vacancies that are now being created in the UK economy are higher-skilled, higher-paid roles that require people who can bring with them considerable experience as well as specific skills. The problem is that the stock of skills in the UK labour market is rather lower. As was pointed out in the government-sponsored **Leitch Report** (2006) and more recently in the OECD's study of skills levels across the industrialised world (OECD 2013), the UK's performance in educating its people to meet the needs of our evolving knowledge economy is 'mediocre' by international standards. In short, over time we are building an economy that has too many opportunities for highly skilled people, and far too few for lower-skilled people – hence the hourglass effect. There are more jobs than there are jobseekers in the top half of the hourglass, even during the recent recession. This means that these labour markets are relatively tight and that employers struggle to recruit and retain strong performers. Wages are pushed up as a result and job-holders are treated well. By contrast, the opposite is the case in the lower half of the hourglass. Here there are many more people with limited skills and experience chasing relatively few jobs.

As a result there is downward pressure on wages and little reason for employers to increase the quality of jobs. They know that when someone leaves they will have no problem filling the vacancy quickly.

From a practical HR perspective it is developments in the top half of the hourglass that pose the greatest challenges. Severe skills shortages emerged in these labour markets in the early years of the twenty-first century, resulting in the evolution of 'a war for talent' as employers fought harder to recruit and retain appropriately qualified people. The heat was taken out of this battle during the recession years, although even then CIPD surveys reported that a good majority of employers struggled to recruit some groups of higher-skilled staff.

As the economy recovers, there are signs to suggest that chronic skills shortages are returning in many growth sectors, pushing effective and smart recruitment and retention back up to the top of the HR management agenda. Importantly, other factors are likely to make these high-skill labour markets even tighter in the future. The retirement of the large Baby Boom generation (born in the 20 years following the Second World War) is now progressing, there being some 3 million fewer people in Generation Y (born 1985–2004) coming into the labour market to replace them.

In addition, we are seeing some quite serious efforts being made by government ministers to reduce net inward migration into the UK. Migration from within the EU continues to grow, but the statistics on migration from the rest of the world into the UK suggest a modest contraction, and ministers are clearly keen where they can to reduce the figures further. It is likely therefore that in the future employers are going to be much less able than was the case previously to rely on overseas immigrants as a supply of skills that are in short supply. In addition, the considerable rise in female participation that occurred during the past 40 years can now be judged largely to have run its course. As many women are now in paid work in the UK as in pretty much anywhere else in the world (75% or so). This is a huge change from the position in the 1950s and 1960s, when the majority of women did not work outside the home. So here we have three reasons – Baby Boomers, overseas migrants and female participation – that can explain how supply of labour kept up with demand for labour in the past, which are going to have much less impact in the future. In short, there are going to be fewer people looking for work in the future vis-à-vis demand and, more importantly, far too few who are qualified to do the jobs that the economy is creating fastest.

?   REFLECTIVE ACTIVITY 3.3

You attend a conference for HRM professionals at which a speaker argues that 'the credit crunch is temporary, but the talent crunch is permanent'. She goes on to argue that employers should not lose sight of this reality when managing people in the tough economic times. Explain what exactly the speaker means in making this statement. Comment on its relevance for your organisation or one that you are familiar with.

3.3 FORMING ORGANISATIONAL AND HR STRATEGIES

In the first parts of this chapter we have tried to explain why HR practice in organisations varies so much, and indeed why it should vary. The business context is different across the private, public and voluntary sectors, resulting in necessarily different approaches to HR. At the same time some organisations are much more affected by increasing competitive intensity than others are, while some have seen their labour markets become much more culturally diverse than others. There is also much variation in the extent to which organisations are affected by skills shortages. In this final section we focus on organisational responses to developments in the business environment. How do business strategies get formed? And what kinds of alternatives are available when shaping HR strategies to support them?

A focus of much academic debate in the field of business strategy has been on the issue of how, in practice, strategy is formulated by organisations. Here it is possible to distinguish three basic alternative approaches:

1   rational/classical

2   emergent/logical incrementalism

3   symbolic/radical.

First there is what is known as the rational approach, which is often characterised as being the 'classical' or 'mainstream' approach. Here the task of strategy-making is entrusted to senior managers. Their job is to undertake a continual appraisal of both the external and internal environments (using tools such as **SWOT analysis**) and to use this information to formulate goals, aims or objectives for the organisation.

Having chosen the strategic direction, the next task is to put it into effect by organising appropriately, and particularly by gathering together the necessary resources (raw materials, technologies, capital, people). Central to the rational model is the idea that organisations should appraise different possible strategic courses of action, evaluate them all and then make a choice. This might involve an organisation which consists of several separate businesses, shedding some in order to focus investment on another. Alternatively, it might involve a business competing in one defined market seeking to increase its share by developing new products, moving existing products up-market or cutting its costs so as to reduce prices.

The idea of emergent strategies originates in the work of analysts such as James Quinn (1980), who studied, in depth, what actually happened in organisations. He found that in practice the rational strategy formulated at senior levels influenced the actual strategic direction an organisation took, but that other factors also intervened, so that the organisation ended up pursuing a rather different strategy. In practice what happens is that a strategy emerges incrementally over time as an organisation responds to the realities of its environmental position opportunistically. Trial and error determines what happens as much as any rationally planned top-down strategy.

The approach is sometimes labelled 'logical incrementalism' in that each step taken is logical and consistent, but is not planned many years or months in advance. Senior managers set general goals, but responsibility in formulating a strategy for getting there lies in the hands of people throughout the organisation, responding to situations as they arise.

The third approach (symbolic) turns the whole process on its head. In practice, it argues, most organisations get on with the business of competing, evolving tactics as they go, trying different things and sticking with things that work well. In other words, they muddle through opportunistically, often succeeding because of luck rather than judgement. They then formulate a written strategy in response. In other words, in reality the tail wags the dog. Implementation precedes the formulation of a strategy. We try things, find which work best and then retrospectively articulate this as our strategy. According to this view, strategy formulation is merely a symbolic action designed to give an organisation gravitas and credibility. In practice, little strategic leadership occurs; what we say is our strategy is actually just a post-hoc rationalisation of what we actually do.

Henry Mintzberg is the most influential thinker in this field of study. He is also well known for having formulated a contingency model which sets out the circumstances when the above types of strategy-formation process are appropriate. He suggests that the key variables are the complexity of the organisation and its environment and the rate of change in that environment (Mintzberg 1994).

These, he states, can be different for different organisations at different times, so the type of approach used for strategy-making which is most appropriate will itself vary over time.

In Figure 3.1, the top left-hand box indicates organisations which operate in relatively stable circumstances and which are themselves either small or relatively uncomplicated. Examples would include most small businesses as well as larger organisations which carry out one or two relatively unsophisticated activities – such as a pizza factory, a retail chain which consists of small stores (bakeries, hairdressers, and so on) or a bus company.

Here a rational strategy is possible because the environment is both stable and very readily fully understood. A small team of managers can thus practically develop a business strategy in the classical fashion and implement it. There is little uncertainty and low risk.

The top right-hand box is where organisations that are complex but operate in stable conditions are placed. They are thus faced with moderate uncertainty which derives from the many different environmental trends that impact on them. Examples are major government departments, hospitals and universities.

Here an emergent strategy is appropriate and it should be one involving all levels in the organisational hierarchy. Senior managers cannot fully understand all the facets of these organisations and cannot impose a single strategy on the whole organisation.

'Moderate uncertainty' is also a feature of organisations in the bottom left-hand box, but here it derives from the speed of environmental change rather than the complexity of the environment. A small hi-tech company such as an independent software house is a good example. The uncertainty in terms of strategy-formation is there because of continual technological developments. Speed of response is what determines survival. There is no time to formulate a rational strategy and it would be out of date quickly. So an emergent strategy is appropriate, but it has to be one which is formulated and implemented by the same people. The manager decides what to do and does it, but the strategy itself develops in response to changes in the environment.

Figure 3.1 Change and complexity

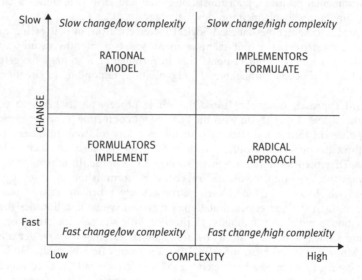

Finally, the bottom right-hand box contains organisations that are both complex and also faced with a fast-changing environment. A large hi-tech organisation is an example, or an international bank – or any large international organisation.

Here the level of uncertainty is high, both because of the organisation's complexity and the speed of change. Rational strategic planning serves no purpose, so an opportunistic, decentralised approach to decision-making is needed. This is then rationalised, post hoc, by senior managers in the form of a strategy document. It impresses investors, but it does not really drive decision-making on a day-to-day basis.

Mintzberg's two big ideas then come together in his argument that organisations are becoming increasingly complex and environments increasingly fast-changing – hence greater uncertainty and 'discontinuity'; hence the 'fall' of traditional, rational approaches to strategy-formation.

3.3.1 CONTINGENCY THINKING

As far as HRM is concerned, it is having a defined strategy to respond to that matters more than how that strategy is arrived at. Where an organisation opts for a classical, rational approach to strategy-making, it is not difficult for HR managers to see clearly what are the organisation's key strategic objectives. This is sometimes a lot less straightforward in the case of emergent or symbolic strategy-making because it is not always clear precisely what the strategic priorities are at any one time and how they are likely to evolve in the future. Nonetheless, it is self-evident that some clarity needs to be established if a meaningful HR strategy is to be developed which supports the wider organisational strategy and enhances the likelihood that it will be successfully achieved.

For many years managers have made use of contingency thinking and contingency models in order to help them align HR strategies with business strategies. Numerous such models have been published over the years, all of which can be very useful tools in helping to clarify the sort of approach to follow.

These are best understood by looking at examples such as Michael Porter's (1985) highly influential model, which focused on the major alternative ways that organisations gain competitive advantage. Here Porter identified three core alternative strategies that firms follow:

- cost leadership (that is, value for money)
- differentiation (via quality enhancement or innovation)
- focus.

The third approach involves using either the cost leadership or the differentiation approaches, but in a niche market, or a specific market segment – one sex, one income group, one geographical area, one age group, one definable type of lifestyle, and so on. So in practice Porter argues that an organisation has a choice of three major strategies to use in order to compete effectively: it can produce goods and services that are cheaper than those of its competitors, it can produce goods and services that are of higher quality (and hence more expensive) or, finally, it can produce goods and services that are more innovative than those of its competitors.

Porter's generic strategy model has been attacked not because it isn't true and useful, but because of his claim that organisations will not gain competitive advantage if they pursue a hybrid strategy. According to Porter, your chances of success are highest when you plump for one of the three and pursue it strongly. Later critics (notably Johnson et al 2010) have argued not only that hybrid strategies can succeed just as well, but that in the modern business environment it is necessary to achieve all three simultaneously – high quality, low price, innovative and able to appeal to niche markets as well as mass markets. But it is accepted that this is difficult to achieve in practice.

From an HR point of view, the kind of policies and practices that need to be in place in order effectively to support each of Porter's three sources of competitive advantage are different (Schuler and Jackson 1987). For example, where an organisation pursues a strategy of cost leadership, the HR strategy will inevitably be focused on keeping the overall wage bill at as low a level as possible. That may mean paying at below-market rates and managing the consequences in terms of recruitment, retention and morale. Or it may mean paying well but requiring staff to be a great deal more productive than those of competitors who pursue different strategies. Cost leadership tends to be associated with bureaucracy, low levels of employee involvement and a lack of sophisticated, cutting-edge approaches to HR that set out to engage staff positively by developing them. By contrast, a strategy that is focused on innovation requires a heavy focus first on recruiting and retaining people with specialised skills and then encouraging them to take risks, share ideas and act creatively. Finally, a strategy that is concerned with quality enhancement is likely to lead to HR policies which enable employees to meet the highest customer expectations. This requires relatively high pay, genuine employee involvement, good training and development opportunities and a consultative management style.

There are numerous other contingency models that take a similar approach. Among the best known and most influential are those derived from the Boston Consulting Model (Purcell 1989), which suggests how HR practices should vary depending on an organisation's relative market share and whether or not its markets are growing or in decline. Miles and Snow (1978), by contrast, focus in their model on identifying the appropriate HR practices for different types of competitive strategy – defensive, prospecting or analysing.

All of these, and several others, have the same strengths and weaknesses. They are effective guides that help the HR function in organisations to think strategically about their activities and about how they can best add value. However, they are also rather one-dimensional and prescriptive, failing to take account of all manner of variables that might actually make a different strategic approach appropriate in a particular case. For example, they take no account of an organisation's competitive position vis-à-vis its labour markets. A company facing severe skills shortages, for example, has no choice often but to push up its wages simply in order to attract and retain the workforce it needs in order to operate – whatever business strategy it is pursuing.

Contingency thinking in HRM has also been widely criticised by the 'best practice school', a group of highly influential thinkers who argue that whatever strategy an organisation adopts, from an HR point of view the same basic bundle of practices needs to be followed in order to enhance its chances of success (Pfeffer 1994, Huselid 1995, Purcell et al 2003). There is no need to differentiate according to wider organisational policy. If you take a sophisticated approach to the management of people, selecting the best staff, paying them according to their individual performance, involving them in decision-making and providing them with job security and career development opportunities, the result is likely to be an effective workforce that is motivated to put in the effort required to deliver wider organisational objectives, whatever they are.

3.3.2 RESOURCE-BASED THINKING

Another widely discussed approach to the formation of HR strategy takes a rather different perspective. Theories developed from **'the resource-based view' of the firm (RBV)** are sometimes described as using 'inside-out' thinking rather than the 'outside-in' thinking that characterises contingency theories. Here the analysis starts with an audit of an organisation's existing resources in terms of their key competitive strengths. This extends well beyond people management concerns to take account of all potential strengths (goodwill, brands, physical resources, and so on), but there is also a very important potential role for HRM to play.

The key to understanding RBV is to appreciate that organisations typically enjoy attributes that are both strengths competitively and that also differentiate them in key respects from their competitors. Having established what these are, resource-based thinking requires that ways are found of protecting, enhancing and reinforcing them so as to build towards sustained competitive advantage over time. Barney (1991) argues that the focus needs to be on understanding which resources (including human resources) are most:

- valuable
- rare

- inimitable (that is, hard for competitors to replicate)
- non-substitutable.

As far as the HRM contribution is concerned, this kind of analysis may lead to the identification of particular individuals whose significance is so great that the organisation simply cannot afford to lose them to a competitor. However, more often there are factors which are not readily defined, such as a type of organisational culture, a body of knowledge that is collectively held, a positive reputation as an employer or simply a stock of skills. Whatever they are, the prime aim of a resource-based HR strategy is to protect, enhance and reinforce these key strengths.

CASE STUDY 3.1

THE NEW COLLEGE OF THE HUMANITIES

In the summer of 2010 the philosopher A. C. Grayling announced that he and a group of other high-profile academics were to found a new university in London.

The New College of the Humanities (NCH) would operate as a private institution, wholly independent of government and funded privately. Each year its students would register, along with 50,000 others from across the world, as members of the University of London International Programmes, sitting existing exams and following existing syllabuses. However, rather than studying overseas using distance-learning materials, NCH students would be based in Bloomsbury, central London, where they would receive outstanding teaching from the world's leading academics.

Despite the project being highly controversial and being much criticised in the press, the college opened in October 2012 offering five degree programmes – economics, English, history, law and philosophy. It had no difficulty attracting applicants and has been able to survive and thrive from a financial point of view. 150 students enrolled each year in its first years of operation, the aim over time being to stabilise total student numbers at around 1,000 once it is able to recruit students from outside the European Union. NCH charges annual fees of £18,000, twice the maximum that universities accepting government funding are able to charge. However,

25% of its places are awarded on a scholarship basis, reducing the fees to £7,200. In return its students are guaranteed a staff–student ratio of 1:10, 13 contact hours each week, one-to-one tutorials and teaching by leading figures in their fields, including major international names such as Richard Dawkins, Niall Ferguson, Steven Pinker and Ronald Dworkin.

Unlike most universities in the UK, the college is run on a for-profit basis. £10 million of initial finance was raised from private equity, a third of the enterprise being owned by A. C. Grayling himself and 13 academic colleagues, who stand to make a considerable amount of money if it is successful and develops a first-rate international reputation.

Questions

1   How would you expect HR policies and practices at the New College of the Humanities to be similar to those in most UK universities? How would you expect them to differ, and why?

2   What trends in the business environment made 2012 a favourable time to launch an institution of this kind?

3   To what extent could contingency thinking and resource-based thinking about HRM be relevant to NCH, and how?

FURTHER READING

Most of the issues covered in this chapter are discussed at greater length and in more detail in some other books published by the CIPD. *Contemporary issues in HRM* by Stephen Taylor and *Human resource management in context: strategy, insights and solutions* by David Farnham are examples. (See back of book for sample chapter).

Texts that focus on the business environment generally, including labour market issues, include *The business environment: themes and issues* edited by Paul Wetherly and Dorron Otter and *The international business environment: challenges and changes* by Ian Brooks and his colleagues.

Global shift: mapping the changing contours of the world economy by Peter Dicken, now in its seventh edition, is an excellent introduction to globalisation and its impact on business in recent decades.

REFERENCES

BACH, S. (2010) HRM in the public sector. In: WILKINSON, A., BACON, N. and SNELL, S. (eds). *The Sage handbook of human resource management*. London: Sage. pp561–77.

BARNEY, J. (1991) Firm resources and sustained competitive advantage. *Journal of Management*. Vol 17, No 1. pp99–120.

BROOKS, I., WEATHERSTON, J. and WILKINSON, G. (2010) *The international business environment: challenges and changes*. 2nd ed. London: FT/Prentice Hall.

CIPD (2002) *Employment law*. Survey report. London: Chartered Institute of Personnel and Development.

CIPD (2007) *The changing HR function*. Survey report. London: Chartered Institute of Personnel and Development.

DICKEN, P. (2015) *Global shift: mapping the changing contours of the world economy*. 7th ed. London: Sage.

EDWARDS, P. and RAM, M. (2010) HRM in small firms: respecting and regulating informality. In: WILKINSON, A., BACON, N. and SNELL, S. (eds). *The Sage handbook of human resource management*. London: Sage. pp524–40.

FARNHAM, D. (2015) *Human resource management in context: strategy, insights and solutions*. 4th ed. London: Chartered Institute of Personnel and Development.

GOOS, M. and MANNING, A. (2003) McJobs and Macjobs: the growing polarisation of jobs in the UK. In: DICKENS, R., GREGG, P. and WADSWORTH, J. (eds). *The labour market under New Labour*. Basingstoke: Palgrave. pp70–85.

HOFSTEDE, G. (1980) *Culture's consequences: international differences in work-related values*. Beverly Hills, CA: Sage Publications.

HOFSTEDE, G. (1991) *Cultures and organizations: software of the mind*. London: McGraw-Hill.

HOUSE, R., HANGES, P., JAVIDAN, M., DORFMAN, P. and GUPTA, V. (2004) *Culture, leadership and organisations: the GLOBE study of 62 societies.* Thousand Oaks, CA: Sage.

HUSELID, M. (1995) The impact of human resource practices on turnover, productivity and corporate financial performance. *Academy of Management Journal.* Vol 38, No 3. pp635–72.

JAMES, P. (2011) Voluntary sector outsourcing: a reflection on employment related rationales, developments and outcomes. *International Journal of Public Sector Management.* Vol 24, No 7. pp684–93.

JOHNSON, G., WHITTINGTON, R. and SCHOLES, K. (2010) *Exploring strategy: text and cases.* 9th ed. New York: FT/Prentice Hall.

KELLIHER, C. and PARRY, E. (2011) Voluntary sector HRM: examining the influence of government. *International Journal of Public Sector Management.* Vol 24, No 7. pp650–61.

LEITCH, LORD S. (2006) *Leitch review of skills: final report* [online]. Available at: http://dera.ioe.ac.uk/6322/1/leitch_finalreport051206.pdf [Accessed 21 January 2016].

MCNAMARA, G., VAALER, P. and DEVERS, C. (2003) Same as it ever was: the search for evidence of increasing hypercompetition. *Strategic Management Journal.* Vol 24, No 1. pp261–78.

MILES, R. E. and SNOW, C. C. (1978) *Organization strategy, structure and process.* New York: McGraw-Hill.

MINTZBERG, H. (1994) *The rise and fall of strategic planning.* New York: Prentice Hall.

NOLAN, P. (2001) Shaping things to come. *People Management.* 27 December.

OECD (2013) *OECD skills outlook.* Paris: Organisation for Economic Co-operation and Development.

PFEFFER, J. (1994) *Competitive advantage through people.* Boston, MA: Harvard University Press.

PORTER, M. E. (1985) *Competitive advantage.* New York: Free Press.

PURCELL, J. (1989) The impact of corporate strategy on human resource management. In: STOREY, J. (ed.) *New perspectives on human resource management.* London: Routledge. pp67–91.

PURCELL, J., KINNIE, N., HUTCHINSON, S., RAYTON, B. and SWART, J. (2003) *Understanding the people and performance link: unlocking the black box.* London: Chartered Institute of Personnel and Development.

QUINN, B. (1980) *Strategies for change: logical incrementalism.* Homewood, IL: Irwin.

SCHULER, R. and JACKSON, S. (1987) Linking competitive strategies with human resource management. *Academy of Management Executive.* Vol 1, No 3. pp207–19.

SENNETT, R. (2012) *Together: the rituals, pleasures and politics of co-operation.* London: Allen Lane.

TAYLOR, S. (2011) *Contemporary issues in HRM*. London: Chartered Institute of Personnel and Development.

TROMPENAARS, F. (1993) *Riding the waves of culture: understanding cultural diversity in global business*. London: McGraw-Hill.

VAN WANROOY, B., BEWLEY, H., BRYSON, A., FORTH, J., FREET, S., STOKES, L. and WOOD, S. (2013) *Employment relations in the shadow of recession: findings from the 2011 Workplace Employment Relations Study*. Basingstoke: Palgrave Macmillan.

WETHERLY, P. and OTTER, D. (2014) *The business environment: themes and issues*. 3rd ed. Oxford: Oxford University Press.

CHAPTER 4

Developing Professional Practice

TED JOHNS AND GRAHAM PERKINS

CHAPTER CONTENTS

- Introduction
- The HR contribution
- The 'thinking performer'
- HR professionalism
- Self-management at work
- Teamworking

KEY LEARNING OUTCOMES

By the end of this chapter, you should be able to:

- understand what is required to be an effective and efficient HR professional
- add value for your organisation through your personal contribution to efficient and effective HRM
- perform efficiently and effectively as a self-managing HR professional
- perform efficiently and effectively as a collaborative member of working groups and teams.

4.1 INTRODUCTION

Developing professional practice drives at the heart of what it means to be a human resource professional. This chapter reviews this subject and its many facets, considering the contribution that HRM as a function makes to our organisations. It is becoming increasingly important for HR professionals to be 'thinking performers', consciously contributing to an organisation's objectives and bringing about change by diplomatically challenging others. Likewise it is also important that HR professionals recognise their professional and ethical responsibilities, and this chapter discusses all of these in depth with reference to CIPD guidance where applicable.

Of course, being a professional also requires us to learn about how we manage ourselves at work. From thinking carefully about how we manage our working time, to our ability to think critically, not forgetting the need to develop effective presentation skills and manage difficult relationships. This chapter covers all these issues, and others, relating to self-management at work in some depth. To begin, let us think critically about the HR contribution within organisations.

4.2 THE HR CONTRIBUTION

Historically, what is now generally known as 'The HR function' played a role that was largely administrative in nature. Its principal purpose was to carry out a range of quite basic tasks that are necessary whenever an organisation employs people, such as issuing contracts, placing job advertisements in newspapers, maintaining absence and training records, running the payroll, setting up selection interviews, designing appraisal documentation and, more generally, drawing up policy statements for line managers to follow when managing their staff. In unionised organisations, the role also used to encompass the maintenance of reasonably strong, trusting relationships with employee representatives. In recent years the role has both changed and developed so that these traditional activities have tended to form a much less significant part of the typical HR manager's activities.

Much more time and energy nowadays is focused on getting the best out of people as corporate contributors. In this context the term 'people' means both individual employees and staff as a collective group. The HR function contributes to organisational success by enabling and encouraging each member of staff to maximise their personal contribution, and more generally by ensuring that people across the organisation are led well. This requires the creative application of a mix of two ingredients, both essential:

'**Infrastructure' factors:** These are the 'hygiene' factors which have to be present if employees are to perform at all, but which don't by themselves generate high levels of commitment and enthusiasm. While the presence of hygiene factors plays no major role in positively motivating people, their absence can demotivate. Making sure that people are paid what they are owed for their contribution, and paid on time, is a good example of an HR hygiene factor. Few are likely to be induced to perform superbly simply because they have received a regular monthly pay cheque, but the absence of payment is very likely indeed to have a seriously negative effect on performance levels.

'**Differentiators' ('motivators'):** These are the elements which turn satisfactory or average performers into good and excellent performers. They include factors such as the opportunity to carry out interesting and stimulating work, the ability to exercise discretion over how that work is carried out, the potential for career development, positive feedback about progress and more generally a sense of feeling valued by the organisation.

Hygiene factors are not difficult to achieve in practice. However, because there are costs associated with getting them right, managers are sometimes tempted to cut back, often leading to negative HR outcomes, such as poor staff morale, active disengagement on the part of employees, high levels of absence, low levels of staff retention, an increased volume of employment tribunal claims and low-trust employment relations.

By contrast, the differentiators are much harder to achieve consistently and to continue achieving over the long term. Some are very specific to an organisation, emanating for example from a particular management culture or approach to doing things which is both difficult to define and even harder for rival organisations to imitate. However, many decades of research into human motivation and effective people management have also demonstrated that no magic ingredient is necessary. We know what the 'secret' of differentiation is, and we also know that it is not at all easy to achieve in practice. This is why some organisations perform much more effectively than others on the people management front. Those that strongly differentiate themselves are able to attract, retain, motivate and engage people much more effectively than those that do not.

The key difference is between those organisations that don't do more than manage their people legalistically, systematically and efficiently, in accordance with the dictates of 'best practice', and those organisations that lead their people positively, inspirationally and imaginatively, in line with their vision of 'next practice'. This is what effective HRM is about – creating an efficient infrastructure and also mobilising an effective set of differentiators that together make an impressive difference to the quality of the organisation and its resulting performance.

A good starting point is to manage people in accordance with some clear and strong core principles:

- Employees are human beings who deserve to be treated with dignity, consideration and sensitivity from the moment they first apply for a job to the moment they finally leave the organisation.
- They are actual or potential sources of 'added value' for the organisation.
- They are all individuals with capabilities that can be developed and utilised for the benefit of the business.
- As employees, they have a right to derive satisfaction from their work and rewards commensurate with their contributions.

? REFLECTIVE ACTIVITY 4.1

On its recruitment website Tesco lists the attitudes and competencies that it wants its employees to have:

Passionate about retail

Focusing on the customer and striving to understand them better than anyone

Driven to achieve results through determination and commitment

Committed to treating people in a fair and consistent way

Willing to roll their sleeves up to get things done

Determined to respond energetically to customer feedback

Motivated to work in partnership with others to achieve individual and team objectives

Adaptable and **flexible** to thrive in a 24/7 business

Devoted to seeking feedback on their performance and investing time in their own development.

Questions

1   How might this list be adapted in order to put together a generic statement of the kinds of attributes needed by an effective HR manager?

2   Can you think of any other attributes which would also be appropriate for today's HR professional?

4.2.1 ADDING VALUE

A key difference between traditional personnel management of the kind we described above and what is required of a successful, contemporary HR function can be summed up by the phrase 'adding value'. In the vast majority of organisations it is no longer sufficient for HR managers simply to carry out administrative tasks; they need to add commercial value – and as importantly, be seen to do so. But how do we go about ensuring that we maximise the value that we add?

One way of thinking about the question of adding value is to divide our activities at work into the following four categories:

1   **Maintenance activities**

Maintenance is about keeping the show on the road. Maintenance activities are necessary, but they don't add a great deal of value simply because they ensure that everything continues to function as it did before.

2   **Crisis prevention activities**

Crisis prevention is about making sure that things don't go wrong or, if they do, that the resultant damage can be contained. This where procedures and processes fit. Here, too, value added is relatively limited.

3   **Continuous improvement activities**

Continuous improvement is where added value really begins, because it focuses on performing current tasks better, faster or more cheaply in ways which are customer-relevant and preferably noticed by the customer. You can introduce and implement continuous improvement in many ways.

4   **Change management activities**

Change management is about proposing, contributing, energising, persuading and/or implementing change. Making change happen is a key added-value performance indicator.

A final requirement, underpinning all four of these active roles, deserves special emphasis. Recent high-profile instances of corporate wrongdoing and managerial misbehaviour have emphasised once again the importance of ethical conduct – for organisations, for directors, for executives, for managers, (especially) for those in the HR function, and for employees in general.

Both maintenance and crisis prevention are essential, but their capacity to add value is limited. A contribution to the achievement of competitive advantage is made when an organisation achieves these things more efficiently and effectively than their competitors can, but that is the extent of any real added value. An HR function can be good maintenance and crisis prevention activities, and respected for this. But it is insufficient as far as adding real long-term value is concerned. For that to be achieved, HR professionals need to switch their energies, as far as is possible, to continuous improvement and change management activities.

In fact, it can be persuasively argued that spending less time on maintenance and crisis prevention is a prerequisite for achieving greater added value. This is because it releases time and resources which can be used for more productive and authentic added-value purposes.

4.2.2 BEING 'BUSINESS SAVVY'

Being what the CIPD refers to as 'business savvy' is increasingly being recognised as one of most important attributes of effective HR practitioners. No longer – as once tended to be the case in some organisations – can HR professionals expect to function in 'professionally-detached ivory towers', issuing edicts and prohibitions for others to follow which have no clear business justification (that is, being based largely on notions of 'good practice' or a highly risk-averse interpretation of employment law). If an HR function is to be successful, the way people are managed needs to enhance rather than restrict an organisation in achieving its objectives. Being 'business savvy' is also important for HR professionals because it helps hugely to enhance our credibility among other managers in our organisations and therefore our ability to influence events rather than simply react to them.

According to CIPD research (CIPD 2012), there are four elements to being 'business savvy':

- *Understanding the business model in depth* – knowing where value is created and destroyed within the organisation, and identifying people-related improvement points which can drive value and enhance organisational performance.
- *Generating insight through evidence and data* – having the courage to ask questions and look for explanations even when the knowledge required seems masked in technical or professional jargon.
- *Connecting with curiosity, purpose and impact* – demonstrating curiosity about why and how the business operates, with the purpose of identifying opportunities for improvement; not waiting to be asked, but taking a proactive approach to making connections across the business and collaborating at all levels.
- *Leading with integrity, consideration and challenge* – serving stakeholders, not power structures, by retaining a strong stewardship role centred on the courage to challenge the pursuit of short-term business goals that are detrimental to an organisation's people and longer-term success.

? REFLECTIVE ACTIVITY 4.2

To what extent do you agree with the following point of view, and why?

In some HR circles a legal and compliance orientation predominates, especially in organisations which regularly face the threat of employment tribunal claims. HR professionals may then suggest that they have added value because the number of such claims and hearings has fallen, or because the business has 'won' more cases. In truth, nobody ever truly 'wins' such cases and no well-managed business should be dismissing people unfairly or discriminating against people unlawfully in the first place. If employees believe they have been treated unlawfully and go to tribunal, it is an indication that an organisation is being managed ineffectively.

It is far preferable, surely, to add value by introducing an effective people-management and people-leadership culture characterised by genuine engagement. Certainly that is much better than trying to claim that we are adding value because we have created a scenario in which the number of costly, reputationally damaging and energy-sapping events has been reduced.

4.3 THE THINKING PERFORMER

The '**thinking performer**' concept is something that sits at the very heart of professional practice and has been promoted by the CIPD through its professional qualifications framework for many years. In the HRM arena, the 'thinking performer' is the person who not only performs operationally, but the person who also thinks about what they are doing. These are two competencies which don't always go together, but when they do, the combination is very impressive – and very valuable both for the individual and the organisation, provided always that there is some resonance between the individual's desire to think and the organisation's wish to perform.

Authentic thinking performers tend to display the following behaviours and attitudes:

- Consciously seeking to contribute to underlying organisational purposes – and therefore taking the trouble to find out what these underlying (strategic) purposes are. Thinking performers are more concerned with ends than with means.

- Reinforcing the legalistic and compliance role of the HR function when it is necessary, yet fully appreciating that to do so is not a sufficient condition for the HR function's genuine added-value effectiveness.
- Diplomatically challenging the way things are done to find solutions that are:
  - better (higher standards of cost-effective quality)
  - cheaper (lower costs, measured financially or via some other means of resource utilisation, including time)
  - faster (improved response times and personal/team productivity).
- Having continuous contact with 'customers' through networking in order to better understand the business, reacting to feedback appropriately and proactively developing their performance.
- Looking not just inside but also outside the organisation to learn about new thinking, new ideas, new practices or new evidence which their organisation might be able to exploit by copying or adapting it for its own purposes.

Conversely, it is relatively easy to spot individuals who are not thinking performers because their behaviour and attitudes will display the following features:

- They do their job but pay minimal attention to what is going on around them.
- They are much more concerned with means than with ends.
- They think that the organisation's strategy is nothing to do with them – and may even believe that the organisation doesn't have a strategy, not because they genuinely know it doesn't have one but rather because they've never taken the trouble to seek it out.
- They see their role, especially within HR, as ensuring that 'the law' is obeyed at all times.
- They believe that the overriding goal of the HR function is to ensure that everyone (whether inside or outside the organisation, employees or job applicants) is treated 'fairly', which for them will mean that everyone is treated the same.
- They pay little or no attention to the opinions of their 'customers' about their performance – indeed, they may even reject the notion that they have 'customers'.
- They never constructively challenge the way things are done.

Consider for a moment an HR professional who has been tasked with updating an organisation's induction process. A non-thinking performer will likely approach this task with a relatively closed mind. While they may well examine literature or HR-related best practice on the subject, the non-thinking performer will likely see this as an HR-centric task. In other words they will pay little attention to organisational strategy, they will focus the induction strongly on the communication of HR policies and processes, and they will not engage with other stakeholder groups. By contrast, a thinking performer will understand the organisation's strategy and seek to embed this into the new employee through the induction. The thinking performer will involve others in the design of the process/system, asking for opinions, feedback and advice. While they, themselves, will use the induction to communicate important HR-related information, they will recognise that this is not the only purpose of induction. In short, the thinking performer will take a broader, business-focused view, consciously seeking to use HR activities to bring about organisational success.

Why is it important to become a thinking performer? Essentially the thinking performer concept has grown in importance because professionals have recognised that it can move both them and their organisations forward intellectually, professionally and ethically. In today's organisations, a thinking performer culture is the optimal mechanism for attaining competitive supremacy and mobilising the talents of the workforce as a whole. Whatever the organisation – manufacturer or service provider, private or public, large or small, profit-making or not-for-profit – all its employees need to understand and be able to implement its strategy. They need to know how their jobs push the strategy forward and, if nobody can show them any link between the strategy and what they do, in all probability their jobs don't need to exist at all.

One way of bringing the concept of the thinking performer to life is illustrated in Figure 4.1. Here the vertical axis represents 'effectiveness' and 'doing the right things' (that is, adding value, making a difference, focusing on outputs, outcomes and results) – in a word, *thinking*.

The horizontal axis represents 'efficiency' or 'doing things right', concentrating on process conformity, legal and ethical compliance, putting things right when they've gone wrong – in a word, *performing*.

Figure 4.1 The thinking performer

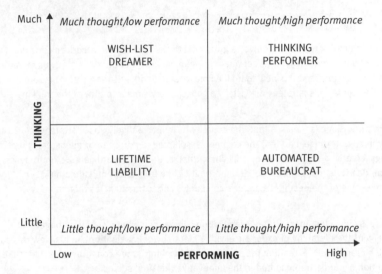

The automated bureaucrat is the non-thinking performer, the person who carries out instructions blindly, without necessarily knowing (or caring) about their purpose. These individuals believe it to be acceptable to be told that a procedure is justified because 'it has always been done that way' and take refuge in plausible arguments about, say, the legal justification for certain HR actions without bothering to check whether indeed the law does actually specify what is being done in its name.

The wish-list dreamer – the thinking non-performer – will privately regard many of the things they are required to do as absurd, indefensible, inefficient, even maybe immoral or corrupt, but will say nothing about these concerns even when invited to do so. The wish-list dreamer often knows a better way yet does not share it with others (apart, perhaps, from those outside the organisation) and therefore loses some valuable opportunities to 'add value' to the business. Wish-list dreamers tend to keep quiet either for fear of 'rocking the boat' or because, rightly or wrongly, they perceive that their views will not be listened to if they express them.

The lifetime liability, as the title suggests, is a non-thinking non-performer. Such people rarely deliver task performance, results, or improvements, yet often devote a good deal of time and energy to the development of 'reasons' for why agreed outputs have not been attained and specified tasks have not been performed. The lifetime liability can be a poisonous influence on others, subverting an organisation's goals and values, interpreting its vision cynically, and infecting others with similar attitudes.

Thinking performers, occupying the fourth quadrant, deliver both everyday performance and added-value improvement, both for and through themselves and for and through their wider accountabilities for the HR function and the business as a whole.

It is important to recognise that thinking performers don't challenge everything that goes on in their organisations, even strategies and practices which are supported by no evidence whatever as to their effectiveness. They understand the need to act in a politically adept fashion and to select battlegrounds carefully. They challenge on fertile ground, when the time is right, preparing a strong case, securing some respected allies and proceeding with caution.

?   REFLECTIVE ACTIVITY 4.3

The thinking performer concept owes a great deal to the ideas of the American consultant and academic, Gary Hamel (1996), as set out in his seminal article entitled 'Strategy as revolution'. In this Hamel expressed the view that all employees of an organisation carry the potential to become what he calls 'strategy activists' – a concept very similar to that of the thinking performer.

A key part of Hamel's thesis is that 'the capacity to think creatively about strategy is distributed widely in an enterprise' and that the common assumption among senior managers is that strategic creativity is possessed by only a few (that is, them). The article goes on to describe how an idea for a multi-million-dollar opportunity came from a 'twenty-something secretary', and how some of the best ideas about a company's core competencies originated with a forklift operator.

In Hamel's view, genuinely strategic innovation can happen where 'senior managers ... supplement the hierarchy of experience with a hierarchy of imagination'. In his view this can be done by 'dramatically extending the strategy franchise' into three constituencies which are conventionally under-represented in the 'innovative thinking' stakes:

Young people – 'or, more accurately, people with a youthful perspective', who do not necessarily have to be young.

People at an organisation's periphery – who are often forced to be more creative because they have fewer resources and also because they are more exposed to ideas and developments that do not conform to the organisation's traditional shibboleths.

Newcomers – 'people who have not yet been co-opted by an industry's dogma'.

Questions

1   Why do you think senior managers are often reluctant to take on board ideas such as Hamel's on strategy?

2   What roles could the HR function play in helping to make Hamel's ideas a reality in organisations?

4.4 HR PROFESSIONALISM

How should we define the word **'professional'**, and do HR managers have a legitimate right to call themselves 'professionals'? These are not straightforward questions to answer because people have a variety of different opinions about how to define a 'profession'.

Lester (2010, p2) sums up a commonly held point of view when he argues that a professional is someone who:

> makes proficient use of expert or specialist knowledge, exercises autonomous thought and judgement, and makes a voluntary commitment to a set of principles. Such a person need not be a member of an easily defined profession or of a professional association; it is possible to work as a professional from a set of expertise and skills that is relatively unique to the individual.

According to this rather broad definition a 'profession' can be distinguished from an occupation due to its having the following characteristics:

- It is based on a body of knowledge (usually comprising theory, knowledge and practice) which can be taught and learned.
- Its practitioners possess appropriate expertise to which they apply their knowledge and judgement.
- It is underpinned by a code of conduct or ethics.

Another definition is narrower and more restrictive, only conferring the label 'professional' to occupations that are controlled to a considerable extent by a governing body which has a formal membership structure with admission barriers and performance criteria that must be met. Professional bodies of this kind not only promote high ethical standards, but reinforce them with a disciplinary procedure. You become a member of the profession when you join the professional body, and can cease to be a member if you fail to meet its standards and are required to leave.

Under either of these definitions there is a case for arguing that HR managers, at least in the UK, can legitimately regard themselves as being professionals. However, there also remain some grounds for arguing against this point of view.

On the one hand there is a definite body of knowledge that has to be learned (such as how to handle disciplinary events or set down reward strategies) and individuals certainly have to apply their judgement in their own organisations. It is also the case that the CIPD acts as a governing body for the profession in the UK and Ireland, and that it has a code of conduct that members are expected to adhere to. On the other hand, unlike some other professions, notably law and medicine, membership of the professional body is not compulsory and so CIPD membership does not constitute a formal 'licence to practise' (as is the case with law and medicine).

A factor that tilts the balance in favour of **'professionalism'** is the fact that a good majority of HR practitioners in the UK are members of the CIPD, and that the CIPD is the only professional body currently operating in the HR arena. Its credibility level is very high, not just as the guardian of HR standards but also, even more importantly, as a forward-looking organisation which consistently sets forth its vision for the future HR profession as well as its standards for the conduct of the HR profession today.

Another way of looking at professionalism and defining it is more concerned with the general approach that people take to their work, the key point being that it is characterised by a high level of quality. Here we are thinking about individuals, the way they carry out their jobs and the approach they take to building relationships with others.

According to this definition, whether you are a member of a professional body or possess some special expertise is irrelevant. A professional is someone who carries out their job – whatever it is – to a high standard. There are professional and unprofessional postmen, professional and unprofessional lawyers and, so it follows, HR managers who act professionally and HR managers who do not.

According to this definition professionalism in HR is not one-dimensional. There are in fact many elements that can be nicely summarised as the following 'four concentric circles of HR professionalism':

- Managing self
- Managing in groups/teams
- Managing upwards
- Managing across the organisation

At the core of professionalism is the ability to manage one's own skills, knowledge and behaviours. Without this ability it is not possible to effectively manage relationships or other individuals. At the second level HR professionals must be able to manage in groups and teams. This might involve working with other HR practitioners to solve problems in an organisational setting or working with other relevant stakeholder groups. The next level is termed 'managing upwards'. HR professionals will be required to work closely with their managers and senior professionals in organisations. Without the ability to manage upwards in an organisation, HR professionals will not be able to integrate their specific strategies and plans with wider organisational strategies.

The final circle of professionalism is given the title 'managing across the organisation'. Once strategies and plans have been agreed and set in place, HR professionals must then be able to set these plans in motion across their organisations. Managing horizontally across the organisation means having the professional knowledge and skills to communicate and influence line managers, highlighting the benefits that can arise from successful and integrated HR activity.

4.4.1 CODES OF CONDUCT AND ETHICS

Ethics and the need to observe high standards of conduct are common to all of these different definitions of professionalism, and we can thus conclude with confidence that a failure to act ethically means that someone cannot claim to be professional and should not be considered to be a member of a profession. This is as true of HRM as any other profession. Despite the importance of ethical behaviour to conceptions of professionalism, there are numerous examples in the press of organisations falling short of expectations. These include the Volkswagen emissions scandal, the collapse of Enron and the allegations of bribery at FIFA.

HRM, as a professional area, has also not been immune to ethical scandal, with the BBC criticised for paying £25 million to 150 outgoing senior employees between 2009 and 2012. In some cases outgoing employees were paid more than their contracts stipulated (BBC 2013). Investigations by the National Audit Office argued that weak governance arrangements had been behind the excessive payouts, which ultimately provided poor value for licence fee payers. Changes implemented after this scandal resulted in the capping of severance payments at the lower of £150,000 or 12 months' salary (BBC 2013), with the corporation reassessing its redundancy policies and arrangements.

For a long time the CIPD has had a code of professional conduct to which its members are expected to adhere. A number of different versions have been published over the years; the current version, downloadable from the CIPD website, having become effective from 1 July 2012. The Code is designed around the CIPD's core aims, namely 'to drive sustained organisation performance through HR, shaping thinking, leading practice and building HR capability'. Moreover, it is written 'to be applicable at all stages of an HR professional's career, working in organisations of every size and type; and in all work roles, for example generalist and specialist, in house and consultancy, in line management, or as an individual contributor'. It has four major parts:

- professional competence and behaviour
- ethical standards and integrity
- representative of the profession
- stewardship.

The following extract highlights key points that appear under these four headings, but HR professionals must ensure that they become familiar with all of the code's detailed stipulations. The full code can be found by following this web link (www.cipd.co.uk/cipd-hr-profession/about-us/code-professional-conduct.aspx).

Professional competence and behaviour

Members of the CIPD shall:

- maintain professional knowledge and competence
- ensure that they provide a professional, up-to-date and insightful service
- accept responsibility for their own professional actions and decisions.

Ethical standards and integrity

Members of the CIPD shall:

- establish, maintain and develop business relationships based on confidence, trust and respect
- exhibit and defend professional and personal integrity and honesty at all times
- demonstrate sensitivity for the customers, practices, culture and personal beliefs of others
- advance employment and business practices that promote equality of opportunity, diversity and inclusion and support human rights and dignity
- safeguard all confidential, commercially sensitive and personal data acquired as a result of business relationships and not use it for personal advantage or the benefit or detriment of third parties.

Representative of the profession

Members of the CIPD shall:

- always act in a way which supports and upholds the reputation of the profession
- comply with prevailing laws and not encourage, assist or collude with others who may be engaged in unlawful conduct
- exhibit personal leadership as a role model for maintaining the highest standards of ethical conduct.

Stewardship

Members of the CIPD shall:

- demonstrate and promote fair and reasonable standards in the treatment of people who are operating within their sphere of influence
- challenge others if they suspect unlawful or unethical conduct or behaviour
- promote appropriate people management and development practices to influence and enable the achievement of business objectives.

As with many other professional codes of conduct, the document developed by the CIPD highlights the ethical and professional responsibilities of members. There is a focus on confidentiality, sensitivity and professional knowledge as well as a need for HR professionals to act as role models in organisations. Broadly speaking, the CIPD's code of professional conduct is a mechanism to prevent exploitation of HR practitioners and is also intended to preserve the integrity of the profession.

4.4.2 CUSTOMERS AND STAKEHOLDERS

For many people, being 'professional' involves taking a stakeholder perspective on the activities of an organisation. This means accepting that a variety of different groups of people have a legitimate stake in an organisation and that their interests must be taken into account by managers when making decisions. This does not mean that a commercial organisation should not seek to maximise its profits or make money for its shareholders, nor does it mean that a public sector organisation should be run to suit the interests of its staff. It means that a reasonable balance has to be struck and that broad principles of fairness must be observed by managers. The major groups of stakeholders are as follows:

- customers
- shareholders/owners
- managers and their staff
- suppliers
- the community.

The adoption of a stakeholder perspective places a particular requirement on HR managers to act as champions for effective and fair people management. It is not our job to take the side of employees against that of management, but it is our job to ensure that genuine employee concerns are communicated to senior managers and that legitimate employee interests are looked after.

It has become fashionable for HR managers to use the term 'customer' when referring to those to whom they supply some kind of internal service, such as professional colleagues, line managers and senior executives. The word 'customer' is also used sometimes to describe people outside the organisation with whom HR managers form professional relationships, such as job applicants. People have different views about the desirability of this trend. Some see it as something of a fad that will pass in time while others argue that it is a misuse of the term 'customer' to apply it to colleagues and would-be colleagues. Many also argue that it is wrong to equate real (external) customers on whom an organisation relies for its survival, with its staff, who are major beneficiaries. The major argument in favour of using the term 'customer' in this internal context is that it serves to remind us of the need to treat our employees and colleagues with due respect, to provide them with a service that is of the highest possible quality and to deliver it with skill and integrity. In other words, it helps to make us act professionally in our dealings with others.

4.5 SELF-MANAGEMENT AT WORK

A key set of skills and habits that underpin effective and professional HRM practice, as well as becoming a 'thinking performer', can be grouped together under the heading 'self-management'. These encompass effective time management, a capacity to manage projects well, analytical and critical thinking, and a range of communication skills. In one short chapter we cannot cover these areas in significant detail, but it is possible to summarise some of the key principles in each case.

4.5.1 TIME MANAGEMENT

Time management essentially revolves around exercising conscious control over the time that is spent completing certain activities. In day-to-day working life HR professionals are faced with competing priorities and there are several methods through which these tasks can be prioritised. One relatively straightforward method is called 'ABC analysis'. Here, tasks are written down into some form of list, perhaps in a notebook or on a computer program, and the professional assigns each task either an 'A', a 'B' or a 'C' depending on their relative level of importance. 'A' tasks are perceived to be urgent and important, 'B' tasks are important but not urgent and 'C' tasks are neither urgent nor important.

HR professionals must find a time management method that works for them. It is important to understand that every individual is different and will therefore optimise his or her productivity in a different way. Having said this, professionals who do not think carefully about time management often become overwhelmed with competing tasks and their productivity subsequently drops as their stress levels rise.

4.5.2 PROJECT MANAGEMENT

Alongside time management, HR professionals must also possess the ability to manage specific projects. The number of projects that HR professionals might need to manage will vary between organisational settings. There may be occasions when individuals are involved with projects for extended periods of time or, alternatively, individual projects may be relatively short in duration. A project can be split into five basic steps or phases that must be completed:

- initiation
- planning and design
- execution
- monitoring and controlling
- completion.

At the initiation stage the nature of the project is determined and a broad idea developed. For instance, an HR manager might want to investigate the effectiveness of an organisation's induction procedure. The second stage of the process takes this broad idea and plans the project to an appropriate level of detail. Keeping with the example above, here the HR manager might state that CIPD guidance is to be reviewed, employees are to be interviewed and retention statistics analysed. The next stage, execution, is all about putting the plan into practice. Our HR manager would now set the plan in motion, collecting the data and drawing conclusions from it.

Monitoring and controlling occurs whilst the execution phase is underway – in other words, the HR manager must monitor the project, identifying any issues and correcting for them. In this example, the HR manager might find that interviews are not providing enough data and he or she might therefore set up some form of organisation-wide survey to ensure the success of the project. At the final stage of the process, completion, the project is evaluated, files are archived and lessons learned.

There are many tools and techniques that professionals can use to manage projects successfully. A key technique that is useful in this regard is milestone monitoring. Successful projects will have milestone or review points built in so that professionals can monitor their progress, making small corrections as and where necessary. In many cases professionals might make use of something known as a 'Gantt chart'. This sort of chart shows the start and end points of a project and highlights the location of different tasks or activities. Gantt charts are useful as they show links between the different elements of projects and highlight where more than one task might be completed at the same time. An example of a Gantt chart is shown in Figure 4.2.

Figure 4.2 A sample Gantt chart

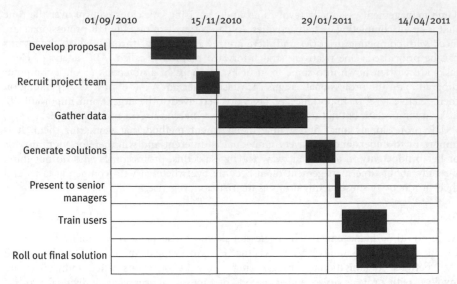

By using a Gantt chart, professionals can see exactly where issues in their project plan might occur. In the example presented in Figure 4.2, it can be seen that if the presentation to senior managers is delayed, this will impact on the training of users and the rolling-out of the final solution. The chart also shows that the training of users and the rolling-out of the final solution can occur at roughly the same time. This information will allow professionals to plan workloads and direct resources to potential problem areas.

4.5.3 ANALYTICAL AND CRITICAL THINKING

The ability to think analytically and critically is fundamental to all professional practitioners, including those who work in the HR field. It is important to understand that the ability to think analytically and critically does not always occur naturally and is something that often develops over time. When thinking analytically, professionals must:

- evaluate how far materials, processes or systems are appropriate
- evaluate whether evidence or examples really prove the points that are being made
- weigh up opinions, arguments or solutions against appropriate criteria
- follow lines of reasoning through to logical conclusions
- check whether evidence and arguments really support conclusions.

Thinking which follows the points above is particularly useful when professionals encounter situations where they need to make decisions based on evidence or ensure that their choices really are suitable or likely to solve specific problems. An example of this might be taking the time to evaluate whether an element of HR strategy really aligns properly with corporate strategy. HR professionals might, for instance, be developing a new reward or pay strategy, and without analytical thinking it might well be difficult to ensure that this strategy links with wider organisational goals.

Let's now turn our attention to the concept of **critical thinking**.

The words 'criticise' and 'critical' are often used in the context that something or someone must be wrong. Being 'critical' in this context means making statements suggesting that theory X is right and theory Y is incorrect. It is very important to understand that this is not what critical thinking is about. Thinking critically involves using 'methods of disciplined, systematic analysis of written or oral discourses'. In other words, a critique is impersonal; professionals are not focusing on an individual. Instead the focus is on analysing the structure of a particular thought, process or system. In order to critique something, HR professionals need to arrive at an informed opinion based on technical knowledge, specific training or their personal or professional experience. HR professionals must recognise that they cannot exercise critical thinking without first having requisite professional knowledge, skills and experience.

> **?   REFLECTIVE ACTIVITY 4.4**
>
> What would happen if HR professionals did not possess the ability to think analytically and critically in organisations?

4.5.4 EFFECTIVE COMMUNICATION

HR managers are required to communicate clearly, effectively and professionally at all times. It is thus a key component of the role and a set of skills that we all have to learn and continually seek to improve. In most cases we become more effective communicators as we gain in confidence and become more practised across the range of communication situations. The major examples are presentations, report writing, networking and difficult relationships.

Presentations

HR professionals make formal presentations very regularly to a variety of audiences. Whether we are briefing senior managers about our activities, leading training sessions for staff, welcoming new starters at induction sessions, opening negotiations with trade unions or summing up after presenting evidence at a disciplinary or tribunal hearing, the same broad principles apply.

Key is the need to tailor the message to the audience. When preparing a presentation it is vital to put yourself in the position of your audience and to speak appropriately. Do not assume that people have knowledge that they may not have, and particularly avoid the use of obscure terminology and acronyms that will mean nothing to them.

Secondly, it is important to get the tone of a presentation right. Sometimes, for example, using humour is appropriate and helpful as a means of conveying a key message. On other occasions it is wholly inappropriate due to the seriousness of a situation.

Thirdly, it is advisable to make as much use as you can of communication aids. PowerPoint slides, provided they are not overcrowded and rushed through at inappropriate speeds, can greatly enhance your ability to get points over in presentations. Handouts written to accompany a presentation are very helpful in many situations, not least because they release the audience from the need to take notes, thus permitting them to concentrate on what you are saying.

Finally, it is necessary to judge the appropriate time to speak. Keeping it short and sweet is often the best advice here. Only say what you have to say and do this concisely and with as much clarity as you are able to. Avoid repeating yourself and saying things that are largely irrelevant to the key message.

Report writing

Many of the skills that underpin effective presentations also apply when it comes to writing effective reports, particularly the general comments made about tailoring your approach and language to the given audience. Being concise is also as important, as is clarity of expression. Here, though, there tends to be a need for rather more formality in the language that is used than is the case with a presentation.

A good report, unlike a written narrative, starts with an 'executive summary', which is, in effect, a brief statement of the contents and its conclusions/recommendations. The reader therefore knows what is coming and should therefore not get any surprises when reading on beyond the summary to the main body of the report. Another key feature of an effective report is the way that evidence is always provided to back up the key points. It should also be possible for someone to quickly read and understand the report, focusing on the summary at the front and the conclusions at the end, while reading the central sections more haphazardly. Signposting helps a lot here. The text should be divided up with subheadings, a full contents list being provided at the start. It also helps if detailed information is placed in appendices at the end of the report so that they can be referred to easily as and when necessary.

Networking

HR professionals, like many groups of people, benefit greatly from building up a network of contacts, both inside and outside the organisation they work for. Being plugged into a wide network of fellow HR professionals means that you have plenty of people to turn to for advice and information. It is also crucial to the development of a career in the profession because it helps you to 'get known' and to be seen as being someone who exercises a degree of professional influence. Effective HR managers also understand that it is vital for them to build up effective networks inside their organisations, the purpose being to develop high-trust relationships with colleagues through whom influence can then be exercised. Only if you are respected and trusted by your fellow managers can you expect to have any say over how they manage the people in their teams.

We plug into networks and build them naturally in the course of our working lives. The skill is to maintain them over time as people who we once worked with closely drift away from us. Maintaining networks requires, above all, effort. It is a question of taking steps to ensure that we do not lose touch with people and that a positive relationship is retained. Social networking websites are hugely helpful in enabling us to achieve these objectives, but they can sometimes be impersonal. So there is a need for regular, direct communication and face-to-face meetings in order to supplement web-based tools. The more relaxed and sociable such meetings can be, the more effective they will be as the basis for maintaining and building networks.

Difficult relationships

In any organisation and in many teams that we work in, relationships become strained. We are often required to work with colleagues we personally dislike or whose values and ways of working we disapprove of. Difficult relationships frequently span organisational hierarchies, resulting in our working for people we perceive as difficult and, very commonly, having to supervise such colleagues.

The first point to make about this is that it is the normal state of affairs. A team of people that operates entirely functionally without clashes of personality and disagreements is very unusual. Relationships in organisations are very often difficult and frequently strain to the point (almost) of breaking, particularly when stress is applied in the form, for example, of change which is perceived as threatening. We may wish that organisational life was not like this, but it is. Complaining about it is no more fruitful than complaining about the weather. We will be better served in these situations by developing coping strategies.

The second key point is to appreciate that relationships can be made to work if the people concerned put a concerted effort into doing so. It is important to try to build good working relationships with all colleagues, even those with whom any relationship is always going to be strained or rocky. As with other forms of communication, building these relationships is something that we learn from experience. Over time, for example, we learn that it is often best to 'bite our tongues' in order to prevent tension from rising unnecessarily. We also learn how important it is to separate disagreements about what needs to happen in an organisation from personal relationships. It should be possible to disagree fundamentally with a colleague and to argue the case passionately without falling out personally at all. Finally, we learn that the best policy is always to treat our colleagues with respect, even when in truth we may not have huge respect for them. This means being as supportive as possible, trying always to understand their point of view and refraining from taking any action which they may see as undermining their position. In short, we need to communicate with others in as mature and emotionally intelligent a manner as we are able to. This often requires us to suppress our natural urges, but that is part and parcel of acting professionally at work.

? REFLECTIVE ACTIVITY 4.5

Consider a 'difficult' relationship that you have experienced either in your personal or professional life. What were the causes of tension in this relationship? How did you attempt overcome the difficulties?

4.6 TEAMWORKING

The dynamics of organisational life means that all professionals must be able to work with one another. HR professionals are no exception to this and must work with colleagues within their function as well as individuals and groups from other backgrounds. There are many academic texts that discuss teamworking and these typically focus on issues such as group dynamics and conflict resolution. It is very important to state that poor teamworking can lead to serious losses in both organisational productivity and individual motivation. This is why it is crucial to understand the various dynamics of group situations.

Huczynski and Buchanan (2010) tell us that teams can take many forms in our organisations, including:

- advice teams (for example review committees or quality control circles)
- action teams (for example negotiating teams)
- project teams (for example planning or research teams)
- production teams (for example assembly teams or manufacturing cells).

Teams vary significantly in their size and structure depending on the specific reasons behind their formation. It is important to understand that HR professionals can be members of different teams at the same time. It is also crucial to remember that HR professionals do not work solely with others in formal teams or groups; they may work with a variety of stakeholders while simply going about their day-to-day tasks.

4.6.1 GROUP DYNAMICS

HR professionals must be aware that the dynamics of group environments are affected by a number of different factors. These include:

- the nature of the individuals in the group
- leadership
- the structure of the group or team
- power and status issues
- communication structures or processes.

In order to operate effectively when working with others, HR professionals must understand that the presence of different individuals with different agendas and needs will affect the balance of group environments. Alongside this important issue, groups are very significantly affected by those in leadership positions. Power and status issues likewise cannot be ignored, and Huczynski and Buchanan (2010) highlight that power-plays and the negative use of political activity can hamper a group's effectiveness.

In order to operate successfully in environments where working with others is the norm, HR professionals must understand the skills associated with collaborative working and conflict resolution. There will, of course, be times where individuals have competing agendas or requirements, and this is when conflict can often arise (Forsyth 2009). In order to successfully resolve conflicts, HR professionals must be clear about the scene and gather relevant information about the other party's needs and wants. The problem situation must then be clearly highlighted (for example, that both parties need financial resources to implement their plans), before both parties brainstorm possible solutions. After coming up with a variety of options, individuals then need to negotiate an effective solution which may involve compromise on both sides in order to arrive at a satisfactory outcome.

?   **REFLECTIVE ACTIVITY 4.6**

Consider a team that you have been a part of. How effective do you think this team was in accomplishing its ultimate goal? In what ways did the various factors discussed above (leadership, structure, power, etc) affect the function of the team?

4.6.2 INFLUENCING

There are many academic textbooks and articles that discuss the concepts of influence and negotiation. Yemm (2008) argues that in order to successfully influence others, HR professionals must spend time thinking about their broad message and how they wish to convey it. It is important to understand that HR professionals often need to influence others in order to bring about some sort of change or to gain buy-in to a new process or way of thinking. An example of this might occur when an HR professional has developed a new employee reward strategy and needs to gain the buy-in of line managers before rolling it out across an organisation.

Yemm (2008) argues that effective influencers possess the following attributes:

- friendliness
- empowerment
- vision
- the ability to build alliances
- expertise and knowledge
- bargaining skill.

In order to influence others, HR professionals must also have requisite knowledge and expertise. Keeping with the reward strategy example discussed above, it is important to understand that without appropriate knowledge and expertise, line managers would no doubt be able to undermine the HR professional's position by asking 'difficult' questions. Alongside knowledge, HR professionals also need to be friendly but assertive. By being open and creating an atmosphere of trust, HR professionals will be better able to communicate their thoughts and listen to the genuine concerns that other stakeholders might have. Another key skill which influencers possess is the ability to strike a bargain. There will be times where compromises have to be made and HR professionals must have the skills to reach agreements in difficult situations.

4.6.3 NEGOTIATING

The purpose of negotiation is to reach a common understanding or viewpoint or produce an agreement upon a common course of action. Effective negotiation skills help all professionals to resolve situations where what one person or group wants conflicts with what another individual or group wants. The best outcome of negotiation is what is known as a 'win–win' situation, where both parties gain or feel that they have achieved a satisfactory outcome.

In order to successfully prepare for negotiation, HR professionals must understand:

- *goals:* what is the aim of the negotiation?
- *trades:* what can be traded between the parties?
- *alternatives:* are there any alternatives if an agreement cannot be reached?
- *relationships:* what history do the parties have? Will this impact on the negotiation?
- *expected outcomes:* what is expected to occur from the negotiation?
- *consequences:* what are the consequences (for both parties) of winning or losing the negotiation?
- *power:* who has power in the relationship?

All of the factors above will impact on negotiation. If HR professionals fail to consider the points above, it is likely that they will be unprepared for negotiation and other individuals or groups may well be able to undermine their position as a result. Style is also an important consideration when negotiating with others. If discussions can be positive and constructive rather than negative and adversarial, there is a greater chance of the parties' coming to a mutually beneficial outcome.

Negotiations often involve a degree of compromise on both sides. Professionals who approach these discussions with the mindset that they will not move from their starting position in any way often cause tension and aggression, extremely negative states from which it is difficult to arrive at positive outcomes. HR professionals must seek to achieve 'win–win' outcomes as often as possible, especially where there is to be an ongoing relationship with the other party.

 FIRST DIRECT

CASE STUDY 4.1

Banking is an industry which has never been noted for its innovative flair, but in 1994 the Midland Bank set up First Direct, initially as a telephone bank and later as also an Internet bank, using approaches which were then revolutionary. For example, it had the courage to ask its customers what they wanted from a bank – which, incredibly, no conventional bank had ever done before. Customers said they wanted five things:

1 Make it easy for me.

2 Leave me in control.

3 Know me as an individual.

4   Treat me as an equal.

5   Give me confidence.

In response, First Direct established a business model arranged around these principles:

Processes designed around the customer – not around the bank's preferences (and certainly not around the preferences of the IT specialists)

Staff empowered to 'manage' interactions with customers – without any reliance on 'scripting' or any form of interactive voice response (IVR) system

Staff treated as respected contributors – with 'people people' as team leaders and managers

Ideas for change and innovation regularly solicited from employees – with their active involvement in continuous-improvement programmes

Staff self-confidence maximised – through extensive training and coaching.

First Direct's initial breakthrough was to find out what its customers wanted from a bank and then give it to them. The second breakthrough was the realisation that if the five fundamental customer needs were to be satisfied, then those same needs had to be met so far as the bank's employees were concerned:

1   *Make it easy for me:* ensure that the bank's systems are as simple and straightforward as possible.

2   *Leave me in control:* empower me to act discretionally with our customers and don't expect me to function mechanically through a repertoire of repetitive scripts.

3   *Know me as an individual:* respect me for who I am, call me by my name, go

some way to respect my need for a reasonable work–life balance.

4   *Treat me as an equal:* allow me to influence decisions on matters that directly concern me, and also to make my own choices.

5   *Give me confidence:* train me, develop me, support me.

First Direct set out to create an organisational culture that deliberately offered a positive contrast to the relatively poor reputations of the traditional and established players in banking circles. Candidates with appropriate personal qualities and attitudes were accepted, irrespective of their level of banking knowledge. Indeed, in most cases the company rejected applicants who had worked for a significant period of time in a conventional bank, because they believed that any capacity for original thinking and imaginative insight would have been destroyed by exposure to an atmosphere of relentless conformity and dogmatic systems.

Questions

What evidence is provided in the case study for:

1   Effective HR management which genuinely adds value?

2   The development of 'thinking performers'?

3   HR policies and practices which are 'business savvy'?

4   Professionalism in the approach taken to managing people?

5   Promotion of effective team-working and communication skills?

FURTHER READING

HARVARD BUSINESS ESSENTIALS (2005) *Time management: increase your personal productivity and effectiveness*. Boston, MA: Harvard Business School Publishing. This text discusses time management in detail and shows how professionals can prioritise tasks, deal with workplace stress and find an effective work–life balance.

SPELLMAN, R. (2011) Don't shoot the boss just yet. *People Management*. 5 July. This article discusses the issues faced by professional managers, including the need for effective time and project management.

THE CRITICAL THINKING COMMUNITY (2015) *Defining critical thinking* [online]. Available at: www.criticalthinking.org/pages/defining-critical-thinking/766. This website provides in-depth information about the concept of critical thinking, highlighting why it is of crucial importance to professionals. The website also provides links to other relevant material.

YEMM, G. (2008) Influencing others – a key skill for all. *Management Services*. Vol 52, No 2. pp21–4. Influencing skills are discussed in detail in this article. Specific tactics for influencing others are highlighted and the development of rapport is also considered.

REFERENCES

BBC (2013) *Q&A: BBC pay-off scandal* [online]. Available at: www.bbc.co.uk/news/entertainment-arts-24013974 [Accessed 13 November 2015].

CIPD (2012) *Business savvy – giving HR the edge* [online]. London: Chartered Institute of Personnel and Development. Available [for members] at: www.cipd.co.uk/hr-resources/research/business-savvy-giving-hr-edge.aspx [Accessed 7 August 2015].

FORSYTH, D. R. (2009) *Group dynamics*. 5th ed. Pacific Grove, CA: Brooks/Cole.

HAMEL, G. (1996) Strategy as revolution. *Harvard Business Review*. July–August. pp69–82.

HUCZYNSKI, A. A. and BUCHANAN, D. A. (2010) *Organizational behaviour*. 7th ed. London: FT/Prentice Hall.

LESTER, S. (2010) *On professionals and being professional* [online]. Stan Lester Developments. Available at: devmts.org.uk/profnal.pdf [Accessed 7 August 2015].

YEMM, G. (2008) Influencing others – a key skill for all. *Management Services*. Summer. Vol 52, No 2. pp21–4.

CHAPTER 5

Using Information in Human Resources

GRAHAM PERKINS AND CAROL WOODHAMS

CHAPTER CONTENTS

- Introduction
- The research project: a roadmap
- Types of data
- Sources of data
- Research approaches and designs
- Collecting data
- Analysing data and drawing conclusions
- Presenting information in a business case
- Understanding the needs of stakeholders

KEY LEARNING OUTCOMES

By the end of this chapter you should be able to:

- effectively identify a relevant area of research within an organisation
- analyse the differences between 'primary' and 'secondary' and 'qualitative' and 'quantitative' data
- critically evaluate various different research approaches and designs
- critically discuss the different ways in which data might be collected in organisations
- evaluate the broad ways in which data might be analysed
- highlight the various components of **business cases** and critically discuss why these documents must be tailored to the needs of different stakeholders.

5.1 INTRODUCTION

This chapter concentrates on the use of information in human resources. It has a primary focus on how HR professionals can undertake small-scale research projects and present their findings in clear, concise business-focused reports. To begin, the chapter highlights how professionals might identify an area of research, exploring the 'roadmap' of a typical project before the various types of data are investigated. It is important to understand that data exists in a variety of forms and that HR professionals must use different techniques to gather and analyse it.

After examining the various types of data, the chapter then moves on to consider sources of data. There are many different places in which we might find information relevant to research projects, including academic journals, online databases, industry reports and the Internet. After thinking about the forms and sources of data, our attention then turns to research methodologies and specific methods of data collection. Please do not be put off by the term 'methodology'; during the chapter we examine the various ways in which we can design our research in simple, straightforward language.

Towards the end of the chapter we reflect on the various ways in which we can analyse data. It is important to understand that without effective data analysis techniques, we are unable to draw firm conclusions and this can hinder the effectiveness of our research projects. These discussions then flow into how we might present information in a business case format, before we close the chapter by considering the needs of different stakeholders.

5.1.1 IDENTIFYING AN AREA OF RESEARCH

There are many different ways in which HR professionals might identify a potential area of research. Horn (2009) highlights that these methods are:

- the 'burning desire' strategy
- the replication strategy
- the practical problem strategy
- the convenient access strategy.

Horn (2009) suggests that the 'burning desire' strategy is born out of a personal interest in a particular area; for some practitioners this might be investigating the causes of workplace stress, while for others it might revolve around assessing the effectiveness of an appraisal process. By contrast, the replication strategy seeks to apply some sort of previous research in a new context. Here the HR professional is seeking to replicate a previous research project in their own organisation, adjusting the scope of the project to fit effectively with the context of their organisation.

The 'practical problem' strategy may be the most common method of identifying an area of research. Perhaps senior managers have highlighted a key area of concern in their organisation or perhaps a staff survey has thrown up an issue which the workforce is concerned about. Either way, there is a practical problem that needs to be addressed through some kind of focused research project. In many ways the practical problem strategy feeds into the convenient access strategy. Within this approach, HR practitioners select a particular area of research because of the access that they have. An example of this might be a pensions administrator conducting some kind of research into the consequences of altering an organisation's pension scheme. The key issue to remember here is that the professional has access to specific data or individuals which will enable the research project to go ahead.

From a practical perspective, Horn (2009) notes that there are several issues which HR professionals need to consider when identifying an area of research. The first of these is searching for similar studies. When embarking on a research project HR professionals need to assess the current knowledge that surrounds their particular topic, whether this is from the academic literature or practical understandings that already exist in their organisations. The second is that HR professionals also need to think about the research process itself and assess whether they have the time, resources and skills to complete their chosen project successfully. It is very important to understand that without necessary time, resources, skills and access, research projects are likely to fail to meet their initial objectives.

Anderson (2013) also advises on the selection of research projects and highlights that HR professionals need to consider the opinions of various stakeholders before settling on a final area of research. From an organisational perspective, Anderson (2013, p41) suggests that key questions worth asking are:

- What is currently bothering me/my boss/my department/my organisation?
- What changes may be occurring in the near future?
- What HR developments may impact on the organisation in the next few weeks and months?

By answering these questions, HR professionals will have a clearer understanding of the specific issues facing their organisations and will therefore be better able to target their research projects. Once an initial area of research interest has been identified, Anderson (2013) then suggests that HR professionals must take time to think carefully about their subject area. It is very important to narrow the scope of research projects so that they can purposefully contribute to organisational performance. While the broad area of a given research project might be 'employee engagement', a more specific aim might be to 'investigate the impact of changing communication strategies on employee engagement'. It is important to understand that by focusing research in this way, HR professionals will be able to target specific issues and gather meaningful information which can then be used to inform strategic decisions.

 IDENTIFYING AN AREA OF RESEARCH

CASE STUDY 5.1

It was a Sunday morning and Ben was stuck behind his computer struggling to think of a relevant idea that could form the basis of his Master's dissertation. He was studying part-time whilst working in his position as an HR Officer for a leading accountancy organisation. He knew that he needed a substantial, original topic, but could not find a spark of inspiration.

In an attempt to develop his ideas, Ben started to map out some of the important projects he was involved with as part of his job. He listed out the various main aspects of his role: employee relations, reward management, recruitment and induction and then started to list out his responsibilities and key problems that

had not yet been solved. While doing this, Ben recognised that his HR team was struggling significantly with its graduate recruitment, the number of unfilled vacancies having risen for three consecutive years.

After making this discovery Ben realised that basing his dissertation on graduate recruitment, seeking to make recommendations for his organisation, would be a very interesting project. Not only was he very interested in the topic himself, but his organisation would be equally interested in the topic as it would, potentially, solve a significant and ongoing problem.

? REFLECTIVE ACTIVITY 5.1

What might happen if an HR professional does not think carefully about the choice of research project? Might this have implications for levels of stakeholder engagement?

This initial part of the chapter has considered the various ways in which HR professionals might identify potential areas of research. It has also highlighted the importance of focusing research carefully to ensure that it provides meaningful information. To build on this introduction to the subject area, the next section highlights the broad roadmap that research projects generally follow. Before sources of data and analysis techniques are discussed in greater detail, it is important to understand how the various steps in research projects interlink and the basic skills that HR professionals need in order to conduct meaningful research.

5.2 THE RESEARCH PROJECT: A ROADMAP

Anderson (2013) notes that unlike in other areas of study or work, research projects and the resulting production of managerial information are often conducted independently. For this reason HR professionals need to ensure that they have the skills to complete these tasks, collecting data and submitting clear reports within given timescales.

The main skills that HR professionals need in order to successfully undertake research projects are those associated with project management. While this chapter does not cover project management methodologies and theories in detail, HR professionals must be able to break large projects down into smaller tasks and then link these effectively in order to produce useful management information. After identifying an area of research, HR professionals must note down the key steps in the research process, including data collection and analysis, and work out which of these can be conducted at the same time and which must follow in a sequential manner. For instance, a reward management specialist, conducting research into perceptions of his or her organisation's benefits package, would need to identify the aims and objectives of the project before starting to collect data. To collect data without first identifying a clear aim would run the risk of missing something important or improperly targeting the research project. Different research projects require different amounts of time to be assigned to the various stages of the research process – for example, one project may require a detailed look at the current literature while another may require more time to be allocated to data analysis.

Helpfully, Anderson (2013) has produced a roadmap which lists the various stages of the research process. This diagram has been reproduced in Figure 5.1. It is important to state here that not all research projects will include all of the steps shown. Figure 5.1 should be seen as a guide rather than a prescriptive 'how to'.

A final key point that is worth mentioning in this section revolves around monitoring. One key benefit of setting out a research roadmap is that it allows for progress to be monitored against initial expectations. Certain aspects of research projects occasionally take longer than expected – for example one-to-one interviews. HR professionals can use project plans and roadmaps to highlight where these issues may occur. By thinking about these issues in advance, HR professionals will be able to plan for contingencies and it will be easier to meet final deadlines as a result.

Having thought about how an area of research might be identified and the importance of setting out a roadmap for this sort of project, attention now turns to the various types of data that may be gathered within research studies.

5.3 TYPES OF DATA

When conducting research projects of any size, HR professionals need to collect and review data that is relevant to their area of research. Figure 5.1 shows that at the very start of research projects, HR professionals must spend time reading around their subject area, evaluating what is already known, before collecting any new data. It is important to understand that there are different types of data that are used in research projects; essentially they fall into the following categories:

- primary or secondary
- qualitative or quantitative.

These bullet points should not be seen as mutually exclusive; in other words, we can have **primary data** which is qualitative or quantitative or **secondary data** which is qualitative or quantitative. Before the latter terms are explored, the differences between primary and secondary data must be clarified.

Figure 5.1 The research project 'journey'

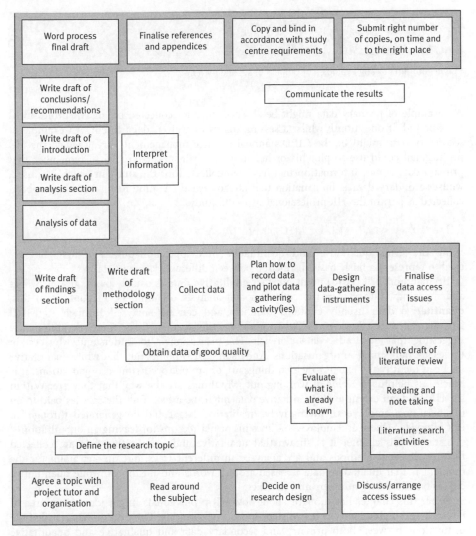

Source: Anderson 2013, p71

5.3.1 PRIMARY AND SECONDARY DATA

Horn (2012) points out that primary data refers to information that has been collected for the study in which it is used. In this sense primary data is 'new' in that it has not been captured by previous research projects. In contrast to this, secondary data refers to information that has been included in or discovered through previous research projects or academic writing. In essence, secondary data is data that already exists and it is often found in books, webpages or professional reports.

Anderson (2013) suggests that effective research projects begin by reviewing secondary data sources before HR professionals start collecting new primary information. Despite making the distinction between primary and secondary data sources, it is crucial to understand that neither is 'right' or 'wrong'; they are simply different sources of information that are relevant in different situations.

?   REFLECTIVE ACTIVITY 5.2

Can you think of any examples of primary or secondary data?

An example of primary data might be absence statistics collected by an HR professional for a period of one month whilst assessing trends in a given department. An example of secondary data might be the CIPD's annual absence management survey which the HR professional could use to plot his or her findings against. It is crucial to remember that primary data is new information that has been collected for the study in which it is used, whilst secondary data is information that already exists in some form that has not been collected as part of the HR professional's specific study.

5.3.2 QUALITATIVE AND QUANTITATIVE DATA

While the terms 'qualitative' and 'quantitative' may appear off-putting at first, they are used to represent a fairly basic distinction between different types of data.

Bryman and Bell (2015) point out that **qualitative data** is usually based around words and meanings, rather than the collection and analysis of numbers. In contrast to this, **quantitative data** usually contains numbers and can be analysed through statistical analysis software. Anderson (2013) goes a little further than these definitions by suggesting that qualitative data can help HR professionals to understand why certain things are happening in organisations. Anderson (2013) points out that while quantitative data can identify the extent to which things are or are not occurring in organisations, it is much less helpful in terms of working out *why* things are the way that they are. Within the HR field, an example of quantitative data might be a list of all the salaries paid to an organisation's employees. Alternatively, qualitative data could be generated through an exit interview, where an employee outlines his or her reasons for leaving an organisation.

Later in this chapter it is shown that qualitative and quantitative data are collected through different methods and are analysed in different ways, but the key point for the moment is that qualitative data is based around words and meanings, while quantitative data is based around numbers and statistics.

So far this chapter has thought about how HR professionals might identify an area of research and highlighted the broad steps in research projects. This section has clarified the distinctions between both primary and secondary data and qualitative and quantitative data. To move on, the following section builds on the territory covered so far by exploring the various sources of data that HR professionals may choose to make use of in their research projects.

5.4 SOURCES OF DATA

Once an area of research has been identified and a research project has been mapped out, HR professionals must gather information which already exists about their area of study. In some 'desk-based' research projects this is as far as data collection goes, but in more involved research projects this data-gathering phase is a precursor to a period of study in one's own organisation. In essence this review of the literature provides the basis of further inquiry and data collection. So, what are the main sources of data?

Anderson (2013) and Horn (2012) suggest that the most important source of data is often likely to be the academic literature on a given subject. If an HR professional is researching an element of employee reward in their organisation, for example, they may wish to consult textbooks or academic journal articles written about their topic. By doing this they will find out what is currently known in a particular field. Academic literature can be accessed through a variety of means, including university or public libraries, academic journals which can be purchased online, or electronic databases which can be searched for key words or phrases. Examples of academic journals relevant to the HR field include the *British Journal of Industrial Relations*, *Employee Relations* and the *Human Resource Management Journal*.

In addition to the sources of data listed above, many professional associations, including the CIPD, the Chartered Institute of Management, or the Institute of Leadership and Management also provide access to libraries of material and these can be very useful sources of data. Aside from physical libraries, some useful online databases for HR research include (Anderson 2013, p90):

- EBSCO
- Emerald
- XPertHR
- Google Scholar
- Science Direct.

Electronic databases such as those listed above can enable HR professionals to quickly assess what is currently known about a particular topic and can be very powerful sources of data. The Internet itself can also be a very useful source of data, although it is important to remember that just because something has been written on a website, it does not mean that it is correct. When searching the Internet for information, it is perhaps best to prioritise well-known organisations and sites such as those listed below:

- The CIPD (www.cipd.co.uk)
- *People Management* (www.cipd.co.uk/pm)
- The Office of National Statistics (www.statistics.gov.uk)
- Companies House (www.companieshouse.gov.uk)

Although this is just a brief selection of websites, the key point to keep in mind is that there can be a large amount of sometimes conflicting data on the Internet. Bryman and Bell (2015) suggest that some sources can be too commercially orientated or very opinionated, and point out that these issues can impact on the quality of final research. They note that key words must be chosen carefully and that HR professionals must take time to think critically about what they are reading. By taking time to assess the relevance of data sources and the quality of information contained within them, HR professionals will produce reports and reviews that stand up to scrutiny.

Finally, in terms of data sources, HR professionals may wish to review media sources such as newspapers, magazines or periodicals such as *The Economist*. These sources of data often include up-to-date, practical examples and case studies and can be used alongside more 'academic' material. In addition to media sources, there are various other commercial and company sources such as labour market reports and commercially published industry reports that may provide useful information that can be used in research tasks.

So how does this process of reviewing various sources of data operate in practice? How can HR professionals ensure that they focus their efforts towards a particular goal rather than adopting a scattergun approach? While Horn (2012) points out that it is very important to assess data from a variety of sources at the beginning of a research project, it is also important to focus this search. In other words, HR professionals investigating the concept of 'total reward', for example, would not review every journal article that mentions the wider field of 'employee benefits'. Instead, HR professionals would concentrate on searching for data sources that mention the impacts of 'total reward' or articles that highlight practical examples of it. The key point to take from this discussion is that HR professionals must focus their search for data by defining their overall aim relatively tightly.

Having now considered the various sources of data that might be used within research projects, the next section of this chapter concentrates on the various ways in which research tasks can be designed. It is important to recognise that different designs are applicable in different situations and the following section considers these 'methodological' issues in detail.

5.5 RESEARCH APPROACHES AND DESIGNS

Having settled on an area of research and thought about the various types and sources of data, HR professionals then need to think about how their projects might be impacted by methodological issues. Although this term may appear complex at first glance, it has a very basic meaning. Essentially, methodological issues are issues connected with how research projects are constructed and carried out. It is important to recognise that there are many different frameworks that HR professionals can use to collect data and these are explored in this part of the chapter.

Before thinking about specific ways in which research projects can be designed, Bryman and Bell (2015) point out that final **research designs** must meet three basic criteria. They must be:

- reliable
- replicable
- valid.

Reliability relates to whether the results of a particular research project are repeatable and whether data collection methods are consistent. Research methods must be replicable; in other words, another researcher must be able to come along and replicate a given study either in the same, or perhaps a different setting. Finally, research designs must be valid, meaning that conclusions that are drawn must be consistent with the data that has been collected. Or, in other words, the data collection instrument needs to measure the item it believes it is measuring to be valid.

Keeping the three basic criteria in mind, Anderson (2013) points out that there are four basic research strategies or 'designs' that HR professionals can choose from. It is important to understand that each of these designs is appropriate in different situations, and so we cannot say that one specific design is 'better' or 'worse' than any other design. The research designs that Anderson (2013, p60) has discussed include:

- cross-sectional
- case study
- action
- comparative.

5.5.1 CROSS-SECTIONAL DESIGNS

The cross-sectional design simply involves the collection of data in a relatively standardised form from groups or individuals at a single point in time. Data might be gathered through surveys or interviews. Cross-sectional research is useful when researchers are attempting to uncover patterns or make comparisons between groups or scenarios. The advantages of this research design include the fact that it is relatively cheap to organise and administer and can achieve a broad coverage. This research design can also lead to the production of a large amount of information. An example of a cross-sectional study would be an HR professional distributing a questionnaire covering a topic, such as employee engagement or work–life balance, to the employees of an organisation, analysing the resultant data for patterns and trends.

Thinking more critically, the cross-sectional design can be inappropriate at times because depth is sacrificed for breadth, and poor survey or interview questions can lead to poor quality data being collected. It is also important to recognise that there is a lack of control over how individuals respond to questions, and that different individuals may interpret questions in different ways.

5.5.2 CASE STUDY DESIGNS

The second design in Anderson's (2013) list is known as the case study design. Whereas the cross-sectional design looks to gather data from individuals or groups at a single point in time, this method involves a detailed investigation into a situation which might be a single case or small number of related cases. The case study design is useful where the issue being examined is very difficult to separate from its wider context. Within the case study design, interviews and periods of observation are often used to collect data. As an example, an HR professional could utilise a case study design when attempting to discover more about an organisation's culture. Needing to explore the issue in significant depth, the HR professional may interview and observe employees, understanding exactly how culture operates and proliferates within the given setting. The resultant data would be very detailed and complex, it would help the HR professional to understand culture within the organisation studied, but would not necessarily help to understand the same issues in other organisations. In other words the data would not be generalisable.

The advantage to this design is its focus on one specific issue and the fact that it can focus on only one department or group if necessary. From a critical perspective, we can argue that case study designs often produce a large amount of qualitative data which can be difficult to analyse. It is also important to note that it is often difficult, if not impossible, to cross-check information. Our ability to generalise – that is, draw recommendations and learning from one context to another – is also limited when there is only a single research setting.

5.5.3 ACTION RESEARCH DESIGNS

Anderson (2013) points out that action research designs are firmly grounded in problem-solving. The overall aim of this research design is to understand and promote change. Within action research, researchers are involved in a continual cycle of planning, taking action and then observing the effects of that action. While this design is useful if the researcher is attempting to solve a specific problem inside an organisation, there are drawbacks to keep in mind. An example of action research could involve an HR professional involving others, ie employees, managers and trade union representatives, in the planning and design of a system to promote employee voice and participation at work. By involving others, the HR professional may be able to change patterns of thinking, contribute to practical action and experiment with different ideas and solutions.

Having said this, a significant drawback to action research is that it can often be descriptive rather than explaining why things are the way that they are. Researchers can state the effects of certain actions but may not be able to tell precisely why these actions have occurred or what has motivated them. It is also important to state that action research involves a significant time commitment and that it can be difficult to justify any value in terms of knowledge and understanding outside of the specific research setting.

5.5.4 COMPARATIVE DESIGNS

The final design described by Anderson (2013) is termed 'comparative'. As suggested by the title, comparative research designs allow for comparisons to be made between different groups or situations, usually internationally. Comparative research often uses standardised surveys or interviews to collect data in different settings, allowing researchers to compare and contrast findings. We could perhaps use comparative research to compare levels of staff engagement at different company sites or within different departments in one particular organisation.

The main drawback to comparative research designs is that they can be difficult to administer and organise. Another difficulty lies in making valid and accurate comparisons. It is important to recognise that not all environments have a sufficient amount in common to enable comparative research to be successful. Despite these challenges, Anderson (2013) points out that comparative designs can tell researchers a great deal about how HR practices and frameworks operate in different situations.

 REFLECTIVE ACTIVITY 5.3

Which research design do you think would be most useful if you were attempting to investigate a single issue in detail within an organisation?

Moving on from research approaches and designs, the next part of the chapter explores the various ways in which HR professionals can collect data. You will remember that surveys, interviews and observation were all mentioned in this part of the chapter, and these (along with other methods) are now discussed in detail.

5.6 COLLECTING DATA

Before thinking about specific data collection methods, this part of the chapter needs to address the concept of **sampling**. What is sampling, and why do researchers use it?

Broadly speaking, sampling is useful where there are large groups and researchers cannot collect data from every individual. Suppose an organisation has 1,000 employees and a researcher wants to collect data through interviews. It is important to recognise that interviewing all 1,000 staff would involve a considerable amount of time and produce an inordinate amount of material. For these reasons, interviewing all employees would be ineffective and inefficient. In this instance, authors including Creswell (2007) and Horn (2012) point out that HR professionals would normally choose to interview a proportion of the employees to speed up data collection and save costs.

Bee and Bee (2005) and Creswell (2007) describe several different sampling strategies that HR professionals might choose from. The primary concern when choosing a sample is that it reflects the wider characteristics of the group. If, for instance, an organisation employs 500 individuals in a production department and 500 individuals in a marketing department, it would be inappropriate to interview 250 production employees and only 50 marketing employees. This approach to sampling would not be representative of the real situation and would thus lead to bias in the data. This is a key point that is worth keeping in mind. Sampling strategies, however they are chosen, must be representative of the wider groups from which the samples are drawn.

CASE STUDY 5.2

SAMPLING

Sarah is employed as the HR Manager at ABC Machining Limited, a large organisation headquartered in London supplying specialist parts to companies around the globe. In total the organisation employs 750 individuals in a variety of positions, located at factories around the UK.

Having recently introduced a new employee reward package, Sarah is keen to understand the impact that this has had on employee satisfaction and retention. Knowing that she wants to gather representative data, but cannot interview or survey the entire organisation due to time and resource constraints, Sarah finds herself in somewhat of a dilemma. How can she gather useful and informative data without involving everyone employed by the organisation?

Helpfully, Sarah's manager suggests that she gather only a smaller set of data from each department and location, a more straightforward task but still representative of the wider whole. Together with her manager, Sarah devises a plan whereby she would interview 10% of the total population, a total of 75 individuals. She puts together a sample selection which ensures that each department, location and job grade is covered, to ensure that there could be no accusation of bias within the data set. Following approval, she implements her plan and collects representative data in a fraction of the time that would have been needed had she set out to interview every member of staff employed by the firm.

Having thought about issues relating to sampling, this part of the chapter can now move on to examine specific methods of data collection. Anderson (2013) and Bryman and Bell (2015) point out that research projects typically make use of one (or more) of the following data collection methods:

- surveys/questionnaires
- interviews
- focus groups
- participant observation.

5.6.1 SURVEYS

Many research projects involve the use of some form of survey or questionnaire. Bryman and Bell (2015) state that surveys involve researchers producing documents which detail specific questions that respondents then provide answers for. Surveys are generally cheaper and faster to administer than interviews and are typically more convenient for respondents as they can complete them when they have a period of free time. Thinking more critically, it is important to understand that surveys do not allow for researchers to prompt individuals to provide more information about particular topics and it is also difficult to ask complex questions. In addition, there is also the risk that respondents might not answer specific questions and that response rates in general might be low.

In order to improve response rates, it is important that surveys are clear and concise so that they do not appear bulky and off-putting. Questions may be either 'open' or 'closed' – in other words, they may require a yes/no answer or a tick to be placed in a box (closed) or they may require a few words or a sentence of explanation (open). The format of questions and the content of the survey will be driven by the topic that the researcher is investigating.

5.6.2 INTERVIEWS

Horn (2012) points out that interviews are normally classified as a qualitative method for gathering data and that the skills required for interviewing are different from the skills required for preparing a survey. While researchers may use similar questions in interviews as they do in surveys, it is important to understand that interviews are predominantly about listening and understanding what the respondent is saying.

Broadly speaking, interviews are useful where researchers need to investigate a small number of issues in a significant amount of detail. While surveys may be useful in capturing broad perspectives and understandings of specific topics, interviews allow researchers to dig into specific details, opinions and views. Interviews may therefore be useful when an HR professional is seeking to gain an insight into complex and multifaceted issues such as organisational culture, employee engagement or the psychological contract. Both Horn (2012) and Bryman and Bell (2015) note that interviews can be either 'structured' or 'unstructured' – in other words, they can follow strict question sets or they can flow in a more discursive way. It is important to recognise that different topics and question sets lend themselves to either structured or unstructured formats.

Interviews can allow researchers to gather a wealth of information about specific topics, although it can be time-consuming to analyse the output and the interviews themselves take a significant amount of time to organise and administer. Researchers need to decide whether the time commitments involved in interviewing are offset by the potential benefits of gathering more detailed data.

5.6.3 FOCUS GROUPS

Some researchers assume that focus groups are just interviews that are conducted with a group rather than with individuals on their own. Walker (1985) points out that this is not the case and that focus groups should be used where researchers are interested in how groups of individuals make sense of specific concepts or ideas.

Building from the points above, it is important to understand that focus groups are relevant where researchers are investigating tightly defined issues or concepts. Focus groups themselves promote dialogue and discussion and allow researchers to find out about a range of attitudes and opinions on a given topic. A practical example of the use of focus groups might be where an organisation is attempting to gauge reactions to a new product or to a new internal reward package. The participants in the focus group can be questioned about specific issues and researchers will be able to see how the group forms its opinions.

It is important to understand that while there are benefits to the use of focus groups, there are also drawbacks. It can sometimes be difficult to get participants together and there is always the risk that one or two individuals might dominate the discussion. It is also important to remember that the focus group participants need to be representative of the group which is the focus of the study.

5.6.4 PARTICIPANT OBSERVATION

The final data collection method to be examined in this part of the chapter is participant observation. Bryman and Bell (2015) indicate that participant observation occurs where the researcher immerses himself or herself in a social setting for an extended period of time. During this time the researcher observes behaviour and listens to what is said in conversation and might ask questions to find out more detailed information about specific events or issues. For instance, an HR professional attempting to understand more about the working practices of a particular department or company site, may wish to observe employees and managers going about their daily activities.

From a positive perspective, participant observation can allow researchers to observe the realities of the workplace and it can also be an efficient way of gathering data about practical problems. Thinking more critically, it is important to understand that researchers may not actually view the 'realities of the workplace' as observed individuals may modify their behaviour or conduct simply because of the presence of the observer. It is also important to think through the ethical considerations of observing others. Nevertheless, this data collection method can provide a useful insight into the inner workings of organisations.

In this part of the chapter, the concept of sampling has been discussed and several methods through which HR professionals might collect data to use within their research projects have been explored. Having now collected this data, the next step in the research process is to analyse this data to search for key themes and issues. The following section considers these issues in detail.

5.7 ANALYSING DATA AND DRAWING CONCLUSIONS

Methods of data analysis vary depending on the type of data that has been collected within research projects. Quantitative data (that is, data which is numerical in nature) is often best analysed through spreadsheets or bespoke statistical software such as SPSS. Qualitative data (that is, data which contains words and meanings) is most often analysed through visual comparison and computer database programmes or specialist software, such as NVivo. The choice of analysis method will very much depend on the nature of research projects. If an HR professional has gathered only a small amount of quantitative data, a spreadsheet package such as Microsoft Excel might be the best analysis tool, whereas a large amount of qualitative data must be analysed through a bespoke piece of software such as NVivo.

Once a data analysis tool has been selected, HR professionals must then examine the collected data looking for patterns, correlations and underlying meanings. Within quantitative research projects it is often easy to produce detailed analyses demonstrating the strength of various factors. For example, if an HR professional was conducting a staff survey, they might find that everyone answered a question concerning their work environment very positively. This finding would be made clear through statistical analysis and the HR professional would be able to draw reasonably firm conclusions.

Analysing qualitative data is often more complicated. Once data has been collected, sorted and perhaps input into a computer system or database, HR professionals must then search for key words or phrases that repeat themselves throughout the data. If patterns are found, HR professionals will be able to draw conclusions about particular issues. For instance, everyone might use specific words or phrases to describe the work environment or their relationship with their line manager. HR professionals will be able to ascertain how 'strong' particular findings are depending on the number of references to specific issues.

? REFLECTIVE ACTIVITY 5.4

Assume for a moment that an HR professional has undertaken a research project investigating the effects that an induction programme has had on overall levels of staff retention in an organisation. The data has been collected through semi-structured interviews and retention statistics.

What type (or types) of data will this HR practitioner have collected, and how might it best be analysed?

Once patterns and underlying meanings have been found, HR professionals must then think about how best to present their data. Anderson (2013) suggests that charts and tables can be useful methods of displaying key findings, while Bryman and Bell (2015) indicate that practitioners might also want to produce bullet lists of more general points. For instance, was one particular phrase repeated on several occasions in a qualitative study? If so, practitioners might want to include this in their findings. Computer software such as Microsoft Excel and SPSS can be used to produce graphs and tables, and in some cases HR professionals might want to produce more detailed analyses using pictograms, histograms or frequency tables. The purpose of this section is simply to provide an overview of the potential data analysis methods rather than full descriptions of techniques, so these particular issues are not explored in more detail here. Follow-up references are provided in the *Further Reading* section for HR professionals who wish to investigate data analysis in greater detail.

Now that the basic issues surrounding data analysis and drawing conclusions have been discussed, the next stage in the research process is to present findings back to key stakeholders.

5.8 PRESENTING INFORMATION IN A BUSINESS CASE

Clarity is perhaps the most fundamental point to keep in mind when presenting research findings in a business case. Many sources including Marchington and Wilkinson (2008) and Anderson (2013), indicate that business cases must be structured effectively so that they communicate findings and put forward recommendations clearly. Anderson (2013) suggests that reports and business cases generally contain the following main elements:

- title page
- summary or abstract
- introduction
- literature review
- methodology
- findings and analysis
- conclusions
- recommendations.

While the above list certainly provides a useful starting point, it does not provide detailed information about the contents of each part of the research report. Helpfully, many business research texts such as Bryman and Bell (2015) and Saunders et al (2016) (and others) provide detailed instructions and guidance in this regard. Table 5.1 contains an overview of each part of the research report and lists the common contents of the various sections.

It is important to understand that different projects will follow different formats, so methods of presentation will vary. In some cases, HR professionals will not be required to construct a written report; instead they may be asked to present their findings verbally at some sort of meeting. Irrespective of whether the final business case is presented verbally or in a written report, it is important to follow the relevant elements of structure highlighted in the bullet list above. If this structure is not followed, key points may be underplayed and, as a result, the overall business case will not be clear.

Table 5.1 The research report

Section	Common contents/coverage
Introduction	• Provides a clear overview of the topic • Should contain the aim and objectives of the research project • Covers any necessary background information – eg company information or history and reasons why the research was considered necessary
Literature review	• Highlights existing work within your chosen area of study, eg academic theories, findings of previous research projects, benchmarking data, etc • Must be written in a critical and analytical rather than descriptive manner • This is the stage at which you introduce your research questions or hypotheses
Methodology	• Outlines and defends your choice of research technique (eg interviews/surveys) and the type of data that you gathered (qualitative/quantitative) • Must allow the reader to understand the rationale behind your selection of methods • Should discuss any potential limitations that your study might have, for example, the size of your sample
Findings and analysis	• Reporting of your results – this is where you will include charts and tables setting out your data • Must include a discussion of the implications of what you have found. For example why might you have found a particular theme or pattern in your data? • Your discussion should, where possible, link to relevant academic and professional literature
Conclusion	• Answers to your research questions or hypotheses • What are the managerial and practical implications of what you have found? • Areas of possible future research and a reflection on the limitations of your study • A summary of your research project
Recommendations	• Linked to your findings and conclusion, here you should highlight practical steps to address the problem that you have investigated • Good recommendations will be action-orientated, describe costs, outline timescales and provide an indication of accountabilities • Recommendations must be accompanied by a short, but compelling justification, again linked to your findings and conclusion

Horn (2012) notes that HR professionals may want to use graphs, diagrams and other visual aids to demonstrate key points within their business cases. If, for example, a research project was exploring the causes of absence in an organisation, an HR professional may be able to produce some sort of chart indicating the absence levels in different departments or divisions. An example of this sort of chart is contained in Figure 5.2.

Figure 5.2 Using charts in business cases

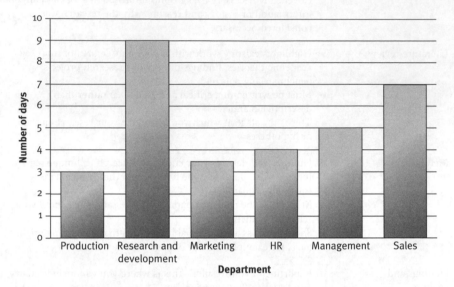

You will agree, I am sure, that Figure 5.2 demonstrates key findings more effectively than paragraphs of text or a list of numbers and is likely to add clarity to a business case. Horn (2012) goes on to point out that effective HR professionals will use their business cases to highlight key trends and present diagrams and charts to support their conclusions and recommendations.

It is important to recognise that the write-up of a research project is arguably the most important stage. Without an effective write-up, our research will not be viewed as credible and our conclusions and recommendations will be dismissed. Saunders et al (2016) provide advice about the writing process and note that we must see writing as a continuous process. In other words, we should write up our research reports as we progress through our research project, rather than leaving the write-up to the end. Furthermore Saunders et al (2016) suggests that we should create allocated portions of time for our writing, such as from 08:00 to 10:00 or from 16:00 to 18:00. Finding a time slot that works for you, when you will not be disturbed and when your mind is fresh, will allow you to make faster progress through your write-up. They also suggest that we should create and use a structure for our writing (such as the structure discussed earlier in this section) and that we should set interim goals for ourselves. For example, during one writing session we may decide to focus on completing our introduction, or developing and justifying our recommendations. Setting clear goals can help to maintain motivation and enthusiasm, allowing us to see that we are making progress with the write-up of our research project.

A final topic to consider in this chapter is the needs of various stakeholders. When compiling business cases and reports, it is vital to recognise that different stakeholders have different needs. These issues are now explored in detail.

5.9 UNDERSTANDING THE NEEDS OF STAKEHOLDERS

Anderson (2013) suggests that a key part of writing effective business cases and research reports is understanding who the readers are going to be and what they are going to be looking for. HR professionals must understand that senior managers have different needs from employees who equally have different needs from professional bodies or educational institutions. Before compiling a research report or business case, HR professionals must ask themselves who will be reading or listening to the information and think about what the stakeholders are going to want to know.

Senior managers as a stakeholder group are likely to be concerned with how research projects will enable them to operate more efficiently and effectively. As a consequence of this, business cases must highlight key findings and how they will feed into the wider strategy of the organisation. Contrastingly, employees are likely to want to know how the research project will improve their working conditions or processes. It should be clear that understanding the needs of stakeholders when writing business cases and reports is of paramount importance.

Once a business case (either written or verbal) has been drafted, HR professionals must take time to review their work and evaluate its likely effectiveness. While going about this analysis, HR professionals must think very carefully about the needs of stakeholder groups and whether their final report will meet these requirements. By thinking carefully about the needs of stakeholder groups, HR professionals will inevitably produce more effective business cases and research reports.

CASE STUDY 5.3

RESEARCHING ABSENCE AT WORK

Tamara is a student in a hurry. She is a distance-learning student fulfilling a demanding role in an important government department in a fairly small overseas location. Tamara's organisation must change rapidly to meet new government modernisation requirements in her country. Absence from work is a big problem in Tamara's organisation. Although certain departments have very low rates of absence on average, others have significant issues. Indeed in some departments the rate of absence is almost triple the organisation's overall average. As a result of this, the government has set challenging targets in this area, so it is in the area of absence management that Tamara has decided to focus her research project.

Tamara and her manager have met to discuss her project and have decided that investigating the specific causes of absence would be useful for the organisation. They agree that a variety of stakeholders will be interested in the results of the project including senior managers, line managers and employee representatives. In broad terms, Tamara and her manager agree that she needs to collect data from the 1,000 strong workforce, focusing in particular on the differences in absence rates between managers and front-line employees. The plan is that Tamara will be able to evaluate the effectiveness of current absence management practices and recommend improvements.

An issue that Tamara is attempting to deal with at the moment is how she will frame the research project as a whole and target specific questions to gather relevant data. Tamara's manager has pointed out that there are many different sources of data which discuss absence management, although Tamara has indicated that she is unsure as to the benefits of reviewing what has gone before. Tamara's manager points out that there are both academic articles and industry reports that might include relevant information, including possible question frameworks and the results of research in similar organisations.

A final question that needs to be addressed is how data will be presented back to various stakeholder groups. Tamara is aware that senior managers will be interested in hearing about the results of her research; however, they do not have much time to read through lengthy reports. The senior management team do meet every Monday to discuss strategic issues, although Tamara is still not sure about how to present information in this situation. These meetings often have a very busy agenda and she is unlikely to be given more than 20 or 30 minutes in which to present her findings and recommendations. Line managers will also want to see the results and Tamara has been told that this group would prefer to receive a report that they can keep for future reference.

Source: adapted from: Anderson (2013, p11)

Questions

1   What methods might Tamara use to collect new data about absence management inside her organisation?

2   Why should Tamara take time to assess the current body of knowledge surrounding absence management before she embarks on her own data collection?

3   Critically discuss how Tamara might effectively present her findings back to the various stakeholder groups mentioned in the case study.

5.10 CONCLUSION

Being able to effectively and efficiently find and utilise information is a key skill that HR professionals need to master. While it is true that research projects differ from one another, all have common aspects and require similar skills and abilities. The HR professional needs to recognise that data can exist in different forms and can be acquired from varying sources, including academic journals and textbooks, industry reports and statistics and finally, organisational documentation. When collecting *primary* data HR professionals also have a number of options available, including surveys, interviews, observation and focus groups. It is crucial that HR professionals recognise that different methods will be appropriate in different situations, and that data collection methods can also be combined to provide a more detailed overview of a situation.

Analysis methods will depend on whether data is either qualitative or quantitative. HR professionals may need to use specialised computer software to analyse their collected data. It is to be remembered that data analysis can take a significant amount of time and that if rushed, the results may not produce meaningful conclusions. The needs of different stakeholder groups may necessitate the HR professional presenting data in different ways. It is important that effective business cases are developed which provide a basis from which actions can be taken or recommendations can be made. Presentations of findings, whether verbal or written, must accurately report the findings of the research project and be presented in a clear, concise and compelling way.

FURTHER READING

ANDERSON, V. (2013) *Research methods in human resource management.* 3rd ed. London: Chartered Institute of Personnel and Development. This detailed text provides HR professionals with information about how research projects can be structured alongside various data collection and analysis techniques. (See back of book for sample chapter).

BRYMAN, A. and BELL, E. (2015) *Business research methods.* 4th ed. Oxford: Oxford University Press. This text considers many of the theories that underpin management research and also discusses practical issues, including various research techniques and sources of data.

FREE MANAGEMENT LIBRARY (2015) *Basic business research methods* [online]. Available at: http://managementhelp.org/businessresearch/index.htm. This website provides detailed information about various methods of data collection and considers how results can be analysed, interpreted and reported.

HORN, R. (2012) *Researching and writing dissertations: a complete guide for business and management students.* 2nd ed. London: Chartered Institute of Personnel and Development. This textbook provides a useful overview of important topics such as finding a research area, constructing an appropriate methodology and analysing data.

IBM (2015) *IBM SPSS statistics* [online]. Available at: http://www-01.ibm.com/ software/analytics/spss/products/statistics/. This website provides information about the statistical analysis tool SPSS.

LESSER, E. (2010) HR analytics: go figure. *People Management.* 20 May. This *People Management* article highlights the importance of collecting data in the HR field so that organisations can make effective strategic decisions.

QSR INTERNATIONAL (2015) *NVivo 10 for Windows* [online]. Available at: www.qsrinternational.com/products_nvivo.aspx. This website provides product information about the NVivo 10 software package.

TAYLOR, N. (2010) How to... write a business case. *People Management.* 2 September. This *People Management* article explores the practical issues around the construction of business cases in human resources.

REFERENCES

ANDERSON, V. (2013) *Research methods in human resource management.* 3rd ed. London: Chartered Institute of Personnel and Development.

BEE, F. and BEE, R. (2005) *Managing information and statistics.* 2nd ed. London: Chartered Institute of Personnel and Development.

BRYMAN, A. and BELL, E. (2015) *Business research methods.* 4th ed. Oxford: Oxford University Press.

CIPD (2015) *CIPD* [online]. Available at: www.cipd.co.uk/ [Accessed 28 July 2015].

COMPANIES HOUSE (2014) *Companies House* [online]. Available at: www.gov.uk/ government/organisations/companies-house [Accessed 28 July 2015].

CRESWELL, J. W. (2007) *Qualitative inquiry and research design.* 2nd ed. London: Sage.

HORN, R. (2009) *Researching and writing dissertations: a complete guide for business students.* London: Chartered Institute of Personnel and Development.

HORN, R. (2012) *Researching and writing dissertations: a complete guide for business and management students.* 2nd ed. London: Chartered Institute of Personnel and Development.

MARCHINGTON, M. and WILKINSON, A. (2008) *Human resource management at work.* 4th ed. London: Chartered Institute of Personnel and Development.

PEOPLE MANAGEMENT (2012) *People Management* [online]. Available at: www.cipd.co.uk/pm [Accessed 28 July 2015].

SAUNDERS, M., LEWIS, P. and THORNHILL, A. (2016) *Research methods for business students.* 7th ed. Harlow: Pearson.

UK NATIONAL STATISTICS (2012) *UK national statistics* [online]. Available at: www.statistics.gov.uk [Accessed 28 July 2015].

WALKER, R. (1985) *Applied qualitative research.* Aldershot: Gower.

CHAPTER 6

Developing the Knowledge and Skill of the HR Professional

Carol Woodhams, Graham Perkins and Krystal Wilkinson

CHAPTER CONTENTS

- Introduction
- The CIPD's HR profession map
- The principles of continuous professional development
- The theory of CPD: reflective practice
- Managing your CPD
- CIPD membership and career progression
- Further resources to support your learning

KEY LEARNING OUTCOMES

By the end of this chapter, you should be able to:

- feel familiar with the range of tools from the CIPD that guide the development of the HR profession
- evaluate the significance of continuing professional development (CPD) to HR and other professionals
- understand how to effectively manage your own CPD
- feel familiar with the content contained in the other textbooks in this series and understand the various sources of information that are available to HR professionals.

6.1 INTRODUCTION

It is noted in the introduction of Watson and Reissner (2014) that 'knowledge, skills and continuing professional development (CPD) are at the top of the twenty-first century human resources agenda'. Returning to themes established in Chapter 5, this final chapter explores the knowledge, skills and behaviours that are central to the work of an HR professional and their development. Important here are the linked concepts of the CIPD's HR profession map, to diagnose areas of developmental need, and continuing professional development (CPD) as a means of meeting those needs. During the course of this chapter we analyse both. We also include a number of suggestions of resources that support learning.

Initially, we prioritise areas for development by exploring the CIPD's 'map' of HR expertise. Then we analyse the principles of CPD, explain its importance in the modern business world and review the theory that underpins it. We then turn to more practical issues and explore the various tools and techniques that can be applied to maximise the potential of CPD in an HR role before we examine the connection between CPD and the CIPD's professional framework. Finally, to support your learning, this chapter summarises material from other titles in this series and provides an indication of the sources of information that you can access to further develop your skills and knowledge.

6.2 THE CIPD'S HR PROFESSION MAP

The CIPD's **HR profession map** sets out in detail the competencies which HR professionals will need in the foreseeable future. The map itself can be thought of as a competency framework and is the product of significant research into what it means to be an HR 'professional'. This section shows how it is useful in guiding development.

Introduced in 2009, the map reflects the belief that the HR profession as an 'applied business discipline with and people a organisation specialism'. This means that HR professionals must work 'from a deep business, contextual and organisational understanding' to deliver sustainable organisation performance, to be made real by using insights to create HR strategies and deliver solutions that stick, taking people with them and staying agile and innovative (CIPD 2015, p9).

The fact that HR professionals must work from a comprehensive understanding of business, contextual and organisational issues is a point which requires special emphasis. It is important to understand that the ten elements in the 'capability framework' of the HR profession map are intended to 'emphasise the contributions that everyone in the profession needs to make, regardless of role, level or specialism'. In other words, these 'professional areas' are not purely aimed at HR managers, HR consultants or HR directors – they are equally applicable to HR practitioners who are just embarking on their professional careers. People just like you.

At the time of writing and as part of the Profession for the Future project, the CIPD are preparing for a refresh of the map and gathering comments on the next version. Access the online map (CIPD 2015) and check out page 3 for details of how you can get involved.

The CIPD's HR profession map is shown in Figure 6.1. Currently it contains ten different areas, which will now be explored in greater detail.

There are two areas at the heart of the profession map:

- insights, strategy and solutions
- leading HR.

The first area details the knowledge, skills and behaviours that are needed to develop understanding of the business and its context and use these insights to tailor strategies and solutions to meet organisation needs now and in the future. Leading HR is built around the need for individuals to act as a role model leader, maximising the contribution that HR, or your own specialist function, makes throughout the organisation both through your own efforts and through supporting, developing and measuring others across the organisation.

Alongside these two core professional areas there are eight additional functional professional areas in which HR professionals implement HR as an applied business discipline. The relevance of these areas will depend on the specific role that practitioners have in organisations. For instance, while performance and reward may be a key area for an employee reward specialist, the learning and talent development area is far more relevant to someone responsible for learning and development in their organisation. The basic content of each functional area is highlighted in this bullet list:

Figure 6.1 The CIPD's HR profession map

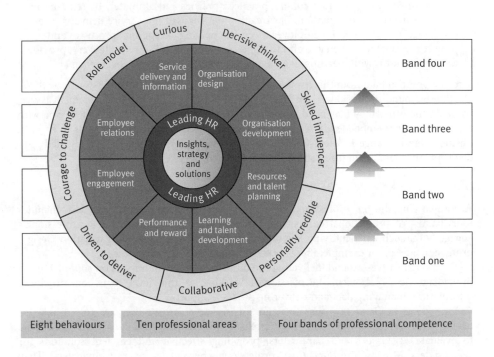

- *Organisation design*: Ensure that the organisation is appropriately designed to deliver maximum impact in the short and long term.
- *Organisation development*: Identify organisational and individual capability requirements and align strategy, people and processes to optimise effectiveness and achieve organisation goals. Design interventions to drive the appropriate culture, behaviours skills and performance and provide insight and leadership on change management strategy, planning and implementation.
- *Resourcing and talent planning*: Ensure that the organisation has the right resources, capability and talent to achieve immediate and strategic ambitions now and in the future.
- *Learning and development*: build organisational capability and knowledge to meet current and strategic requirements, and create a learning culture to embed capability development.
- *Performance and reward*: Help create and maintain a high-achieving organisation culture by delivering programmes that reward and recognise key employee capabilities, skills behaviours, experience and performance, and ensure that reward systems are market-relevant, fair and cost-effective.

- *Employee engagement*: Work to strengthen the connection that all employees have with their work, colleagues and to their organisation so that employees are more fulfilled by their work and make a greater contribution towards organisational objectives; give particular attention to good leadership and management.
- *Employee relations*: Ensure that the individual and collective relationships between the organisation and its employees are managed appropriately; within a clear framework underpinned by organisation culture, practices, policies and ultimately by relevant law.
- *Service delivery and information*: Ensure customer-focused HR service delivery excellence across the entire employee lifecycle, applying exceptional processes and project management to enable effective and cost-efficient HR service delivery; provide the organisation with meaningful analytics to enable business improvements.

The key point to take from this list concerns the diversity of the HR profession as a whole. On the one hand professionals can be tasked with sorting out reward management issues, while on the other they may need to advise on elements of contract law. And, in line with themes that were embedded in Chapter 4, there is a need for HR professionals to be both business- and change-focused. This is an important point, which should be fed into development plans – but more about them later in the chapter.

6.2.1 THE BANDS OF PROFESSIONAL COMPETENCE

Accompanying the ten professional areas, the CIPD's HR profession map also includes four 'bands' of professional competence. Alongside each activity that HR professionals engage with, such as 'identifying key organisation processes' in the 'Organisation Design' professional area, for example, there are four distinct levels of competence.

Band one revolves around 'delivering the fundamentals', with a focus on supporting the immediate needs of clients. Professionals working at this level focus on providing information, managing data and delivering process support.

Individuals at *Band two* operate at an 'adviser' level, where they are responsible for dealing with current or near-term priorities. Professionals operating at this level must be able to evaluate HR issues and parameters, providing effective and efficient solutions for stakeholders. Moving into *Band three*, professionals become 'co-operative partners'. They will be expected to lead the professional area and deal with medium- to long-term challenges. Professionals must understand functional and business realities, provide ideas and insights, and challenge decisions as and where appropriate. Finally, *Band four* professionals operate as 'leadership colleagues'. They lead the function as a whole and develop strategy.

They must understand industry and organisational dynamics and be able to partner strategically with key stakeholders and/or clients of the function. Early career professionals will normally operate at one of the first two bands. The CIPD's HR profession map provides very useful information about how professionals can develop their skills so that they can prepare themselves for roles at either Band three or four. To illustrate, Table 6.1 provides a brief extract from the CIPD's HR profession map. This extract has been taken from the 'Organisation Design' area of the map. The topic here is organisation change. In the first column of the table, the activity that HR professionals need to engage with can be seen – that is, 'assess current need and operating model' – while the four columns to the right show what professionals are expected to be able to do at each of the four career-stage bandings.

Table 6.1 An extract from the CIPD's HR profession map

Area of competence	Band one	Band two	Band three	Band four
Assess current need and operating model.	3.4.1 Help managers/ individuals to see the rationale for design change.	3.4.2. Work with managers to complete tools and frameworks which will help define the case for change.	3.4.1 Identify and engage with senior managers around the purpose, principles and benefits of change.	3.4.1 Lead discussion on the core processes the organisation will follow and the structuring of resources that will best deliver those processes.

The content of Table 6.1 is not the most important point to be made here. The key learning point to keep in mind is that the CIPD's HR profession map not only defines activities in ten different functional areas, but it also highlights the progression from junior to senior roles.

? REFLECTIVE ACTIVITY 6.1

In what ways do you think the CIPD's HR Profession Map will help you to guide your professional development?

6.3 THE PRINCIPLES OF CONTINUOUS PROFESSIONAL DEVELOPMENT

There are many varying definitions of **continuous professional development (CPD)**, but they all contain similar points and themes. In many ways, CPD is a very basic concept – it is all about ongoing learning and improvement in the specific professional requirements of an individual's role. CPD is concerned with improving specialist knowledge, ensuring adherence to legislative and regulatory process and a general awareness of developments within a field. One of the early definitions of CPD was offered by Madden and Mitchell (1993, p12). Here's how they defined the term:

> the maintenance and enhancement of the knowledge, expertise and competence of professionals throughout their careers according to a plan formulated with regard to the need of the professional, the employer, the profession and society.

Madden and Mitchell (1993) make specific reference to the 'maintenance and enhancement of knowledge, expertise and competence'. This resonates clearly with the initial description of CPD presented in the previous paragraph. An important point is that Madden and Mitchell suggest that CPD must relate to the needs of the professional, the employer, the profession and wider society. It is very important to remember that CPD is not something which solely benefits HR professionals; there are wider benefits which can be realised from effective practice.

CPD is not a one-off activity; it is a lifelong commitment to continually improving your knowledge and skills. It is a very personal business, and no one else can do it for you. When it comes to CPD, you will be your own objective setter, implementer, funder (perhaps in money, certainly in time) and evaluator.

The fact that you are currently completing a CIPD qualification suggests that you probably understand the value of CPD and may well have already made a commitment to it.

6.3.1 THE IMPORTANCE OF CPD

There are a number of important reasons for you to undertake CPD. The main reason is that it is a means of developing yourself continually in terms of your professional competence, and keeping track of your progress. In addition, many professional bodies view the activity as a prerequisite of continued membership.

The Law Society, for example, stipulates a set amount of CPD hours per member per year – which must be logged ready for inspection if required. Also, a CPD record can prove to potential and current employers your skills, competence and suitability/readiness for new roles and challenges.

As an HR professional, the CPD of the organisation's workforce will also be of importance to you. An organisation in which everyone is actively engaged in continual personal and professional improvement constitutes a 'learning organisation' – one which is innovative and responsive to change. You will have a duty to support the CPD of the whole workforce via appropriate training and development policies, job design, and so on.

The reason that CPD is becoming ever more important to organisations and professional practitioners is that the business world is continuously changing. Due to this continuous and often rapid change, professionals in all fields who don't engage with continual learning and improvement will quickly find that their skills and knowledge fall out of date. CPD focuses on the development of transferable skills that not only help you to achieve the objectives of your current employer, but also help you obtain work elsewhere if you need to. CPD is a necessity, not a luxury.

6.3.2 WHAT IS THE FOCUS OF CPD?

There are a number of different levels on which CPD can, and should, be targeted:

- Personal, which means asking yourself how you, as an individual, can improve your effectiveness. This entails improving your self-awareness, your understanding of your values and personality, working on your time and stress-management, and so on, as well as keeping up to date with key developments in your organisation, sector and profession.
- The external context (organisation, sector and profession) is always developing, and in order to make effective decisions, you will need to be aware of these changes and how they affect your role. To be an effective HR professional, you will need to keep abreast of political and legislative developments; demographic and labour market trends; technology developments; environmental concerns; and social trends.

6.3.3 SOURCES OF CPD

CPD can be found in any event, activity or encounter from which you have learned something. But the most obvious sources include:

- formal study (such as your CIPD programme)
- vocational training courses – internal and external
- seminars (employment law updates, and so on)
- CIPD local branch events (and the Annual Conference, if possible)
- sector/industry events

- literature (*People Management*, reputable newspapers, and so on)
- CD-ROMs, e-learning courses, Learn Direct courses
- networking events
- company committees and projects, especially where cross-departmental
- shadowing and role-modelling
- coaching and mentoring at work – from both sides of the relationship.

? REFLECTIVE ACTIVITY 6.2

Given what you know, what risks might there be for individual HR practitioners who do not engage in CPD?

CPD can also be generated from reflection and learning within your day-to-day work and, of course, informal opportunities. At the heart of CPD is 'reflective practice'. While this term may seem a little daunting at first, the underlying concept is relatively straightforward. Essentially, reflective practice is the capacity to reflect on action so as to engage in a process of continuous learning. The key phrase here is 'reflect on action'. CPD revolves around thinking carefully about what has been done or experienced in order that we can facilitate further learning. Without reflective practice, development activities will be poorly targeted and will therefore be of little use to professional practitioners.

 DEVELOPING HR SKILLS: AN EXAMPLE OF A CPD ACTIVITY

CASE STUDY 6.1

I work as part of the HR team for a medium-sized company operating in the service sector. Being relatively new to the role, I have limited experience of practical HR issues, such as how best to manage 'difficult' disciplinary or grievance interviews or how to manage an effective selection process. Despite having an undergraduate degree in HR management, I do not have significant practical experience to draw on. It is important to my development that I take advantage of opportunities to add this experience to my knowledge base.

An example of just such an event occurred recently when I participated in a role-playing activity with other members of the HR department. My manager had devised a scenario whereby I needed to conduct an investigation/disciplinary interview with a colleague who had been persistently late for work. In setting up the scenario my manager had devised a series of unexpected obstacles for me to

navigate, such as the member of staff revealing that he had been suffering from stress and marital problems, thus contributing to his absences from work. I therefore had to 'think on my feet', investigating the issue in order to draw out the necessary details, before coming to an ultimate decision on the way forward.

As a source of CPD this event was valuable to me for a number of reasons. Firstly, it introduced me to the difficulties that can arise during disciplinary interviews in a 'safe' environment. In other words, by using a role-play format I could make mistakes and perfect my skills without this having wider consequences. Additionally, I was able to discuss the activity at length with my manager following its conclusion, whereupon she indicated how she would have dealt with the situation and conversation. Finally, aside from an hour or so of working time, this event did not cost either myself or my organisation money to arrange. It was therefore very cost-effective and very useful in terms of passing tacit knowledge from my more experienced colleagues to myself.

? REFLECTIVE ACTIVITY 6.3

Recall a few events in your career, and specifically within training events, that you have been involved in that have either caused you considerable satisfaction or considerable anxiety, or both. Answer the questions below, or as many of them as are relevant:

● With regard to the balance between satisfaction and anxiety, how satisfied are you with your current levels of performance, and why?
● Do the tasks that you perform well have anything in common with each other? What about the tasks that cause you anxiety?
● What actions have worked for you when undertaking these activities?
● Where and when could you try out using these practices again?
● What didn't work in these situations, and why didn't it work?
● How could you have changed what you did to make it more successful?

6.4 THE THEORY OF CPD: REFLECTIVE PRACTICE

One of the earliest writers on the usefulness of **reflective learning** was Schön (1983). Schön expresses the view that many professionals seem to stop learning as soon as they leave graduate school, but those who become lifetime learners practise what he called 'reflection in action'. This is the ability to reflect on one's thinking while in the process of carrying out the activity. Schön believed that 'reflection in action distinguishes the truly outstanding professional'.

The following quote is taken from Schön so it cannot be changed, but please note that the masculine context is misleading and the quote applies equally to women. Schön states of reflective practitioners (Schön 1983, p69):

> In each instance, the practitioner allows himself to experience surprise, puzzlement, or confusion in a situation which he finds uncertain or unique.

> He reflects on the phenomena before him, and on the prior understandings which have been implicit in his behaviour. He carries out an experiment which serves to generate both a new understanding of the phenomena and a change in the situation... When someone reflects-in-action, he becomes a researcher in the practice context. He is not dependent on the categories of established theory and technique, but constructs a new theory of the unique case.

> His inquiry is not limited to a deliberation about means which depends on a prior agreement about ends. He does not keep means and ends separate, but defines them interactively as he frames a problematic situation. He does not separate thinking from doing (...) Because his experimenting is a kind of action, implementation is built into his inquiry.

What does all this mean? Schön is identifying the limits to the use of prescribed best practice 'theories', suggesting instead that we all create our own best practice rules and theory in action through trial, error and reflective learning. It is common sense really, and it forms the theoretical basis of CPD.

Reflecting on your learning enables you to link your professional development to practical outcomes and widens the definition of what counts as useful activity. Quite simply, you need to keep asking 'What did I get out of this?' As a reflective learner, you'll think about how you'll use new knowledge and skills in your future activities – so learning is always linked to action, and theory to practice.

It is also useful to reflect on how you learn best. This may be through private study, networking with peers, formal courses, mentoring or a combination of techniques.

6.5 MANAGING YOUR CPD

Now we have defined continuous professional development, considered its importance in the modern business world and examined what it covers and its potential sources, turn your attention to your own CPD and the strategies you can employ to manage the process effectively. We address each of the following in turn: identifying your learning needs; making **personal development plans**; embedding reflective practice (learning logs); identifying support; and overcoming barriers.

6.5.1 IDENTIFYING YOUR LEARNING NEEDS

There are a number of approaches and techniques that you can use to identify areas for development. These include:

- *Situational approach* – consider where you have been, where you are now, where you want to be in the future, how you can get there, and how you will know when you have arrived. This is especially useful if you are considering a significant change.
- *Benchmarking* – against national professional standards or role-models. Observe the behaviours of people you consider to be very successful, or who are doing what you would like to be doing in the future. Identify the behaviours that you think make them successful and measure yourself against them. You could talk to the individual about the values, beliefs, emotions and attitudes that inform their behaviour. You could also ask how they developed themselves and what advice they would give. They may even consider acting as a mentor through your development.
- *Request feedback* from as many different sources as possible. Try to ensure that feedback relates to areas of your job, that it is precise and that it uses measurements (time, quantity and cost wherever possible). Your formal appraisal with your manager especially should provide useful information on areas for development.

6.5.2 MAKING PERSONAL DEVELOPMENT PLANS

It is important to take a structured and formalised approach to personal development planning. This is so that all needs are covered, objectives are set, learning activities are focused and take place in a logical order, and outcomes can be measured (against objectives). It also enables you to build up a portfolio of evidence, which could lead to exemptions towards a qualification or contribute to a CIPD membership upgrade (which we address later).

There are six steps to successful personal development planning:

Step 1: Personal skills audit and identifying learning needs (as detailed in section 6.5.1).

Step 2: Setting objectives. Once you know what you want to improve, you can set a clear objective for each area. You will surely have come across the acronym SMART – indicating that every objective should be specific, measurable, achievable, realistic and timebound. By keeping these key points in mind HR professionals will be able to set clear objectives within their CPD plans. If these points are not considered, objectives are likely to be ill-defined, meaning that HR professionals will not be able to track their progress or guide their CPD activities effectively. An example of a poorly defined objective might be:

'To stop leaving important pieces of work until their deadline'.

This objective is not very specific and there is no measurable outcome. There is no time component to the objective and its achievability is debatable. Here is a much better way of phrasing a CPD goal or objective:

'To increase the time I have for planning and managing (as opposed to fire-fighting) by 10% within three months'.

This objective specifies a clear goal and there is a measurable output. We can see that the objective has a relevant timescale and that it should be achievable and realistic depending on the individual's access to relevant development experiences.

Step 3: Selecting opportunities. Once your objectives are set, you need to identify opportunities for development in each area, both inside and outside the workplace. For the objective above, opportunities may include:

- understanding my use of time, and where I waste time
- delegation
- learning from others
- practising outside the workplace.

Step 4: Actions. You should now develop an action plan of precise activities to be undertaken over time. This should include details of WHAT activities, HOW they will be carried out, WHERE (workplace, classroom, and so on) and WHEN. For the example above, activities might include:

- attending a time management workshop (venue and timing as dictated by course availability)
- observing/shadowing colleague X, who seems to manage his time more effectively (timing according to mutual availability)
- keeping a time log for a week, and assessing where you waste time, and so on.

Step 5: Implementation and progress. During the implementation phase, it is important to have someone that can give you support and guidance. A mentor who can provide input and help to monitor your progress is a valuable asset.

Step 6: Assessment. It is important that there is a formal assessment of your development by an objective party – such as your manager, tutor or a colleague. Assessment can come from numerical measurement (time saved, money saved, database accuracy, number of customer complaints, and so on); observation of your performance/behaviour (interviewing, delivering training, and so on); a review of documentation you have prepared; and so on.

6.5.3 EMBEDDING REFLECTIVE PRACTICE AND THE LEARNING LOG

As we have seen in section 6.4, one of the key skills required for successful continuous professional development is reflective practice, which is closely linked to the notion of experiential learning. You will have been carrying out reflective practice as you have worked through this chapter – especially when responding to the Activity sections, which encourage you to reframe past experiences; consider what skills you possess, and at what level; assess your strengths and weaknesses; and identify specific areas for development. The trick now is to get into the habit of taking moments to reflect in your everyday job –

turning every experience into a formal learning opportunity on which you can draw in the future. You can do this by asking yourself a simple question: 'What did I get out of this event or experience?'

One of the key tools used in reflective practice is a learning log. Some professional study courses require the submission of a formal learning log, and many people use them to demonstrate learning and competence to current or potential employers.

Keeping a learning log does more than just provide a record of development activities undertaken; it forces you to adopt a more structured approach to learning and to reflect on each experience – reducing the usually haphazard nature of learning experiences in everyday life.

There are a variety of different formats that you can use, but each entry should include the following: the date; details of the learning experience (something significant that happened that you learned from); a brief conclusion – what you learned; actions that you will now take; and a deadline for actions.

The principles are that entries should be brief (a log should not be seen as a burden), timely (as soon as possible after a learning event) and honest, and that further actions should be realistic. HR professionals must also recognise that there are differences between 'descriptive' and 'reflective' writing. Learning logs require us to not only describe, but more importantly, reflect on events in order to draw out relevant learning points. Here is an example of 'descriptive' versus 'reflective' writing.

DESCRIPTIVE VS REFLECTIVE WRITING

Example One: A Descriptive Account of a CPD Event

I recently attended an employment law update briefing run by a local legal firm. At this meeting we were told about the implications that auto-enrolment legislation would have for pension schemes and advised about the content of several interesting legal cases concerning holiday pay. The event was therefore valuable in terms of keeping my employment law knowledge up to date.

Example Two: A Reflective Account of a CPD Event

I recently attended an employment law update briefing run by a local legal firm. The briefing covered a number of topics relevant to my role including pension legislation and important legal cases surrounding holiday pay. During this briefing I thought carefully about the implications that the changes outlined would have for HR practice within my organisation, and recognised that I must work closely with our pensions specialist with regard to developing appropriate communications, and ensuring all employees are enrolled successfully. After the event I discussed the issues surrounding holiday pay with our Finance Director and agreed that we should review our processes and procedures to ensure that we are legally compliant. Doing this will ensure that we avoid potentially costly legal action. These activities will be ongoing but I will review progress in two months to ensure that plans remain on track.

Can you see the difference between the two entries? The first is essentially a summary of the event, while the second seeks to translate the event into actions relevant to the individual's role. In example two there are clear actions that will now be taken, a broad timescale within which activities will be conducted and monitored, and the individual is much clearer about *what* was learnt. In terms of the learning log, example two is significantly more informative and therefore significantly more beneficial within the CPD process.

?   **REFLECTIVE ACTIVITY 6.4**

Reflect on something that you have done recently that resulted in you learning something. Write a learning log entry, structured as follows:

Learning experience:

Conclusion:

Actions:

Deadline:

You may wish to keep a portfolio of evidence (of your development). This can supplement your reflections (your learning log) with documentary evidence and third-party testimonials of your competence. Documentary evidence can include things such as letters, emails, reports, PowerPoint presentation slides, meeting minutes, surveys, budgets, and so on. Third-party testimonials should come from someone who is able to comment critically and directly on your skill or behaviour. This may be your line manager, other managers, colleagues, suppliers/customers, college tutors, and so on. Testimonies need to be written and explicit: 'I have always found Carla Conrad to be a very efficient manager' may be gratifying to hear but does not provide much in the way of evidence; 'I can confirm that Carla Conrad led the successful negotiation with ABZ Direct' does.

6.5.4 IDENTIFYING SUPPORT

Support can be very useful in helping you identify appropriate development opportunities, sustaining you through the development, and providing you with opportunities to put your learning into action after completion. Personal and professional support can be drawn from a number of sources, including your line manager, a workplace mentor, colleagues, subordinates, college tutors, your training and development department, professional or sector networks, family and friends.

Gaining support will be easier in a company that values and invests in CPD. The Rolls-Royce case study (adapted from Simms 2005) illustrates the difference such an approach can make.

   ROLLS-ROYCE

CASE STUDY 6.2

HR is often too busy looking after other people's development needs to attend to its own. But thanks to a pioneering professional development scheme, that's no longer the case at Rolls-Royce...

Back in 1999, it had become apparent to John Rivers, Company Director, Human Resources, that managers in other functions such as engineering, procurement and finance were looking to HR to help them support a growing focus on continuous professional development (CPD). This prompted Rivers to accelerate the drive towards greater professionalism within HR too – a case of 'Physician, heal thyself'.

Although HR professionals already participated in regular training programmes and many of them sat CIPD exams, Rivers felt the function needed a company-specific framework of standards and competencies and a more structured approach to CPD...

Rolls-Royce involved the CIPD from the outset in designing its professional development framework for HR. In a stroke of good timing, it came as the Institute was looking for companies to pilot the internal professional upgrading of practitioners to membership or fellowship.

'We saw a real opportunity to make an explicit link between individual personal development, business development and development of the Institute itself,' says Ken Boyle, who is Vice-President, Membership and Education at the CIPD.

'Many people don't upgrade, partly because of the paperwork involved in compiling portfolios of experience and qualifications, and partly because they feel it wouldn't make much difference to their career prospects. But we were keen to encourage upgrading activities as part of our drive for professionalism,' says Boyle. He argues that if you use CPD as a learning opportunity rather than a box-ticking exercise and put it into an organisational context, both the company and individuals take it more seriously...

The scheme involved setting up an in-house upgrading panel... and training internal mentors covering eight company sites to help people eligible for upgrading to put their portfolios together. 'They coach people through the process and act as sponsors,' explains Martin Shipley, CIPD Education and Development Adviser...

Within Rolls-Royce itself, one reason for the success of the scheme is the development diaries that members of the HR team now keep. These record

evidence of their training and professional development in a format that is consistent with the Institute's upgrading process.

To support the upgrading scheme, Rivers, Boyle and their colleagues created an internal competency framework that categorised all HR jobs into four groups: HR director, HR manager, HR adviser and HR administration. For each, the framework set out a series of required competencies, the appropriate professional grade (CIPD or its overseas equivalent) and a series of education and development programmes, including CIPD courses and qualifications as well as internal seminars and master classes.

'You quickly get to the stage where there is an expectation that people will be operating at these specified professional levels, which helps to make the link between the value of CPD and internal career progression more obvious,' says Boyle...

Questions

1   You have been asked by your local CIPD branch to give an input to an annual event for new CIPD students in your area on the benefits of CPD. As you are aware, students need to provide evidence of CPD in order to progress their career. It is advisable that they start this at the beginning of their studies and see it as a lifetime journey.

2   Based on the material in the case study and in this chapter, what personal and professional benefits of CPD would you include?

6.5.5 OVERCOMING BARRIERS TO CPD

Despite the commentary presented in this chapter thus far we do need to recognise that some employers do not 'buy into' the concept of HRM, which can present one potential barrier to engagement with CPD activity. Sources such as Pingle (2014) emphasise that the HRM function can have a poor standing in some contexts, limiting its influence and the resources that it controls. In these situations it can be difficult to win support for investment in HRM-related activities. Any business cases must be very well argued and convincingly linked to an organisation's wider strategy if they are to be successful.

Despite an upsurge in interest in continuous professional development for all professional groups in academic and practitioner literature, and for the HR profession in particular, evidence of CPD in practice is somewhat patchy. The following extract (Rothwell and Arnold 2005) reports on research that has been done with CIPD members on engagement with CPD:

> We found that the value attached to CPD was high, but this did not necessarily translate into levels of participation. ...The most popular updating strategies were informal, related to job role, emphasising organisational–procedural aspects rather than professional knowledge. Some widely promoted strategies, such as reflective diaries or online media, were hardly used, and there was little emphasis on courses and qualifications. Respondents were more positive about targets and recording than previous research had indicated, but some highlighted challenges in identifying CPD opportunities, especially if self-employed.

> Twenty per cent of respondents identified 'strategic HRM' as a CPD priority. Only two variables had an impact on the perceived value of CPD: professional commitment and gender. The more professionally committed the respondents – especially women – are, the more likely they will value CPD. Other variables, such as past career success, perceptions of future employability, position in the company, graduate status, and professional membership, hardly had any influence.

While these comments are rather disappointing from the perspective of encouraging engagement with CPD activity, we must recognise that CPD can have a significant impact on professional competence (Megginson and Whitaker 2007). New developments occur frequently within the HRM field and the best HR professionals will recognise that learning and updating professional knowledge is a continuous process. Those failing to engage with CPD activity will quickly find that their knowledge becomes outdated, with significant implications for their future employability.

With this in mind what factors might hinder your ability to engage with CPD activities? Table 6.2 contains a list of common barriers and suggested strategies for overcoming them.

Table 6.2 Factors acting as barriers to CPD

Barriers	Strategies
Lack of time	Put a little time aside on a regular basis for learning. Consider alternative types of learning that can fit around commitments.
Lack of support	Be assertive with your managers about the importance of CPD. Be prepared to ask others for support and offer to support others in return.
Lack of opportunities	Look for these yourself; don't wait for others to offer them. Be prepared to undertake voluntary work or duties to get experience, and to attend events in your own time.
Lack of resources	Try to link personal learning needs to organisational needs and then argue a case for resources.
Low expectations	Don't just think about short-term extrinsic rewards; identify the long-term and intrinsic rewards that can be gained via learning CPD activities.
Previous bad experience	This is usually associated with a learning activity, rather than with learning as a whole. Treat this experience as a learning point in itself – what did it tell you about how you learn? See if you can find alternative activities.

Barriers	Strategies
Lack of enthusiasm	CPD puts you in the driving seat; make sure you are working to your own agenda and that there is something in it for you.
Personality factors	Certain activities may be incongruent with your personality. An introvert, for example, may not relish the idea of a networking event. Consider alternative learning activities where possible, but do try to experiment with moving out of your comfort zone.

6.6 CIPD MEMBERSHIP AND CAREER PROGRESSION

CIPD membership is a key indicator of professional competence, and CPD is a key requirement for CIPD membership. There are a number of different levels of membership and your aim should be to work up the levels throughout your professional career. The three main professional levels are:

- *Associate*: working in a support role to key HR areas
- *Chartered Member*: able to demonstrate the expertise needed to plan and manage generalist or specialist HR operations
- *Chartered Fellow*: holding a strategic position and able to demonstrate the expertise to lead the key areas of HR.

To apply for an upgrade to a professional level of membership (Associate, Chartered Member or Chartered Fellow), you will need to apply using the CIPD's online membership assessment process. This will assess your knowledge (based on qualifications), activities (based on a self-assessment impact report) and behaviour (based on workplace questionnaires) against the membership criteria you are applying for.

It is in the impact report, workplace questionnaire and other associated correspondence that you will have the opportunity to provide evidence of your CPD. The CIPD advice for compiling CPD records is to consider questions based around past and planned learning, as shown in Table 6.3.

Table 6.3 CIPD's recommended approach to recording CPD

Last year	Next year
What were the three most important things you learned last year? How did you learn them?	How do you identify your learning and development needs?
What value did you add (to your organisation, clients or colleagues) through professional development?	What are your three main development objectives, and how will you achieve them?
What were the tangible outcomes of your professional development over the last 12 months?	What differences do you plan to make (to your role, organisation, clients and colleagues)?
Has anyone else gained from your professional development? How?	When will you next review your professional development needs?

There is a section of the CIPD website dedicated to CPD. A guidance and support page is available, which includes a policy, advice, examples, templates and case studies. This can be accessed at: www.cipd.co.uk/cpd/guidance.aspx. There is also a CPD online page www.cipd.co.uk/cpd/my-cpd-map.aspx, where you can enter and edit your own CPD plans and records, ready to submit them to the CIPD as required.

6.7 FURTHER RESOURCES TO SUPPORT YOUR LEARNING

As you read in Chapter 1, this textbook covers the core elements of the CIPD's level 5 programme. In addition to this textbook, two further texts have been produced which are relevant to the human resource development (HRD) and human resource management (HRM) streams. These books are *Studying Learning and Development: Context, Practice and Management*, edited by Jim Stewart and Patricia Rogers, and *Human Resource Management: People and Organisations*, edited by Stephen Taylor and Carol Woodhams. Each contains chapters by a number of expert writers.

6.7.1 *HUMAN RESOURCE MANAGEMENT: PEOPLE AND ORGANISATIONS,* SECOND EDITION

The second companion textbook in this series is called *Human Resource Management: People and Organisations*. Chapter 1 by Gail Swift explores how contemporary organisations are using a variety of different models of HR service delivery, highlighting how they have evolved and changed to suit the needs of different organisations. This chapter asks why organisations might want to change the structure and/or location of HR service provision and discusses the challenges involved in maintaining and managing HR services.

One of the areas of HR practice that is a CPD priority is employment law. Chapter 2 provides an overview of employment law written by Stephen Taylor and Krystal Wilkinson. It is important to understand that this chapter only provides a brief synopsis of the main issues and developments in employment law, for the territory is vast. The chapter will nonetheless enable learners to understand the purpose of employment regulation and the various ways that it is enforced in practice. After examining the purpose of employment regulation, attention switches to how HR professionals can manage a range of issues lawfully.

These issues include recruitment and selection, change and reorganisation, pay and working time, and performance and disciplinary matters. The chapter also discusses the principles of discrimination law and highlights how HR professionals can ensure that employees are treated fairly at work.

Another key area of practice is resourcing and talent planning. This is covered by Krystal Wilkinson and Stephen Taylor in Chapter 3. The purpose of this chapter is to provide an overview of the way different organisations effectively manage resourcing and talent planning activities within the context of diverse and distributed locations. A fundamental part of HR management is the mobilisation of workforces, ensuring that organisations can access relevant skills at the time and in the places that they need them to drive sustained performance. This chapter explores key labour market trends, highlighting their significance for different types of organisations, and demonstrates how HR professionals can forecast demand and supply of skills. One of the major aims of this unit is thus to introduce learners to the strategic approaches that organisations take to position themselves as employers in the labour market and to plan effectively so that they are able to meet their current and anticipated organisational skills needs.

To this end, the chapter highlights how HR professionals can contribute to the development of effective resourcing strategies, including recruitment, selection, retention and dismissal issues.

Chapter 4, by Ted Johns and Cecilia Ellis, explores the concept of employee engagement. This chapter covers the components of employee engagement and highlights how it can be linked to and yet be distinguished from other related concepts. Specific attention is focused on how employee engagement links with relevant HR policies, strategies and practices and learners will see how employee engagement can be a contributor to positive corporate outcomes. The chapter shows how HR professionals can evaluate the findings of employee engagement surveys and demonstrates how strategies and practices intended to raise levels of employee engagement can be implemented. Learners will also understand the future for employee engagement, both in the UK and the wider world.

Chapter 5, by Cecilia Ellis, is called 'Contemporary Developments in Employee Relations'. The chapter is designed to encourage learners to assess and understand broader developments that influence the effective management of the employment relationship in organisations. It outlines key developments in the theory and practice of employment relations, the main sources of employment relations legislation, and the approaches that organisations can adopt, such as unitarism and pluralism. It also highlights the effect of management style and trade unions on employment relations and explores the concepts of employee involvement and participation. Conflict resolution is discussed in this chapter and learners are given guidance to understanding different forms of conflict behaviour and different methods of dispute resolution.

Chapter 6 in this textbook explores the concept of reward management. The purpose of this chapter, by Graham Perkins and Carol Woodhams, is to provide the reader with a wide understanding of how the business context influences reward strategies and policies. It locates reward management in the wider business context and highlights key issues that drive reward strategies and policies. Learners are introduced to the main theories that underpin reward strategies, and the concept of 'total reward' is discussed in some detail. Specific reward initiatives and practices such as job evaluation are briefly discussed, as is the role of line managers in reward management. The chapter ends with an outline of how HR professionals can evaluate the impact of reward management.

Three new chapters have also been included in the new edition of *Human Resource Management: People and Organisations*. In her chapter on organisational design and development Claire Roberts introduces readers to current thinking in these areas, explaining how they can contribute to superior organisational performance when managed creatively and thoughtfully. The same aims are addressed by Stephen Taylor in his chapter on performance management. The focus here is on high performance work practices and on ways in which the HR function can help to facilitate improved performance across an organisation. The third new chapter, by Graham Perkins, provides a good, general introduction to the field of learning and development in business organisations. It has been written to meet the needs of students who are studying this subject as an elective, but who are not planning to specialise in human resource development more generally.

6.7.2 SOURCES OF INFORMATION

Each of the chapters in the companion books has a section of additional resources to support learning that is specific to the topic. There are a number of other generic sources of information that early-career HR professionals can access and that will be useful.

Academic journals can be very useful sources of information and research data because, in order to get published, any article is first subjected to 'peer review'. That means that it must first be scrutinised anonymously by reviewers who are specialists in the field. They typically suggest that amendments must be made before publication is possible. As a result, before you read an account of any research findings, the article concerned will have been rewritten, resubmitted to the journal and re-reviewed, often extensively and on a number of occasions.

In the UK the most respected peer-reviewed journals in the field of HRM include:

- *Human Resource Management Journal* (endorsed by the CIPD)
- *Human Resource Management*
- *British Journal of Industrial Relations*

- *Work, Employment and Society*
- *Employee Relations*
- *Personnel Review*
- *Gender, Work and Organisation.*

It is important to state that HR professionals should not limit themselves to purely HR-related journals because research findings relevant to HR can come from a variety of fields, including sociology, employment law and occupational psychology, to name just a few.

If you are studying at a college or university you will usually be able to access many types of journal through your library's online resources. If this is not the case, many can be accessed through the CIPD's website. To do this you need to click on the EBSCO link on the CIPD library pages at www.cipd.co.uk.

Textbooks can also provide good summaries of academic research, setting out key findings and often debating different interpretations. Some recent well-respected publications in the field of HRM include:

- *The Sage Handbook of Human Resource Management*, edited by Adrian Wilkinson and Nick Bacon (2013).
- *Strategy and Human Resource Management*, 3rd ed., by Peter Boxall and John Purcell (2011).
- *Contemporary Human Resource Management: Text and Cases*, 4th ed., by Tom Redman and Adrian Wilkinson (2013).

Some of the websites that you might find useful in continuing your learning are outlined in Chapter 1. Other useful statistics and reports are available.

Labour market data can be found by visiting websites such as the Office for National Statistics (www.ons.gov.uk) and UK National Statistics (www.statistics.gov.uk). The CIPD produces a number of very useful reports. From the CIPD's website HR professionals can access annual reports on issues such as absence management, reward management and recruitment. The CIPD's website also includes useful factsheets on a variety of topics, including performance management, employee engagement and dismissal.

Government department websites constitute another useful source of information. Examples of these departments include the Department for Business, Innovation and Skills (www.bis.gov.uk) and the Department for Work and Pensions (www.dwp.gov.uk). Here HR professionals are able to find valuable pieces of information, such as new government policies or practical advice.

Another website that is particularly useful to HR professionals is *People Management* (www.peoplemanagement.co.uk). This website provides a wealth of current HR news, case studies and 'how to' documents and is therefore useful to HR professionals at various stages of their careers. A similar website is *Personnel Today* (www.personneltoday.com). HR professionals can also access a wide variety of information through newspapers, such as:

- *The Times*
- *The Independent*
- *The Guardian*
- *The Daily Telegraph.*

HR professionals should be reading a broadsheet newspaper regularly. Periodicals including *Management Today* or the *Training Journal* are also very useful sources of information. Newspapers and periodicals (either printed or online) often provide case studies, benchmarking ideas, insight into new thinking in the HR community and practical tips. Further useful sources of information include specific trade journals that are relevant to different professions (for example, accountancy) or sectors (for example, construction).

Finally, ACAS (www.acas.org.uk) provides a significant amount of information, including guidance on employment contracts and disciplinary and grievance procedures. It is a very useful source of information. HR professionals can download a number of guides from the ACAS website free of charge or can call its advice line if they have specific queries or questions.

The key point to take from this part of the chapter is that there are many different sources of information that HR professionals can make use of when attempting to develop their skills and knowledge. Successful HR professionals will make sure that they review a wide range of material because it means that their final strategies, policies and/or plans are as comprehensive as they can be.

6.8 CONCLUSION

The purpose of this chapter has been to discuss, with tips and advice, the paths for your future learning and development and the means by which it can be accomplished. We hope this chapter has given you a sound understanding of the concept of continuous professional development (CPD) and its importance in the modern business world. You should be able to effectively argue the case for CPD to others and have a good understanding of the strategies that can help CPD be carried out effectively. You should be aware of the CIPD's membership criteria and HR profession map as well as the various sources of data that HR professionals can use to expand their skills and knowledge. We hope that you enjoy your learning.

FURTHER READING

CIPD (2015) *HR profession map* [online]. Available at: www.cipd.co.uk/binaries/the-cipd-profession-map_2015.pdf . This website provides a wealth of information about the CIPD's HR profession map, including information on the key professional areas and the bands and transitions.

CIPD (2015) *Research report: L&D evolving roles enhancing skills* [online]. Available at: www.cipd.co.uk/binaries/l-d-evolving-roles-enhancing-skills_2015.pdf. Places the concept of CPD into an L&D framework alongside other development initiatives. The book sets out useful case study examples.

CIPD (2015) *Podcast 101 CPD for HR*. Available at: www.cipd.co.uk/hr-resources/podcasts/101-CPD-HR.aspx. This podcast interviews three professionals to discuss key issues around CPD, including the value that they attach to it, how they undertake it and the implications of this for their career development.

MEGGINSON, D. and WHITAKER, V. (2007) *Continuing professional development*. 2nd ed. London: Chartered Institute of Personnel and Development. This text provides an excellent guide to the concept of continuous professional development, highlighting its key principles and showing how professionals can effectively engage with it.

ROTHWELL, A. and ARNOLD, J. (2005) Continuing professional development: how has it worked for you? *People Management*. 8 December.

WATSON, G. and REISSNER, S. C. (2014) *Developing skills for business leadership*. London: Chartered Institute of Personnel and Development. Chapter 1 is dedicated to skills for professional development and practice.

REFERENCES

BOXALL, P. and PURCELL, J. (2011) *Strategy and human resource management.* 3rd ed. London: Palgrave Macmillan.

CIPD (2015) *CIPD profession map* [online]. London: Chartered Institute of Personnel and Development. Available at: www.cipd.co.uk/binaries/the-cipd-profession-map_2015.pdf [Accessed 18 October 2015].

MADDEN, C. and MITCHELL, V. (1993) *Professions, standards and competence: a survey of continuing education for the professions.* Bristol: University of Bristol, Department for Continuing Education.

MEGGINSON, D. and WHITAKER, V. (2007) *Continuing professional development.* 2nd ed. London: Chartered Institute of Personnel and Development.

PINGLE, S. S. (2014) A comparative study of the HRM practices in small and medium enterprises. *The IUP Journal of Management Research.* Vol 13, No 1. pp55–65.

REDMAN, T. and WILKINSON, A. (2013) *Contemporary human resource management: text and cases.* 4th ed. London: Pearson.

ROTHWELL, A. and ARNOLD, J. (2005) Continuing professional development: how has it worked for you? *People Management.* 8 December.

SCHÖN, D. (1983) *The reflective practitioner: how professionals think in action.* New York: Basic Books.

SIMMS, J. (2005) High rollers. *People Management.* 14 July.

WATSON, G. and REISSNER, S. C. (2014) *Developing skills for business leadership.* London: Chartered Institute of Personnel and Development.

WILKINSON, A. and BACON, N. (eds) (2013) *The Sage handbook of human resource management.* London: Sage.

Glossary

Bachelor's degree with honours: Usually an academic degree awarded for an undergraduate course or major that generally lasts four years, but can range anywhere from three to six years. Undergraduate degrees are differentiated either as pass degrees (also known as ordinary degrees) or as honours degrees, the latter sometimes denoted by the appearance of '(Hons)' after the degree abbreviation. An honours degree generally requires a higher academic standard than a pass degree.

Benchmarking: The use of data that has been collected on current performance to compare performance, either internally or externally.

Best-fit HRM: Akin to a best practice approach, an approach that also identifies a link between human resource management practice and the achievement of competitive advantage. In contrast to a best practice approach, HR practices are not applied universally to all; instead, all is contingent on the particular circumstances of each organisation. HR policies and practices are required to 'fit' the situation of individual employers. What is appropriate (or 'best') for one will not necessarily be right for another. Key variables include the size of the establishment, the organisation strategy and the nature of the labour markets in which the organisation competes.

Best practice HRM: Best practice perspective of HRM of which adherents believe that there are certain HR policies and practices which will invariably help an organisation achieve competitive advantage, no matter which organisation applies them. There is therefore a clear link between HR activity and business performance, but the effect will only be maximised if the 'right' and 'best' HR policies are pursued.

Biotechnology: The bringing together of computing technologies and biology, leading to the manipulation of living organisms in order to create useful products such as drugs, biofuels and GM crops.

Black box studies: Research studies which were conducted by John Purcell and a team at Bath University for the CIPD and which examined the impact of people management on organisational performance. The study was conducted within a framework which claims that performance is a function of people's ability (knowledge and skills), their motivation and the opportunity they are given to deploy their skills.

Bureaucracy: In HRM a style of management and organisation design associated with Weber (1925) and Fayol (1949) (see Chapter 1). Key features of bureaucracy include centralisation and unity of command, consistency of purpose, a widespread sense of order with a place for everything, the operation of 'equity', where management operates not just within the law but within the spirit of the law, treating employees both fairly and kindly, and long-term employment at all levels leading to a sense of order and stability.

Business cases: Documents which set out the reasoning behind projects and which detail key findings together with what they mean for future plans and strategies.

Centralised: Describing an approach to organisation structure whereby operational managerial decisions are made by a single overall controlling power. This type of structure is frequently associated with a bureaucracy. Decision-making is slower, but also more consistent.

CIPD HR profession map: An extensive and highly beneficial tool which can be used for many purposes, and which sets out in a user-friendly format eight 'behaviours', ten areas of professional practice and four 'bands and transitions' that provide a structure for the study and practice of professional HRM.

Collective bargaining: A method of determining pay and conditions in an industry or organisation that involves annual negotiation between trade unions and employers.

Continuous professional development (CPD): The ongoing learning and improvement related to the specific professional requirements of an individual's role. CPD is related to improving specialist knowledge, ensuring adherence to legislative and regulatory processes and a general awareness of developments within a given field.

Critical thinking: The systematic analysis of a document, process or system by an individual who possesses specific professional knowledge and expertise.

Decentralised: Describing an approach to organisation structure associated with flatter or divisionalised structures. Operational decision-making is delegated to individual units, away from centralised control.

Decentralised bargaining: A collective bargaining arrangement that involves negotiations which take place at the local level in business units. It represents a shift away from traditional national-level bargaining through which terms and conditions are established across a whole industry.

Differentiators: Aspects of people management which are able to encourage outstanding performance from a workforce and thus achieve superior results that exceed expectations. Part of becoming an employer of choice.

Ethics: Rules of conduct recognised as morally appropriate to a particular profession or area of life.

Evidence-based HRM: Form of HRM which involves taking HRM decisions, developing HRM policies and, when debating with colleagues, taking up positions all of which are informed by robust evidence.

Expatriates: Members of staff, mostly managerial, who are seconded by their companies to work in an overseas subsidiary or sister company abroad for a period of time. Assignments of three to five years are the most common.

Flexibility: In HRM, an integrated capacity for organisations to respond to change rapidly and efficiently. It is associated with part-time working, fixed-term working, flexible hours, multi-skilling and performance-based payment arrangements.

Foundation degree: A vocational qualification introduced by the UK Government in September 2001 similar in level to the higher national diploma but below the Bachelor of Science/Bachelor of Arts level of education. Courses are typically two years' full-time study or three to four years' part-time study and are offered both by universities and by colleges of higher education. Foundation degrees are intended to give a basic knowledge in a subject to enable the holder to go on to employment or further study in that field.

Globalisation: Process widely observed in recent decades whereby greater levels of international trade and international exchange are serving to bring diverse countries closer together.

HR business partner: A senior HR professional working closely with business leaders or line managers, usually embedded in the business unit, influencing and steering strategy and strategy implementation.

HR generalist: An HR professional who has knowledge of, and involvement in, all areas of the HR function.

HR profession map: Document produced by the CIPD which sets out the competencies that HR professionals require in professional practice.

HR specialist: An HR professional who has advanced knowledge of a particular area of people management (such as resourcing, reward or organisation development) and limits their focus to strategy development and operational activities in that particular field.

Humanist: In HRM, describing principles derived from the work of Elton Mayo (1933, see Chapter 1) in which the primary argument is that employees achieve higher levels of motivation, satisfaction and performance if the jobs they do are made more interesting and challenging. While it must be accepted that many jobs are never going to be highly enjoyable, it can be argued that the key to higher levels of performance lies in managers' designing jobs and managing people in such a way as to maximise the satisfaction, enjoyment and well-being that job-holders derive from their work.

Human resource management: A debated term formerly meaning a new way of managing people that was clearly distinct from 'traditional personnel management', but now used simply to refer to an overall body of management activities rather than any particular approach to carrying them out.

Infrastructure factors: People management activities which involve organising the work of other people and creating a working environment that can help a business or group to achieve its objectives.

'Knowing–doing gap': Jeffrey Pfeffer and Robert Sutton's (2006) term (see Chapter 1) describing the challenge of turning knowledge about how to enhance organisational performance into actions consistent with that knowledge. Put simply, it is about converting knowledge about improving organisational performance into action.

Knowledge economy: Type of national economy in which most organisations are concerned with the production or manipulation of some form of knowledge. It is often argued that the UK economy is steadily evolving into a knowledge economy over time.

Leitch Review: Comprehensive government-sponsored investigation into the state of skills in the UK carried out between 2004 and 2006 which has informed government policy since. The final report is published on the HM Treasury website along with much of the research which informed its key findings.

MacLeod Report on Employee Engagement: Report commissioned by the Department for Business, Innovation and Skills (BIS) and produced by David MacLeod and Nita Clarke in 2009 to take an in-depth look at employee engagement and at its potential benefits for organisations and employees. The researchers found evidence of a clear correlation between engagement and performance – and most importantly between improving engagement and improving performance. They concluded that a wider take-up of engagement approaches could impact positively on UK competitiveness.

Nanotechnology: Technology which involves manipulating matter at the nano-scale to produce new materials. It has been made possible by advances in miniaturisation through optical magnification. The development of the material known as 'graphene' is a recent example.

Office for National Statistics: Publicly funded national statistics authority of the UK, which publishes a vast amount of data on employment matters on its website. This includes regularly collected statistics alongside articles and larger research reports on particular topic areas.

Outsourcing: Purchasing a service from an external source rather than performing it in-house. It can lead to cost savings and a better quality of service.

Personal development plan: A structured document that lists an individual's goals, relevant learning activities and the expected outcomes. Personal development plans can be used to build up a portfolio of evidence of CPD activity.

Pluralists: In HRM, people who believe that not only do employers and employees have different interests, but that they also have multiple different interests. What employees seek – for example, high wages, limitations on hours – is different from what employers are looking for: flexibility, low labour costs, a high degree of management control, improved productivity, and so on. The result, inevitably, is tension and an 'us and them' conflict.

Pragmatism: In HRM, a style of management whereby managers assess the usefulness of an approach as opposed to its 'rightness'. Pragmatic managers are therefore free to treat good performers more favourably than poor performers and manage their teams by 'gut instinct'. This can lead to problems associated with inconsistent practice.

Primary data: Information that has been collected specifically for the study in which it is to be used. In this sense, primary data is 'new' in that it has not been captured by previous research projects.

Privatisation: Process by which governments sell off public sector organisations – particularly publicly owned corporations – so that they become part of the private sector. Privatisation is associated with the creation of markets in which companies compete with one another for business.

Professional: Person who earns a living by the proficient use of expert and specialist knowledge, who exercises autonomous authority and who makes a commitment to a set of ethical principles.

Professionalism: Qualities or typical features displayed in a profession or by professionals, especially competence, skill, and so on.

Public–private partnership: Form of organisation increasingly common in recent years that represents a hybrid of the private and public sectors, often involving a private company operating part of a public service under some control by ministers or local authorities.

QAA for Higher Education: Quality Assurance Agency for Higher Education. Its job is to uphold quality and standards in UK universities and colleges. It guides and checks the quality of teaching, learning and assessment in UK higher education.

Qualitative data: Data based around words and meanings. It can usually show why certain things are happening in organisations.

QUANGO: Quasi-autonomous non-governmental organisation – a body that carries out functions on behalf of government and is funded by government. However, most quangos are independent of direct ministerial control.

Quantitative data: Data which usually contains numbers and can be analysed through statistical analysis software.

Reflective learning: Learning that involves sitting back and thinking carefully about past events, pulling elements together to aid future performance. Reflection involves 'deeper' learning which enables professionals to expand their personal understandings of concepts, applying theories and knowledge in a wide variety of situations.

Research design: Term used to refer to frameworks for the collection and analysis of data.

Resource-based view of the firm (RBV): A way of thinking about organisational strategy-making which focuses on building on existing internal strengths rather than on adjusting to meet the needs of the external environment.

Sampling: Method through which researchers select a proportionate number of individuals from a given population to participate in a research project.

Scientific management: In HRM, an approach historically based on the premise that the fully regulated organisation of the workforce and work methods improves efficiency. Work should be a co-operative effort between managers who manage and workers who work. Work organisation should be such that it removes all responsibility from the workers, leaving them only to carry out their particular task. By specialising and training in this task, the individual worker would become 'perfect' in its performance; work could thus be organised into production lines and items produced efficiently, and to a constant standard, as a result.

Secondary data: Data that has been included in or discovered through previous research projects or academic writing.

Shared service centre: A means of providing a common corporate service across a large organisation, or sometimes, across several partner organisations. There is a clear service focus, enabling each of the centre's customers to specify the level and nature of the service required.

SWOT analysis: Simple mental mapping tool which encourages managers to think systematically about their organisation's strengths, weaknesses, opportunities and threats. Traditionally, the S and the W relate to internal issues, the O and the T to developments in the external business environment.

Taylorist: Describing the tenets of scientific management.

'Thinking performer': An HR professional who has relevant, theoretical knowledge and who, through reflection and application, can make sense of some of the practical complexities and ambiguities inherent in the management of people.

Three-legged stool model: Way of structuring the HR function in an organisation advocated by Dave Ulrich, making use of HR business partners, centres of excellence, and a shared service centre for routine transactional services.

Unitarism: In HRM, a perspective that assumes employers and employees share the same fundamental, long-term objectives as far as their relationship with one another is concerned. For example, both have an economic interest in the financial success of their organisation: the employer in order to maximise profit, and the employee in order to maximise job security and career opportunity. According to this view, harmonious relations between employer and employee are normal and conflict is abnormal.

Workplace Employment Relations Survey (WERS): Nationwide study carried out every few years into many aspects of employment practice in UK workplaces, including the very smallest. Summaries of the findings are published on the Department for Business, Innovation and Skills (BIS) website.

World Trade Organization (WTO): International institution that hosts near-continual international negotiations aimed at reducing formal and informal barriers to trade.

Index

Human Resource Management and its External Contexts

LEARNING OUTCOMES

By the end of this chapter, readers should be able to understand, explain and critically evaluate:

- the changing nature and forms of contemporary HRM and HR practices in the UK
- the principal factors driving these changes
- some key issues in HRM, such as HR strategy and delivery of HR
- the external contexts affecting organisations and the HR function
- developments in international HRM.

In addition, readers should be able to:

- evaluate the impact of these changes on HRM practices in organisations
- review the impact of external contexts on HR work and HR practice
- understand how these changes affect their own organisations
- relate contemporary HR practices to the CIPD Profession Map.

1.1 INTRODUCTION

This chapter provides the theoretical and practical backgrounds to the rest of the book. It does this by giving an outline description, analysis and overview of contemporary human resource management (HRM) within the United Kingdom (UK) and the external contexts driving it. These contexts are identified within the framework of the insights, strategy and solutions professional area of the CIPD Profession Map (CIPD 2012). HRM, loosely defined as the managing of people at work, has undergone significant changes in its purposes, structures and activities in recent years. This chapter starts by examining the factors influencing these developments and considers the changing nature of HRM and how it has developed historically. The chapter then identifies and discusses some key issues on the HRM agenda. These include: how the human resources (HR) function is organised, HR and performance, line managers and HR, outsourcing HR, HRM and ethics, and HR strategy. Next, the chapter summarises the major institutional, external contexts impacting on the HR function that influence HR strategy and practices; issues that are revisited in greater depth later in the book. Finally, the chapter puts these developments into a global context by discussing some trends in international HRM.

1.2 DEFINING AND UNDERSTANDING CONTEMPORARY HRM

Providing a definitive definition of contemporary HRM is problematic. This is because there is no generally agreed framework for understanding and analysing the HR function; there are only competing models. In practice, the HR function within organisations in the UK (and elsewhere) is infinitely flexible, organisationally contingent over time and driven principally by the external contexts of the age; and these often change within short periods of time. Indeed, the history of HR in the UK and elsewhere shows that it has had to change its priorities and focus its activities by reinventing itself continuously. This has been largely in response to external socio-economic factors beyond the immediate control of HR practitioners or senior managers. For these reasons a variety of definitions, frameworks and models can be found in any of the basic (or not so basic) texts and in the wide range of articles examining and exploring the functions, roles and antecedents of contemporary HRM in organisations. However, some understanding of the differing frameworks and intellectual underpinnings of HRM is necessary, if readers are to identify, understand and analyse the major external and internal contexts within which HR professionals operate today. It is these dynamic contexts which provide a continuing theme throughout the text.

One major text in the field, Marchington *et al* (2012), defines HRM curtly as the management of employment. Another standard text provides no agreed definition of HRM but distinguishes between 'soft' and 'hard' versions of it. These writers, drawing upon Guest (1987) and Storey (1992), claim soft HRM 'recognises employees as a resource worth investing in, and tends to focus on high commitment/high involvement human resource practices'. Hard HRM 'identifies employees as a cost to be minimised, and tends to focus on "flexibility techniques" and limited investment in learning and development' (Beardwell and Claydon 2007, pp671, 675). Boxall and Purcell (2011) regard HRM in the English-speaking world as all those activities associated with the management of employment relationships in the firm.

1.2.1 FROM PERSONNEL MANAGEMENT TO HRM

For Torrington *et al* (2008, p6), the term HRM is used in two ways. They provide a useful distinction between 'HRM mark 1' and 'HRM mark 2'. The first is a *generic term* used to describe the body of management activities which have been traditionally labelled 'personnel management'. The second is regarded as a *distinctive approach* to HRM and suggests a specific philosophy towards carrying out 'people-oriented organisational activities'. Generic HRM seeks to achieve four key objectives: staffing, performance, change-management and administration. These organisational objectives are delivered primarily by personnel/HR specialists or personnel/HR generalists. HRM as a distinctive approach to managing people delivers organisational objectives by HR professionals in collaboration with line managers.

Guest (1987), in turn, has identified a number of 'stereotypical' features distinguishing the personnel management tradition (HRM mark 1) from the distinctive HR tradition (HRM mark 2). Personnel management is specialist and professionally driven. Its features include: a short-term, *ad hoc* time perspective; a pluralist, collective approach to managing employment relations; bureaucratic, centralised, organisational structures; and cost minimisation evaluation criteria. The distinctive, 'new' HR tradition (HRM mark 2) is largely integrated with line management. Its features include: a long-term, strategic time perspective; a unitary, individual approach to managing employment relations; more organic, devolved, flexible organisational structures; and maximum utilisation of human resources.

Interestingly, Torrington *et al* identify six main periods or 'themes' in the history of personnel management and its transition into contemporary HRM. Indeed, as Gennard and Kelly (1997, p31) have perceptively observed, delivery of the personnel/HR function has always been flexible and has adjusted its dominant values historically 'as macro circumstances change'. Legge (1995, pxiv) argues, however, that the apparent overshadowing of personnel management by the distinctive HRM tradition lies in its function as 'a rhetoric about how employees should be managed to achieve competitive advantage [rather] than as a coherent new practice'. Keenoy (1990) goes further in his critique of the new HRM, viewing it as 'a wolf in sheep's clothing'. For him, HRM is more rhetoric than reality and simply supports ideological shifts in the employment relationship, driven by market pressures.

Torrington *et al* (2008) describe the first theme in the evolution of personnel management and HRM in the UK as 'social justice'. This originated on a limited scale amongst a few enlightened employers in nineteenth-century Britain. These employers promoted a welfare approach to managing people by attempting to ameliorate working conditions and avoid adversarial industrial relations. Second, in the first half of the twentieth century, 'humane bureaucracy', influenced by managerial practitioners and observers such as Taylor (1911), Fayol (1916) and Mayo (1933) came to the fore in management practices. Taylor's 'scientific management' principles adopted a work study, incentive-based approach to managing people. This was followed by the 'human relations' school, originating in Mayo's works reported in the Hawthorne experiments, and later others, which aimed at fostering good 'human relations', high morale and efficiency at work. Third, in response to strong trade unions in the 1960s, a period of 'negotiated consent' was fostered by personnel and industrial relations managers. This aimed at containing union power and managing workers by representative systems and collective agreements. Fourth, from the late 1960s, the focus was on 'organisation' provided by personnel specialists. They did this by developing career paths, opportunities for personal growth and workforce planning. Fifth, the recent 'HRM' theme, with its focus on performance management, planning, monitoring and control, flexibility and employees as individuals, emerged and grew in the English-speaking world throughout the 1980s, 1990s and 2000s. This was in response to what is loosely described as globalisation and neo-liberal economic policies.

A sixth theme claimed by some observers, such as Bach (2005, pp28–9), is a 'new HR'. Driven by employer demands for competitive advantage, this theme is characterised by a 'new trajectory' in response to significant long-term trends in the business context. These include a global perspective, issues of legal compliance, the emergence of 'multi-employer' networks (or 'permeable organisations'), engagement of individual employees emotionally at work, and a customer-centred focus in business. This trend or theme seems to reflect a shift away from the 'management of jobs' by organisations to the 'management of people' within them (Lepak and Snell 2007).

In their summary review of the HR literature, Beardwell and Clark (2007) identify five comparative models of personnel management and HRM. They describe these as: the planning perspective, people management perspective, employment relations perspective, structure/systems perspective, and role perspective. In each case, practices and theories of managing people within each of the personnel management and HRM traditions differ. In outline, personnel management in the planning perspective is reactive and marginal to corporate plans. In the people management perspective, people are a variable cost, subject to compliance and organisational control. In the employment relations perspective, personnel management accepts that self-interest dominates at work and that conflicts of interests among stakeholders are inevitable. Personnel management in the structure/systems perspective imposes control of staff from the top and control of information flows downwards. In the role perspective, personnel management is specialised, professional and driven by personnel specialists.

Within the HRM tradition, HRM is strategy-focused and central to the corporate plan in the planning perspective. In the people management perspective, HRM views people as social capital capable of being developed and committed at work. In the employment relations perspective, HRM supports coincidence of interests among stakeholders and de-emphasises conflict in the workplace. HRM in the structure/systems perspective promotes employee participation and informed choice by staff, with open channels of communication to management aimed at building employee trust and commitment. In the role perspective, HRM is largely integrated into line management.

Clearly from this brief outline of some of the recent literature in the field, there is no universally agreed definition of contemporary HRM or the practices it incorporates; an issue which is explored more fully in Chapter 5. However, two observations can be made. First, HRM in the UK, as elsewhere, is historically 'path dependent'. This means, and explains how, institutions, social structures or patterns of behaviour in the present are limited by what has happened in the past, even though past circumstances may no longer apply. Second, as Guest (1997, p266) has argued, this lack of consensus about HRM arises from the 'absence of a coherent theoretical basis for classifying HRM policy and practice'. In examining the key literature in the area, Guest identifies three broad categories of general level theory about contemporary HRM. These are: *strategic* theories, such as those of Miles and Snow (1984) and Schuler and Jackson (1987); *descriptive* theories, such as those of Beer *et al* (1985) and Kochan *et al* (1986); and *normative* theories, such as those of Walton (1985) and Pfeffer (1994). Each theoretical category originates in different sets of assumptions about HRM. These are contingency theory, systems theory and motivation theory respectively. What these theoretical schools have in common is that contemporary HRM is deemed to be distinctive in some way or other from traditional personnel management; debates that are revisited later in this book.

A summary of the main features of personnel management and HRM is provided in Table 1.1, as well as 'contextual' HRM. Contextual HRM or 'comparative HRM' challenges universalist models of HR function of management. It explores the importance of culture, ownership structures, labour markets, the role of the state and trade union organisation as aspects of the subject rather than as external influences on it (Brewster *et al* 2011).

Table 1.1 Personnel management, HRM and contextual HRM

The personnel management paradigm	The HRM paradigm	The contextual HRM paradigm
Driven by employer needs to treat people fairly in organisations	Driven by employer needs for competitive advantage in the market place at firm level	Driven by factors such as the role of the state, legislation, unions and patterns of corporate ownership that impact on HRM at national level
Operates in stable market conditions	Operates within competitive markets and a change agenda	Operates within regulated market conditions
A traditional approach to managing people, with a strong administrative purpose	A distinctive approach to managing people, with a strong strategic purpose	A comparative approach is used to understand the factors influencing HR decisions within firms
Short-term, with an *ad hoc* perspective	Longer-term, with a strategic perspective	A contingent perspective
Incorporates a pluralist frame of reference to organisations and people management	Incorporates a unitary frame of reference to organisation and people management	Incorporates a pluralist frame of reference to organisation and people management

Involves negotiation with trade unions where they are recognised	Involves managing employees individually rather than collectively	Involves managing employees contingently
Delivered, monitored and policed by personnel specialists	Delivered by HR professionals in collaboration with line managers	Delivered in line with national circumstances

ACTIVITY 1.1

What do you understand by the 'strategic theories', 'descriptive theories' and 'normative theories' of HRM? Which approach is the most useful for HR practitioners and why?

1.2.2 THE CIPD PROFESSION MAP

It is useful to conclude this introductory section by drawing upon the CIPD Profession Map and its commentary on contemporary HR practices (CIPD 2012). The outcomes of the Map are based upon in-depth interviews with senior practitioners across the main economic sectors in the UK. Five issues stand out:

- The Profession Map describes what HR professionals need to do, what they need to know, and how they need to do it within each of ten professional areas (outlined below) and eight behaviours, organised into four bands of professional competence.
- The Profession Map covers not only the technical elements of professional competence required in the HR profession but also the behaviours required in the HR profession.
- The Map is organised around areas of professional competence, not by organisation structures, job levels or roles.
- The scope of the Map covers the breadth and depth of the HR profession from small to large organisations, fundamental to sophisticated practices, local to global levels, corporate to consulting, charities to public services, and traditional to progressive activities.
- The Map has the versatility to be used in part or viewed as a whole, with the core professional areas acting as the key or centre that is relevant to all.

The CIPD's approach to contemporary HR practice in the Profession Map is a normative, competence-based one. A major conclusion is that a significant shift has taken place in the focus of HR. There has been a move away from a primary focus on supporting line managers and helping them manage people well to one ensuring that the organisation has the sustainable capability it needs to deliver its aims both today and in the future. The Map seeks to do this by examining what HR people do and what they deliver across every aspect and specialism of the HR profession. The professional areas identified within the Map are the core of the Profession Map: 'insights, strategy and solutions' and 'leading HR', 'organisation design', 'organisation development', 'resourcing and talent planning', 'learning and development', 'performance and reward', 'employee engagement', 'employee relations' and 'service delivery and information'.

Three observations emerge from the CIPD's analysis. First, the Profession Map identifies the underpinning knowledge, skills and behaviours that HR professionals need to have if they are to be successful. Second, it creates a clear and flexible framework for career progression, recognising that both that HR roles and career progression vary.

Third, the Map also provides a comprehensive view of how HR adds sustained value to organisations in which it operates, now and in the future (CIPD 2009, 2012). CIPD's Profession Map, in short, places HRM at the heart of promoting improved performance, the effective managing of people at work and sustainable capability.

ACTIVITY 1.2

To what extent is your organisation practising HRM or personnel management? Provide indicators justifying your judgement.

1.3 SOME KEY ISSUES IN HRM

Given the changing contexts of HRM and HR practices, some key issues in contemporary HRM have emerged out of these developments. These contexts have affected the nature and structure of the HR function, its links with performance, HR and line managers, outsourcing HR, ethics and HRM, and HR strategy.

1.3.1 DEVELOPMENTS IN THE HR FUNCTION

A number of developments have taken place within the HR community and HR work in recent years. First, research by the CIPD (2008) as part of its study on the changing HR function agenda has identified some major changes in the structure of HR in large private and public sector organisations. This reveals that many large organisations are adopting variants of Ulrich's (1997) multi-legged model of HR structures, rather than having centralised HR departments as in the past. This has resulted in HR functions becoming more specialised and being divided between 'shared services', 'business partners', 'centres of excellence' or 'vendor management', overseen by 'corporate HR'. These roles are illustrated in Figure 1.1.

- **Shared services**. Those working in shared services undertake a lot of HR administrative tasks and provide information and advice through intranets and call centres to clients. Staff are often employed for their good interpersonal, customer service and team-management skills, which can be prioritised over their HR knowledge.
- **Corporate HR**. Those working in corporate HR have responsibility for developing HR and people strategy. Corporate HR players increasingly have a governance role, ensuring that organisations uphold corporate values, comply with their legal requirements and follow 'good practice' HR.
- **Business partners**. This HR role varies widely. Some business partners report to senior HR managers, others to senior line managers. Research shows that business partners are expected to work with business units or line managers on strategic development, organisational design, business performance or change management.
- **Centres of excellence**. Other HR practitioners provide support to business partners, develop detailed policy for corporate HR, and act as reference points for shared services when dealing with complex queries. The most common centres of HR expertise are people resourcing, employment relations, pay and rewards, learning and development, and organisational development.
- **Vendor management**. These staff provide third-party services, such as pension administration, managed through service-level agreements.
- **Outsourcing**. This is where organisations subcontract HR work externally.

According to CIPD (2008), the separation of transactional, generalist HR roles from transformational specialist ones within large organisations has led to changing skill requirements, and some recruitment problems, within the HR profession. In small and medium-sized enterprises, in contrast, HR is still likely to take on more traditional people management and development activities, based on generalist roles.

Figure 1.1 Current roles in the HR function

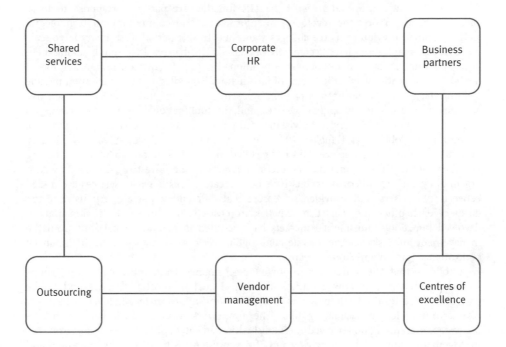

A second development within HR is continuing delegation of some HR activities to line managers. The HR areas that line managers typically deal with include recruitment and selection, pay and reward, performance management, grievances and discipline, coaching, and learning and development. It is generally accepted that some line managers have skills gaps in people management and development activities and therefore have difficulties implementing HR policies effectively. Devolving HR activities to line managers has implications for HR professionals who need to be facilitators, help line managers carry out their HR/people management and development activities effectively, and support line managers in getting the most out of the people resources. In designing and developing HR policies and procedures, HR practitioners also need to be aware that these will be delivered by line managers and that line managers need ownership of them; a theme developed further later in this chapter.

A third set of developments is in learning and development (L&D), where the focus is on 'learning' rather than 'training' and where the skills of those working in the field have changed. Today, business awareness and consultancy skills are highly valued among L&D practitioners. They provide solutions to business problems and support organisational change. There has also been a professionalisation of those delivering work-based learning, with staff working in these areas being increasingly certificated and well qualified.

E-learning and blended learning have become important as technology develops, in a field where virtual learning environments, podcasts and gaming technology are increasing popular. Coaching line managers has also been identified as a very effective L&D practice.

1.3.2 HRM AND PERFORMANCE

Since the 1980s and 1990s, there have been fundamental changes in the structures and management processes of organisations in the private and public sectors. Adjustments to the functions, structures and roles of the HR function are partly in response to these changes but also reflect the revolution in information and communication technologies (ICTs) outlined previously. Three changes stand out. In this period, first, many large-scale hierarchical organisations have become divisionalised. This has resulted from breaking them up into a number of semi-autonomous operations or quasi-businesses, responsible for all the business activities within their areas of jurisdiction. Examples of divisionalisation include splitting large companies into separate, independent organisations, creating executive agencies and trusts in the public services and, in multinational businesses, setting up international product (or services) divisions with responsibility for individual products on a European or global basis (Hughes 2003, Geppert and Mayer 2006). Second, budgetary devolution is now commonplace. This has resulted in allocating responsibility for managing activities within planned financial resources or targets to the lowest possible levels within organisations. Third, internal markets have been created. This is where services are traded between 'purchasers' and 'providers' to ensure that different groups are responsive to the needs of each other and that such activities are cost-effective. In short, divisionalisation, devolved budgeting and internal markets have resulted in a fundamental shift from the management of tasks in the private and public sectors to management by financial performance (Sisson and Storey 2000b).

It follows that the search for improved performance from individuals and groups within organisations is now a crucial managerial goal in most businesses and public enterprises. Customised HR practices and promoting appropriate employee behaviours play critical roles in facilitating this. The framework within which performance is organised, measured and reviewed is established in dedicated, organisational, performance management systems. The underlying aim of these systems is to get the best outcomes and highest efforts from individuals, teams and organisations, in pursuing corporate goals.

A principal feature of performance management is that it connects the objectives of an organisation with the job targets of individuals and focuses on work improvement, learning, development, motivation and reward. A performance management system starts with the induction of new staff when they join an organisation and has four elements: defining performance standards and setting targets, reviewing and appraising performance, reinforcing performance standards, and supporting individuals through counselling and other means to meet performance standards. The review process then identifies the learning and development needs of individuals and allocates rewards for measured outcomes (Armstrong and Baron 2005).

Leading organisations seek therefore to develop, in collaboration with HR professionals, systematic frameworks designed to improve individual and organisational performance in ways that can be measured and reviewed. Analysing claimed links between HRM and performance is now a major area of interest for both researchers and policy-makers. A wide range of studies has attempted to demonstrate the positive relationship or links between certain 'bundles' of HR practices and high organisational performance (Appelbaum *et al* 2000, West *et al* 2002, Godard 2004).

Guest *et al* (2003) provide a useful theoretical framework guiding this analysis, as illustrated in Figure 1.2. In outline, their model suggests possible links between a series of managerial inputs and performance outputs. The inputs are business strategy, HR strategy, and HR practices. The HR practices include induction, job design, recruitment

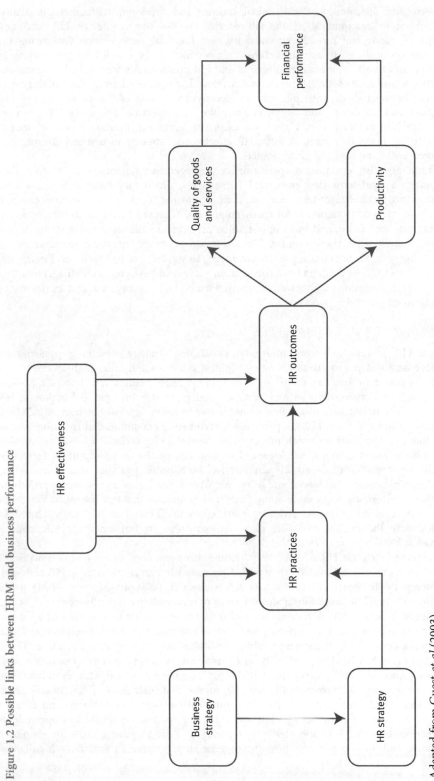

Figure 1.2 Possible links between HRM and business performance

Adapted from Guest *et al* (2003)

and selection, appraisal, pay and reward, training and development, financial flexibility, harmonisation, communication, and job security. The outputs are effective HR outcomes, quality of goods and services, productivity, and financial performance. Evaluating the effectiveness of these HR activities allows an assessment of how well they are working in practice. In this study, managing directors and HR professionals were asked to assess the effectiveness of each of the HR practices described. There were relatively few differences of opinion between them, with job security deemed to be one of the most effective HR practices and job design and appraisal being the least effective. The more HR practices used, and the more effectively they are used, the better organisational performance is likely to be. From this study at least, HR effectiveness appears to demonstrate the link between HRM and business performance.

There are also critiques of performance management systems. One is that they encourage a short-term view amongst UK managers, which may hamper organisational performance in the longer term. Second, there is growing concern that these systems add unduly to stress in working life for many employees, because of their focus on improving the bottom line. Third, and most importantly, performance management systems do not always deliver what they promise. The main driver of performance management is improving overall organisational effectiveness. However, writers such as Bevan and Thompson (1992) and others have found from surveys of performance management that there was no relationship between high-performing UK companies and performance management systems.

1.3.3 HRM AND LINE MANAGERS

Where HR professionals concentrate on developing strategy, designing performance management systems to match changing business priorities and other high-level business activities, line managers take on an important role in implementing HR strategies, policies and practices. Divisionalisation and devolved budgeting also promote delegation of HR activities. The importance of the line manager role in delivering HR has been highlighted by Hutchinson and Purcell (2003, p-ix), amongst others. They found that the behaviour of first-line managers was the most important factor explaining variations in job satisfaction and job discretion amongst employees. 'It is also one of the most important factors in developing organisational commitment.' It has been noted too that strengthening the relationship between managers and their employees results in a positive approach to employee performance and motivation. Such studies indicate that line managers can make real differences to employee attitudes and behaviour (Purcell et al 2003). They also demonstrate the critical role that line managers play in implementing HR policies (Renwick 2003).

To undertake their HR role successfully, line managers need to work closely with HR practitioners to maintain consistency and effectiveness in carrying out their HR activities. A survey by Industrial Relations Services (Industrial Relations Services 2004) asked respondents in 62 organisations about the areas of responsibility typically exercised by line managers. This reported, first, that they had major responsibility in absence management, performance appraisal, team briefing and staff development. Second, line managers and HR professionals had shared responsibility in induction, training and discipline. Third, line managers had little responsibility in recruitment, performance pay, promotions and welfare. Another, later, survey by CIPD (2007), however, which also examined line management and HR responsibility for HR, found, first, that 39% of line management respondents had main responsibility for recruitment and selection decisions and 10% for training and development. Second, HR was a shared responsibility for 84% of respondents in recruitment and selection, 59% in training and development, 46% in employee relations, and 35% in pay and benefits. In general, successive surveys have highlighted increasing HR responsibilities being devolved to line managers in organisations, normally in conjunction with HR professionals as partners.

Devolving HR activities to line managers, however, is not without its difficulties. As Renwick (2003) points out, there are several problems in doing this. First, line managers do not always have the skills and competencies to manage people effectively. The low technical and educational bases of many UK line managers provide barriers to the effective devolution of HR activities in some organisations. Second, in other cases, line managers are not interested in HR work, believing that competence in the field is gained from a mixture of common sense and experience rather than from training. Line managers think they know how to manage people, motivate them and deal with their problems, but have problems doing this (Cunningham and Hyman 1999). Third, line managers have more pressing priorities than managing and developing the people working for them. HRM is low on their list of management priorities. Moreover, they need support, recognition and rewards from top managers to become motivated to deal with HR issues effectively (Marchington *et al* 2012). Fourth, the ways in which HR practices are implemented by line managers are often inconsistent and contradictory, resulting in often subjective and discretionary decision-making, unless HR support is provided (Hutchinson and Purcell 2003). Training line managers in their HR responsibilities and working in partnership with HR professionals appear to be key issues here.

1.3.4 OUTSOURCING HR

In addition to delegating HR responsibilities to line managers, organisations commonly outsource some HR activities to outside bodies or agencies. Outsourcing HR is where organisations subcontract HR activities (and in some cases general commercial activities such as catering and maintenance) on grounds of cost savings, the need to draw on specialist external expertise not available internally, and obtaining independent HR advice from outside people who have greater knowledge, skills and experience in their fields of competence than insiders. Cost factors, for example, often cause managers to consider whether support functions can be provided more cheaply externally. Moreover, subcontractors commonly seek to provide a better service by drawing upon expertise unavailable to their client. Other factors increasing the incidence of outsourcing include the argument that firms gain competitive advantage by focusing their efforts on core business activities and distinctive areas of HR competence. There are also benefits associated with flexibility and leanness. Thus where a core activity is outsourced, suppliers can be changed when they perform badly or their prices become uncompetitive.

Outsourcing takes various forms, such as a shared service centre working for a single organisation, a joint venture between organisations combining HR resources or a multi-client call centre providing HR advice to several organisations (Cooke *et al* 2004). The sorts of HR activities typically outsourced include payroll administration, recruitment and selection, learning and development, executive search, and outplacement and redundancy counselling. Research carried out in the United States indicated four main areas of HR covered by outsourcing arrangements: general HR, transactional work, human capital activities, and recruitment and selection. This study shows that reliance on outsourcing varied with organisational size and complexity, product market uncertainty and the importance of HR strategy to the business (Klass *et al* 2001).

A number of HR implications arise from outsourcing. There are legal issues to consider when an in-house activity is subcontracted, such as transfer of undertakings regulations. There may be issues associated with control of the subcontracted activities. There are implications regarding the regulation of performance levels. With outsourcing, performance is not regulated through a typical contract of employment, but is managed through commercial contracts and service-level agreements. There are also implications for job security and work intensification within outsourced organisations (Taylor 2008).

1.3.5 ETHICS AND HRM

Ethical organisations have always existed although most businesses have traditionally been driven by economic not ethical goals. In the nineteenth century, for example, Quaker companies operated on distinctive ethical principles and firms such as Cadbury incorporated welfare policies into their business philosophies, which benefited their workforces. This was in contrast to most other firms at the time that were driven solely by the profit motive. Today examples of successful businesses noted for the ethical principles they promote include the Co-operative Bank, Scott Bader and Traidcraft.

Some argue that business organisations cannot have 'ethics' or be 'ethical', as they are not agents of morality and are not driven by moral imperatives. However, organisations have sufficient structural complexity to be agents, so they can be called to account for their actions and the consequences of them. If a body can take decisions and implement them, then it must be responsible for those decisions (Kaptein and Wempe 2002). Indeed, as corporate legal entities, business organisations are accountable in law for some of their actions. Therefore part of corporate responsibility stems from legal requirements – such as employment law, health and safety and consumer protection – but part of this responsibility is moral or ethical. Being profitable is a virtue of business organisations but it is not their only virtue. As Kitson and Campbell (1996, p98) argue: 'We can expect organisations to be socially responsible because that is part of the contract out of which they were created.' It is a 'condition of the permission that society granted that they exist in the first place'.

Until recently, there was relatively little mention of ethics in the HRM literature in the UK, although it is growing, stimulated by the growth in ethical investment and ethical consumerism discussed earlier. A different picture emerges in the United States, where ethics and ethical behaviour feature prominently in both HR practice and academic research. Yet almost every HR decision and issue poses ethical questions, since they deal with people issues covering recruitment and selection, managing performance, equal opportunities, learning and development, employee relations, pay and rewards, and termination of employment. Marchington and Wilkinson (2008) argue persuasively that ethical and socially responsible HR practices may become even more elusive as organisations devolve HR activities to line managers, who are required to meet corporate targets that stress production and service targets as their first priorities. However, ethical recruitment and selection, for example, demand properly drafted job descriptions and person specifications, candidates only being invited to interview where they meet the essential requirements and unsuccessful candidates having their applications returned to them, with the selectors' reasons for their decision. Applicants can also be given the results of any assessments made of them. Perhaps the underlying argument for ethical HR practices is that companies adopting them benefit by gaining employee commitment, the trust and loyalty of their workforce and improved organisational performance.

Winstanley et al (1996, p5ff) have written that 'the relationship between ethics and human resource management is emerging as a subject of serious academic enquiry'. They have identified three main issues: ethical concerns, ethical frameworks and putting ethics into practice. They raise concerns about the lowering of employment standards, for example, where several types of undesirable change have been identified. These are, first, job insecurity and risk at work. Second, new forms of work organisation and management control are giving rise to surveillance and control of employees at work. Third, deregulation of management decision-making in firms is leaving little scope for power-based employee participation in the workplace, and this element in contemporary HRM 'is at best unsympathetic to the exercise of democratic rights by employees or to stakeholder models of corporate governance'. Fourth, the rhetoric of HRM, with its themes of commitment and identification, fits poorly with the trend towards less secure employment and evidence of diminished employer commitment to employees, with 'a relentlessly instrumental orientation to the employment relationship on the part of employers'.

Winstanley *et al* (1996, p9ff) also claim that the prevailing common-sense ethical framework justifying contemporary HRM policies based on their utilitarianism to organisations is a weak principle for ethical action. They identify a number of alternative ethical frameworks lending themselves to analysing HRM. These are:

- **Basic human, civil and employment rights**. This seeks greater job security, openness, and transparency, and aims to avoid making scapegoats at work.
- **Social and organisational justice**. This aims to provide procedural principles for evaluating current employment practices.
- **Universalism**. This emphasises the Kantian principle of treating individuals as ends in themselves and not just means to ends.
- **Community of purpose**. This seeks to adopt a stakeholder and more communitarian view of the firm rather than just a stockholder one.

Another level of engagement with ethics is for HR professionals to utilise appropriate frameworks that help to explain and analyse the nature of changes taking place in the employment relationship and to use the frameworks 'more prescriptively'. In seeking ways of putting ethical principles into practice in HRM, Winstanley *et al* (1996, p11) propose the use of employment charters, legal regulation, innovation in good practice and challenging 'the inevitability thesis' on the demise of job security. They are unconvinced that the 'ethical stewardship' role of HR professionals in raising awareness of ethical issues is a viable one. 'There is the risk that assuming ownership of the "ethical" issues and conscience in the organisation might yet again serve to decrease their status.' Drawing on Connock and Johns (1995), they conclude that ethical leadership must come from the top of organisations. It must 'not be part of the ghetto of human resource management'. In their view, growing interest in stakeholding, ethical consumerism and international labour standards are some of the most significant developments putting ethics and HRM on the political agenda.

1.3.5 HR STRATEGY

A key feature of HRM mark 2, as indicated previously, is its role in and contribution to HR strategy formulation and implementation, which Tyson (1995, p3) describes as the intentions of an organisation towards its employees. He defines HR strategy as 'a set of ideas, policies and practices which management adopt in order to achieve a people-management objective'. Rather than consisting of a detailed document, covering all areas of people management, HR strategy is now conceived as an incremental process. It is aimed at influencing key HR practices promoting improved performance and competitive advantage at work, taking account of organisational politics and what is possible in the circumstances. A main characteristic of an effective HR strategy, whatever form it takes, is its integration with business strategy. There are a number of models of HR strategy, which are fully examined in Chapter 5, but each is underpinned by the idea that HR policies and practices need to support the goals of a business, whatever sector it is in, if they are to be effective. HR strategies, in other words, need to have 'external fit' with business strategies and be vertically integrated with them (Fombrun *et al* 1984, Guest 1987, Schuler and Jackson 1987, Pfeffer 1998). Vertical integration thus refers to the links between business strategy, the external contexts and HR policies and practices.

In addition to 'external fit', it is also argued that there needs to be 'internal fit' between different aspects of HR strategy. This 'horizontal integration' of HR means that HR strategy needs to achieve a high level of compatibility of its various elements, not creating policy conflicts between them. One common critique of HR specialists is that they fail to co-ordinate their HR policies and practices to promote consistent and unambiguous messages from management to employees. For example, an HR policy aimed at reducing headcount may be contradictory to another promoting learning at work. Similarly, an incremental pay system without an incentive element, say, may work against a recruitment and selection policy that seeks to attract self-motivated people expecting personal rewards for good performance. A number of studies show that clear benefits accrue from organisations having an appropriate 'mix' of internally consistent HR practices, integrated together and supporting rather than negating one another (Huselid 1995, Wood 1995).

In the managerial literature on HR strategy, then, it is argued that the greater the degree of vertical and horizontal integration within an organisation, the more effective its HR strategy is likely to be. The nature and feasibility of the possible links between business strategy and HR strategy, and the internal consistency of HR strategy, are consistent themes in the strategy literature (Boxall and Purcell 2011).

There is a body of critical literature, however, that challenges these assumptions and questions the links between HRM and its strategic integration with business policy. Legge (1995, p116), for example, argues, first, that the 'matching' approach is based upon a classical, rational approach to strategy that assumes a top-down, unitary planning process which is simplistic and not congruent with reality. She highlights the conceptual problems and 'fuzziness' permeating the major strategy models used to match HR policies with business strategy. Second, this raises doubts 'about their operationalisation in empirical research and the consequent validity of such studies' findings'. She sees these matching models being mainly employed at the normative level, rather than being empirically tested (Golden and Ramanujam 1985). According to one study, an examination of the processes of strategic and HRM change called into question whether managers actually have a genuine free choice in strategic stance anyway (Storey and Sisson 1993). Third, Legge (1995, p124) questions whether the close matching of strategy and HR policies is even desirable. She asks, for example, whether it is possible to have corporate-wide, mutually reinforcing HR strategies, where an organisation operates in highly diversified product markets and, if not, does it matter in terms of organisational effectiveness? Lastly, she questions, in terms of internal integration, whether developing an organisational culture supportive of a particular business strategy stops employees adopting different behaviours in response to changing market demands. In other words, there can be inflexibilities resulting from too close a match between HR strategies and business strategies.

ACTIVITY 1.3

Identify any *three* of the developments in HR that affect your organisation, showing why they are important within it. What sorts of problems arise from these HR developments and how does your organisation address them?

1.4 THE EXTERNAL CONTEXTS OF HRM

To summarise the debate so far, contemporary HRM provides a distinctive approach to managing people at work. Although traditional personnel management approaches remain in some organisations, what Torrington *et al* (2008) describe as the 'HRM theme' is the dominant trend in people management in firms and public organisations today. Contemporary HRM by this analysis has a strategic focus, is integrated with line management and is individualistic in its orientation. The work that senior HR professionals commonly undertake, certainly within leading-edge organisations, is scanning their environments in response to external change, working closely with senior managers as business partners, and building HR capability at individual and organisational levels.

HR practitioners also work in complex, changing organisational contexts. In order to address the HR issues arising from these circumstances, HR professionals have to understand these contexts and try to manage them by developing and implementing appropriate HR strategies and practices, in the short, medium and long terms. In this section, what HR professionals 'need to know' to perform effectively in responding to the major *external* contexts impinging on organisations is briefly explored. The external contexts of HRM are important because HR practices, in any country, are socially embedded in their wider, institutional, external contexts. This means that organisations are affected by external forces that require managers to adapt their internal organisational structures and behaviours to deal with them (Berger and Luckman 1967). As Pfeffer and Salancik (1978) argue, organisational activities and outcomes are accounted for by the contexts in which the organisation is embedded. For illustrative purposes, a summary of these external contexts, known by the acronym STEEPLE, and some key drivers within them, is provided in Table 1.2. The *internal* contexts facing HR practitioners are considered in Chapter 3 and the *business and managerial* contexts in Chapter 4.

Table 1.2 The external contexts of organisations: some key drivers

Field	Examples of key drivers of strategy
Socio-cultural	Demography by size, age, other social characteristics and geographical distribution, working population, gender, ethnicity, education and training, religion, social values and beliefs
Technological	Information and communication technologies, biotechnology, medical advances, nanotechnology, robotics, technological change, research and development
Economic	Macro-economic policy, markets and prices, price levels, global trends, market structures, size of firms, profits, public spending, taxation, consumption and investment spending, wages and salaries, public services, imports and exports, exchange rates, balance of payments, employment and unemployment, labour and capital markets
Environmental	Global warming, conserving natural resources, sustainable development, pollution, carbon footprints, protecting the eco-environment
Political	Party politics, government, opposition, public administration, public policy, devolved assemblies, local government, pressure groups, public opinion, EU institutions, international organisations
Legal	Contract law, employment law, health and safety, consumer protection law, company law, codes of practice, regulatory bodies, the legal system and the courts, the European Court of Justice
Ethical	Balancing stakeholder interests, ethics in the workplace, ethical business relations, ethical production, ethical consumption, ethical purchasing, promoting employee welfare, human rights, corporate social responsibility

1.4.1 INSIGHTS, STRATEGY AND SOLUTIONS

Drawing upon the Profession Map in the professional area of insights, strategy and solutions, a range of prescriptive, underpinning knowledge has been identified that HR practitioners with the highest levels of professional competence 'need to know' to perform effectively. A selection of these are summarised and described in this section.

First, HR practitioners need an understanding of their own organisation's strategy, its performance goals and drivers, and the sector in which they work. These cover the market factors impacting upon performance, including demography, customers, competitors and globalisation. They need to know, understand and speak the language of the business they work for and the 'full range of human resources levers' driving organisational performance. Second, HR practitioners need a broad understanding and technical capability of all ten HR professional areas, with in-depth knowledge in one or two of them, including insights, strategy and solutions. Third, they need to know or access relevant employment and discrimination law in both their local and international jurisdictions. Fourth, they need to know the external and internal influences, including political and economic ones, impacting on the directions, shape and performance of their organisations and the HR levers that can be applied within them. Fifth, HR practitioners need to be able to shape and lead change programmes and know how to develop organisational strategies and operating plans in response to these forces. Sixth, they need to know how to determine organisational capability and resourcing levels to support the delivery of HR strategy and plans. Finally, HR professionals at the highest levels of professional competence need to know 'what external human resources thought leaders and benchmark companies are doing in a variety of areas'. They also need to consider how these lessons 'may apply to [their] own organisation', which necessitates developing 'fit-for-purpose (though stretching) human resources solutions and anticipation of need' (CIPD 2009, p9).

1.4.2 THE SOCIO-CULTURAL CONTEXT

In the social sphere, population trends are a key driver. There are, however, counter-cyclical shifts in population trends. On the one hand, there is rising population growth in the UK and globally, although this is offset by falling birth rates in west and east Europe generally. Higher immigration into the UK and Europe results in increases in the size of the potential labour force, depending on the ages of the migrant populations and their age distributions. It also affects the supply and demand for goods and services in product markets and public services. On the other hand, a generally ageing population, as is the case in most of west and east Europe, results in not only losses of skills, knowledge and competencies from the labour market, but also increased demand for different kinds of goods and services by both younger and older people. It places greater demands on pension funds and social services for the elderly, as opposed to fashionable consumer goods for younger people delivered by leading-edge, hi-tech businesses. Another mega-social trend is increasing socio-economic inequality, with rising affluence for wealthy people and elite groups. This is accompanied by increased relative deprivation for others, rises in asset prices (such as housing stock) and rises in private debt. All these social developments have both strategic and HR implications for organisations in terms of demand for labour, supply of labour and demand for products or services.

At the micro-social level, there are a number of distinctive social trends, all of which impact on organisations, employees, the customers they serve and the HR function. These developments include changing sources of social identity, increased dependency on drugs and alcohol, rising divorce rates, and rising numbers of single-parent households. One social consequence emerging out of these trends is increased solo-living (or single-person households) amongst all age groups. Other social trends include increased self-satisfaction and personal narcissism, with reduced interest in social conformity as well as greater preparedness to take personal responsibility for the self. Underpinning these trends is increased individualism and reduced collectivism at home, at work and in society. The impacts of these developments on working life are wide ranging. These include rising demand for flexible working arrangements and contractual flexibility, more individually oriented HR policies and practices, a lower propensity to unionise and take organised industrial action, and more job mobility within the workforce (Office for National Statistics 2009b).

1.4.3 THE TECHNOLOGICAL CONTEXT

There have been ground-breaking technological innovations in society during the past decades. These have implications for organisations, managers and workers. The most obvious examples are the World Wide Web, email, intranets, the BlackBerry, videoconferencing and, in HRM particularly, the introduction of HR databases, electronic payroll systems and electronic record systems, all linked with innovatory ICTs. During the past ten years or so, ever-newer forms of ICTs have been launched, most of which have implications for how people construct their identities and how they are managed at work. These include Google's search engine; Wikipedia, an online free encylopaedia; Twitter, claimed to be one stage on from Google by applying human intelligence and recommendation to the ordering of information; and, since 2007, the BBC iPlayer. Other technological communication innovations include the smartphone, with its touch screen, rotating screen and zooming screen; craigslist, the classified advertising database now operating in over 70 languages; and Facebook with over 1.32 billion people active on the website. Developments in medical and health technologies are also extending life expectancies and how long people work and remain in the labour market. Other important technological drivers include improvements in biotechnology, hi-tech medicine and a remarkable range of complex pharmaceutical products.

As Soete (2001) points out, a number of implications arise out of the applications of these new technologies. First, there has been the dramatic reduction in the costs of digital information and communication processing, which is not showing any sign of decreasing returns and is unlikely to do so in the future. Second, there has been the technologically driven 'digital convergence' between communication and computer technology at all levels, which is rendering feasible any combination of communication forms. Third, there has been the rapid growth in international electronic networking, both terrestrial and through satellites. Fourth, these developments affect communication between individuals, within organisations, amongst organisations, and increasingly between individuals and machines. They affect all aspects of society, including work, business and the public sector. Fifth, these technologies render physical space and distance irrelevant in many business, working and human transactions. This effectively makes ICTs the first global, technological transformation process. They radically affect how people work, what they do at work, and how people are managed within organisations.

1.4.4 THE ECONOMIC CONTEXT

In the economic sphere, a number of indicative trends are discernible. One is market uncertainty arising out of recession and slow macro-growth in the 2010s. This, in turn, is likely to be offset eventually by an economic upturn and, most probably, the continued globalisation of business activities. The economy is also affected by government macro-economic policies, such as fiscal policy, monetary policy and its own economic activities, as well as by international economic forces. On the business front, for example, an increased role played by international or multinational companies in national economies, and more intense international competition for goods and services, contributes to falls in demand in domestic markets and a rise in unemployment. These and other economic forces impinge on demand for labour, the types of labour required by firms and public organisations, and labour supply. They determine how people are recruited, trained or retrained. On the other hand, with hyper-competitive conditions in some markets, pressure is put on competing firms to retain labour, reskill it or make it redundant. Firms have to adjust their HR policies and practices accordingly.

In the wider labour market, there continues to be increased demand for higher-skilled workers by UK employers and reduced demand for lower-skilled ones. Certainly in the UK, there appears to be limited growth in skills levels. These create recruitment, training and general HR issues for many organisations. At micro-level, there are indications of greater willingness by some workers to switch jobs and employers, resulting in higher labour turnover, increased transaction costs for employers, and personal disruption for the individuals concerned (Office for National Statistics 2009a). There are also significant changes in the structure of the economy, with the manufacturing and extractive sectors being much less important than a generation ago, with increased activity in private and public services today. This has implications for education and training policy generally and for the employment prospects for existing and potential workers particularly, such as graduates in higher education.

Within the European single market, people, goods, services and money move around as freely as they do within one country. People travel across the European Union's (EU) internal frontiers for business and pleasure. Alternatively, they stay at home and enjoy a vast array of products being imported from all over Europe (and beyond). Some argue that the single market is one of the EU's most important political achievements. The single market is certainly at the core of the EU today. Ever since the Single European Act, which established a single market in 1992, the EU has swept away the vast array of technical, regulatory, legal and bureaucratic barriers that formerly stifled free trade and free movement of goods, services and people. In terms of the free movement of goods and services, the single market relies largely on the regulatory authorities to guarantee competition. In terms of the free movement of labour, one consequence is that skilled professional workers can work anywhere in the EU, resulting in firms having to adjust their recruitment and HR policies to this market situation. Thus the UK's economic prosperity, its job creation prospects, and the opportunity for firms and their workforces to benefit from it, are intimately linked with general levels of economic activity in mainland Europe. Indeed, according to the European Commission (2009a), the single market has created several million jobs since its launch and generated more than €800 billion in extra wealth during this time.

1.4.5 THE ENVIRONMENTAL CONTEXT

To protect the ecological environment, there are a number of issues on the business agenda. These include increased interest in sustainable development, sustainable investment and sustainable consumption by producers, investors and consumers respectively. For individuals wanting sustainable production and investment, for example, this means avoiding not only activities likely to cause illness, disease or death, or to destroy and damage the environment, but also those organisations that treat people dishonestly or with disrespect. For firms, it means choosing methods of working and investing that focus primarily on the effects of the company's products or services on the environment, people and communities. Another positive strategy is listing the environmental benefits that producers would like to see their organisations promote. For workers, this can mean good working conditions and for investors the need to articulate what they would like to see their money support. Environmentally sensitive consumers, in turn, may seek to buy products (or services) which are produced ethically, do not harm the environment and promote the well-being of people at work. From an HR viewpoint, sustainable producers, investors and consumers expect companies to act decently in their dealings with staff. This means acting ethically in their relations with suppliers and local communities and managing their businesses with all their organisational stakeholders.

One outcome of this growing interest in environmental issues has been the emergence of 'green HR policies' by a number of environmentally conscious businesses. These companies are noted as developing strategic environmental management policies, especially in the United States. In one survey of 93 US companies, it was reported that some companies were undertaking common green HR initiatives, whether as part of a strategic business plan or a one-off practice. These included 78% which were using either the World Wide Web or teleconferencing to reduce travel, 76% promoting reduction of paper use, and 68% implementing wellness programmes fostering employees' proper nutrition, fitness and healthy styles of living (Bucks 2009). Clearly, this trend is likely to continue, given the shift to 'green' the economy by some leading politicians and pressure groups. All these environmental developments have implications for the HR function and the ways in which people are managed at work.

Although green advocacy is limited, employees can have a key role in building a business's reputation for green HR, and contented workers can become 'green' advocates. A number of initiatives are possible. First, 'green' businesses can get the support of their stakeholders in promoting a sustainable business model. Second, a variable pay element can link pay to 'eco-performance', with the concept of eco-performance being an extension of a common HR practice used in environmentally friendly businesses. Third, employees can help customers understand the importance of 'green living', by highlighting the green practices of their own businesses. Fourth, rewards can be provided to employees who follow green practices established within their firms. These include: recycling office paper, turning off lights and appliances when staff are not in a room, and convincing customers they should recycle their packaging. Employees, in short, can be ambassadors for everything good about their company. An important one is advocating sustainability just as naturally as promoting their business over the competition.

1.4.6 THE POLITICAL CONTEXT

In the political context and in a global age, political support for free-market economics and centre-right government remains generally strong amongst the electorates of the UK, Europe and internationally. National, European and international policy-makers follow this pathway. Within the UK, there is continuing public support for increased government promotion of a competition-and-choice economic agenda. The main political institutions impacting on HR in the UK are Parliament, devolved assemblies in Scotland, Wales and Northern Ireland, and local authorities, including large bodies such as the Greater London Assembly. In Europe, there are the political institutions of the EU (see Chapter 10).

Organisations in both the private and public sectors have to plan responses to the political pressures emanating from these bodies, using appropriate strategies, policies and practices if they are to prosper or at least survive. They do this by drawing upon the support of organised pressure groups, political lobbying or campaigning publicly. Another ongoing political development is privatisation and marketisation. These are normally offset by increased state and European regulation of private and public businesses on the grounds of accountability and the public good. Both the corporate and public sectors have to address the legal requirements arising out of regulation, such as employment legislation or health and safety law. Most importantly in the political sphere, there is increasingly active government involvement in labour markets. This too provides both opportunities and threats to organisations as employers. On the one hand, they have to reward, train and develop existing staff to retain them. On the other, they have to compete with one another for scarce skills and competencies in the open labour market.

1.4.7 THE LEGAL CONTEXT

The legal landscape of employment has expanded exponentially in the last 30 years and there is no sign that this trend will diminish. This is especially the case in regulation of the individual employer–employee relationship, encapsulated in the contract of employment, employment protection, discrimination legislation and health and safety at work. In terms of the contract of employment, unfair dismissal and redundancy laws are the major areas of legal intervention. Discrimination law now ranges across sex, equal pay, ethnicity, disability, religion, age and atypical employment. Health and safety incorporates working time and related working issues. Legislation covering a statutory national minimum wage, statutory sick pay, family friendly policy, human rights and transfer of undertakings are all now recognised fields of employment law. HR departments have to comply with these legal rules, monitor and evaluate them.

In terms of regulatory activity by the UK government, devolved assemblies in Scotland, Wales and Northern Ireland, and local authorities, there is no simple explanation why such an extensive regulatory regime has emerged on a piecemeal basis in the past 20 years. However, a number of factors appear to have influenced the rise of the regulatory state. These include UK membership, first, of the European Common Market and, latterly, of the EU, the decline of trade unionism and collective bargaining, macro-economic policy promoting employment (or at least not increasing unemployment), and political expediency (Taylor and Emir 2009). As Moran (2003, p7) concludes, the private character of the UK's former self-regulatory system has been transformed 'to be replaced by tighter state controls; and the institutions and cultures bequeathed to us by the Victorians have either disappeared or are embattled'. Many HR issues are intrinsically linked with these developments.

1.4.8 THE ETHICAL CONTEXT

Creating, exchanging and distributing wealth in market economies like that of the UK is full of moral ambiguities. In the private sector, for example, businesses exist primarily to make profits. To earn profits, businesses produce goods or services and engage in the buying and selling of goods, services and other factor inputs. If profit making is the first claim on business activities, supporters of stockholder theory (ie that businesses exist primarily for those owning 'stock' or 'shares' within them) argue that there is no need for businesses to act ethically towards their stakeholders, other than shareholders, because the prime responsibility of business is to make money. Others argue, in contrast, that producers should consider the effects of their actions on their wider stakeholders and take their interests into consideration. Producing goods like tobacco and alcohol for profit, for example, is explicitly unethical because of the dangers to the health of people. Some also argue that it is unethical for top business executives to receive excessive reward packages (the 'fat cats' syndrome), when their company's employees are on low wages, non-permanent contracts and are doing what many would perceive as demanding, stressful, low-quality work. Those arguing for social responsibility and ethical responses in business organisations, therefore, say business is not exempt from ethical concerns but must recognise, respond to and manage them appropriately (Mellahi and Wood 2003).

There is, however, no universal model of corporate ethics. Business ethics, or ethical corporate practices, are both subjective and contingent upon those pursuing or evaluating them. Corporate ethics raises questions about how firms should deal with those business issues that have implications for their stakeholders. But firms do not produce universalistic answers to these questions. Chryssides and Kaler (1993, p3) claim that business ethics has two aspects. 'One involves the specific situations in which ethical controversy arises; the other concerns the principles of behaviour by which it is appropriate to abide.' These include: ethics of employment, including pay, unions, workers' rights, equal opportunities and non-discrimination; ethics of accounting, finance, restructuring and investing; and ethics of information technology and whistle-blowing.

Central to the study of corporate ethics is the assumption that 'moral rules' apply to business behaviour, just as they do to individual behaviour and that certain actions are wrong or immoral and others are right or moral. Thus it is generally agreed that employers expect their employees not to steal from them, parties to a contract expect each other to honour it and suppliers expect the businesses dealing with them to pay them promptly. The problem is that there is no universal benchmark of morality. Different people resolve moral dilemmas in business using different approaches and alternative frames of reference; this is the case with HR issues too (Sternberg 2004).

ACTIVITY 1.4

Undertake a STEEPLE analysis of your organisation. Identify the main drivers impacting on HR strategy and HR practices within it. Describe and analyse how any *three* of these drivers impact on your organisation's HR strategies/practices. Give examples of the HR strategies/practices used to respond to them in each case.

1.5 DEVELOPMENTS IN INTERNATIONAL AND COMPARATIVE HRM

This section addresses briefly the extent to which HRM is a universal model of 'good' HR practice or whether it is culturally and country specific. A second issue is trends in international HRM and whether there is convergence in HRM internationally.

1.5.1 THE ORIGINS AND PROGRESS OF HRM

As noted earlier in this chapter, the origins of HRM as a distinctive way of managing people (HRM mark 2), which has a strategic focus, is integrated with line management and is individualist in orientation, were laid in the United States during the 1980s. By this time, the scientific management, human relations and human capital schools of management theory about managing people had been largely rejected by many management practitioners. Scientific management had been based on effective job design and payment systems; human relations on social and psychological insights promoting harmony in the workplace; and human capital theory on investing in labour as an asset in firms, not viewing it as a cost, to raise labour productivity (Schultz 1971). Interestingly, most of these studies about managing people had also originated in the United States.

The next stage, debated first within the United States, was to move on from the flawed studies of the so-called 'in search of excellence' literature (Tiernan *et al* 2001). The crucial issue was to find a framework through which organisations could link their strategic goals with the people they employed, so as to promote organisational effectiveness in conditions of market competitiveness and technological innovation. In 1984, two seminal works on HRM were published. One, promoting a 'soft' version of HRM, was developed at Harvard Business School by Beer *et al* (1985). This model of HRM starts with analysing stakeholder interests in the business and the business's situational factors. As indicated in Figure 1.3, the Harvard model provides a 'map' of the determinants of HR policy choices and HR outcomes for developing employee commitment within organisations. HR policy choices include employee influence and rewards. HR outcomes include employee commitment, competence, congruence and cost-effectiveness. Within the model, business strategy is developed in relation to employee needs, with the long-term consequences of HRM being individual, organisational and societal well-being.

The other important work at this time was the Michigan model of HRM promoted by Fombrun *et al* (1984). This is a 'hard' version of HRM, emphasising the importance of having a tight 'fit' between HR strategy and business strategy, which defines and determines the types of employee performance required by organisations. The aim of this model is to improve overall organisational performance, with the underpinning goal of creating a strategically based value system promoting high employee performance. It is based on an

'HR cycle', as illustrated in Figure 1.4. The focus of this cycle is employee performance. The search for performance is reinforced by adopting HR selection processes that appoint employees with appropriate aptitudes, knowledge and values. Effective selection is supported, in turn, by an appraisal system enabling employee performance to be reviewed regularly and a development system aiming to improve performance shortcomings. Finally, the reward system is designed to distinguish and compensate different levels of performance. The HRM cycle then restarts through an iterative process.

Figure 1.3 The Harvard model of HRM

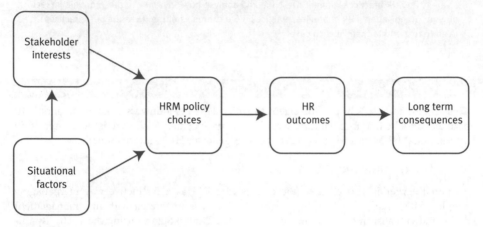

Adapted from Beer *et al* (1985)

Figure 1.4 The Michigan HR resource cycle

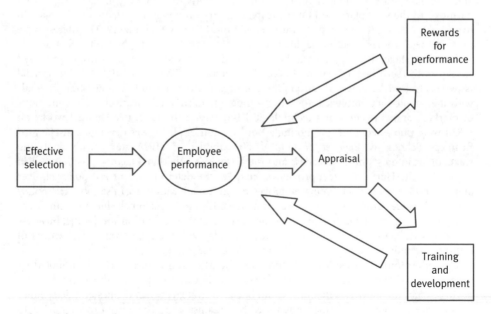

Adapted from Fombrun *et al* (1984)

As a result of these path-finding and subsequent studies, the concepts of strategy and strategic HRM were, by the 2000s, firmly incorporated in both the literature and practice of HRM. This was despite problems regarding the nature, significance, consequences and possible applications of the concepts involved. However, a major debate in the field remains: is the North American HRM paradigm resulting in a convergence of HRM practices universally? Basically, convergence theory or the convergence thesis has a long history (Kerr *et al* 1960). It argues that factors specific to organisations explain HR strategies and policies, with country-specific factors being less important. Thus the US convergence thesis posits that HRM practices are converging internationally as a result of globally driven market and technological forces which affect all firms. Because these forces are universally self-evident, the HR practices associated with them will be transferred around the world (Locke *et al* 1995). In short, the 'market forces model' of convergence posits that market forces generate convergence in HRM within firms towards a US model of HR (Gooderman and Brewster 2003).

The divergence thesis, in contrast, argues that HR systems are determined by national, institutional contexts, not by market and technological forces. This is because national institutions are unique and do not respond readily to market and technological imperatives. Indeed, it is argued, institutional contexts are slow to change, because they derive out of deep-rooted value systems and beliefs. Moreover, change is path dependent and can only be understood in relation to the specific social contexts within which it takes place (Maurice *et al* 1986). Supporters of the divergence thesis argue that, because of its North American origins, HRM is a culturally specific model, largely relevant to Anglo-Saxon business cultures only. The basic assumptions underpinning the Anglo-Saxon approach to HRM are identified with, first, a strong tradition of 'free enterprise' and the 'right to manage'. This means that government intervention in business is expected to be either residual or supportive of it, and that firms are largely autonomous bodies within the market system. Second, the preferred pattern of employment relationships within Anglo-Saxon HRM is individually rather than collectively based; they are not generally subject to trade unionism and collective bargaining. Third, businesses exist primarily to enhance narrow 'shareholder' value, not broader 'stakeholder' interests. The divergence model, in short, suggests that deep-seated differences exist among countries, resulting in continuing divergence in HRM and no convergence in HRM amongst firms.

1.5.2 EUROPEAN AND INTERNATIONAL HRM

Other writers suggest that HRM in places like mainland Europe is essentially different from Anglo-Saxon HRM for a number of cultural, legal and institutional reasons. First, the culture of mainland Europe is far less individualistic than that of North America, the UK and many Commonwealth countries. Above all, the United States is an exceptional case and atypical of the rest of the world (Trompenaars 1985). Second, legislation in Europe protecting individual employment rights, promoting collective employee communication and information channels such as works councils, and providing extensive social security provisions is far more extensive than that found in the United States and elsewhere. Third, the 'Rhineland' model of business enterprise, despite recent reforms within it, contrasts with Anglo-Saxon capitalism by its promotion of the 'stakeholder economy'. Thus whereas the Anglo-Saxon model of 'shareholder' capitalism is characterised by the drive for short-term returns for investors, the Rhineland model is a regulated market economy based on political consensus and comprehensive systems of social security. Fourth, trade union rights are normally incorporated in the Rhineland model but not so strongly within Anglo-Saxon states. Fifth, public ownership is more widespread in mainland European countries than in the United States, whilst in countries like Germany interlocking shareholdings and close management of companies result in less pressure for short-term profits and fewer incentives to drive competitors out of markets (Randlesome 1993).

This analysis gives rise to a corresponding convergence thesis in the European literature, just as in the Anglo-American literature. This is called the 'institutional model of convergence', which suggests that institutional forces generate convergence in HRM amongst European firms towards a common European model of HR. As in the case of the United States, European management and European HRM are claimed to be specific in their nature and common in their culture. This is highlighted by Thurley and Wirdenius (1989), who claim that European management has three main characteristics. First, it is broadly linked to the idea of European integration. Second, it reflects key values such as pluralism and tolerance, although it is not consciously developed out of these values. Third, it is associated with a balanced stakeholder approach and the concept of 'Social Partners' in business.

Katz and Kahn (1978) argue, in turn, that cross-national analyses need to take account of the wider societal variables determining how organisations operate within their external contexts. The national institutional arrangements most affecting national business systems include their employment relations systems, political institutions, the legal framework of corporate governance, education and training systems, the legal system, and product, labour and capital markets. Thus, scope for corporate decision-making on employment issues in countries such as Belgium, France, Germany, the Netherlands and Spain is relatively low, because of the comprehensive labour market legislation in these countries. In the UK, Ireland and the Nordic countries, on the other hand, the state traditionally plays a more limited role in this area, so scope for independent corporate decision-making is greater. In terms of HR practices, the societal contexts of European (and other) countries are likely to explain differences in the extents to which multinational corporations are able to pursue distinctive HR policies within them.

Table 1.3 Directional convergence in HRM in 23 European countries

Strong evidence	Considerable evidence	Weak evidence
Reduced size of HR departments	Some increases in flexible working practices	Little decentralisation of policy-making; more centralisation
Increased investment in human capital		No general decentralisation of HR responsibilities to line managers; slight centralisation
Increased communication with employees		
Increased use of variable and performance-related pay systems		

Adapted from Brewster et al (2004)

A study by Brewster et al (2004, p434) of 23 European countries in the 1990s examined these issues of convergence and divergence, drawing on a large-scale empirical dataset. Table 1.3 summarises this study's findings in terms of 'directional convergence' of HR practices amongst countries. This shows that there was strong evidence of directional convergence in four HR areas, considerable evidence in one area and weak evidence in two areas. The authors conclude that: 'From a directional convergence point of view, there seems to be a positive indication of convergence.' In terms of 'final convergence' of HR practices (ie whether countries are moving towards a common endpoint), however, the answer was not so conclusive. None of the HR practices converged 'at the end of the decade'. There were therefore some signs of HR convergence amongst European countries in the direction of trends. But there were very substantial differences, even continuing divergence, in final convergence. Differences amongst countries, in other words, appeared to be increasing. What this research appears to demonstrate is that whilst some directional convergence in European HRM is apparent, 'there is no unequivocal trend towards final convergence'.

1.5.3 MULTINATIONAL CORPORATIONS

A multinational corporation (MNC) is a business organisation with headquarters in one country and operations in a range of others. There are numerous examples of US, UK, European and Asia-Pacific MNCs. These firms, by their very nature, are large organisations and their size means that they often have considerable power and influence globally and locally. The reasons why MNCs expand into different countries vary: reducing transport and distribution costs, avoiding trade barriers, securing supplies of raw materials or markets, and gaining cost advantages such as low labour costs. MNCs also bring benefits to host countries in terms of economic growth and employment opportunities, improvements in production techniques and the quality of human capital, availability of quality goods and services locally, government tax revenues, and improvements in local infrastructures. MNCs also have distinctive HR policies and practices in managing their multinational workforces.

An important characteristic of MNCs and their HR practices is the notion of 'embeddedness'. This suggests, despite the process of globalisation, that economic activity is firmly embedded in distinct national or regional settings or national business systems. The persistence of different national business systems means the contexts in which firms manage their workforces differ markedly. How MNCs manage their workforces across national borders is related to the national business systems of their countries of origin. The evidence relating to MNCs in the United States, for example, indicates that there is a strong 'country of origin' effect in areas such as performance management, diversity and employment relations. However, as MNCs spread geographically, the embeddedness of their original business system declines. Another characteristic of MNCs is that they have scope to tap into the HR practices of their countries of operation, besides their original one. Through the process of 'reverse diffusion' MNCs are able to draw upon HR practices in their foreign subsidiaries and spread these around their international operations subsequently. Since MNCs are embedded in distinct national business contexts, HR practices that are transferred across countries are amended when they are implemented in their new settings.

It is also argued that evidence of convergence across countries is most evident in relation to MNCs and that globalisation is driving a process of convergence of HR practices within them. Ferner and Quintanilla (1998) claim that the internationalisation of French, German and Swiss firms has coincided with them adopting many HR practices common amongst US and UK companies. These include devolved business units and performance-related pay. But other evidence indicates that marked differences amongst MNCs remain. For example, employment regulations differ between countries and there continues to be centralised collective bargaining in some countries but not in others. Thus what is considered normal or accepted practice in HRM continues to vary across national boundaries. One explanation is that while globalisation causes changes in national models of HRM and at firm level, 'these changes are not all occurring at the same pace, nor are they all in the same direction'. Another observation is that pressures of globalisation are not felt evenly across sectors within countries. So there probably is 'no neat process of convergence'. HRM comes in different national styles but none of these 'is free from pressures to change' (Edwards and Rees 2006, p293).

1.5.4 COMPARATIVE HRM AND THEORIES OF CAPITALIST DIVERSITY

Hall and Wailes (2009, p116) refer to a revival of the 'institutionalist turn' in comparative and international HRM in recent years. They argue that during the last decade there has been an emergence of an increasing body of knowledge that draws on 'institutional theory to explain similarities and differences in HR practices across countries'. These are used, for example, to explain the extent to which MNCs reproduce the HR strategies and practices used in their home countries in their subsidiaries overseas. Thus Whitley (2000, p457) and others reject any cross-national universalist explanations of economic and HR behaviour. For these observers, national differences in managerial and firm behaviours are attributed to differences in national business systems. He argues that national business systems are distinguished along three main dimensions: ownership relations, non-ownership relations, and employment relations and work management. He then identifies six types of business system: fragmented, co-ordinated, compartmentalised, state organised, collaborative, and highly co-ordinated. In Whitley's analysis, these differences are a product of the institutional arrangements within nation states. In particular, it is variations in the nature and policies of the state, 'the financial system, the education and training systems and prevalent norms and values' that have helped structure 'qualitative differences between business systems'. Because the characteristics of national business systems are so deeply embedded in institutional arrangements, their impact on economic behaviour is likely to be persistent and enduring in each nation state.

In rejecting the view that there is any single way to organise market capitalism, as well as the managing of human resources, theories of capitalist diversity draw on the 'rediscovery' of the role of institutions in the social sciences. For Crouch (2005, p10), institutions are 'patterns of human action and relationships that persist and reproduce themselves over time', where these patterns are independent of the individuals performing them. It is these institutional arrangements, as products of past decisions, which play independent roles in shaping political, economic and social outcomes. 'Viewed in this way, institutions establish the rules of the game and act as a constraint on [human] agency' (Hall and Wailes 2009, p119). Thus although all capitalist societies face common pressures associated with globalisation and the international economy, differences in national institutional arrangements determine what happens in practice in each capitalist state.

The distinguishing feature of theories of capitalist diversity is their emphasis on the inter-connections amongst institutional arrangements within nation states, such as political constitutions, individual pay determination or collective bargaining, and training and education systems. Thus Hall and Soskice (2001) distinguish between the institutional arrangements for determining the co-ordination problems of firms in market economies. They identify two systems: 'liberal market economies' (LMEs) and 'coordinated market economies' (CMEs), each of which is the product of specific institutional complementarities. This is where one set of institutional arrangements enhances the efficiency of others. Thus Anglo-Saxon LMEs, for example, such as Australia, the UK and the US, are likely to enhance the effectiveness of financial participation schemes. CMEs, such as those of Belgium, France and Sweden, in contrast, are likely to enhance the effectiveness of collective bargaining systems of pay determination.

1.6 CONCLUSION: HR INSIGHTS, STRATEGY AND SOLUTIONS

From the evidence provided in this chapter, to be effective in the business world today HR professionals need to understand the external contexts (STEEPLE) in which their organisation operates and the levers driving change within it. Appropriate and relevant HR strategies, operational HR activities and HR solutions are important factors in meeting organisational needs to promote competitive advantage in the marketplace. The underpinning argument is that people make a difference to organisational performance. Recruiting, selecting, deploying, rewarding, appraising and developing the 'right' people in organisations are necessary conditions for organisational effectiveness, efficiency and business success. Having the 'wrong' people lacking the knowledge, skills, attitudes, and customer-focus to match organisational expectations and requirements is seen to be antithetical to these objectives.

Current good practice indicates that the HR function is critical to formulating and delivering these business and HR objectives and promoting appropriate HR activities. To achieve this purpose, HR specialists have to understand the business they work in, its markets and the forces driving it in the sector where the business operates. They also need to understand their organisation's business strategy, its performance goals and drivers. More specifically, HR practitioners have to draw on insights to lead and influence decisions at strategic, tactical, team, and individual levels across the organisation. They feed these insights and observations to senior managers to influence strategy, as well as developing prioritised HR plans aiming to deliver the needs of the organisation in line with its overall HR strategy. Other roles for HR include: partnering line managers to address sensitive HR issues; advising and coaching managers on the implementation and delivery of HR plans; and, where change is on the agenda, developing project plans to support the implementation of change initiatives, for example during restructuring and mergers.

In carrying out their roles, HR practitioners have to understand the market factors impacting on performance, customers, competitors, globalisation, population change and other factors. Most importantly, in today's competitive business climate, they are expected to speak the 'language of their business' and be able to draw upon the range of HR toolkits available that influence organisational performance.

To be effective, the HR function has to build relationships with internal and external specialists, taking account of current good practice and emerging HR trends, as well as understanding the external HR market. HR is expected to oversee compliance with regulation and corporate policy and to ensure that the organisation has the right people in sufficient numbers, in the right places, with the right experience and capabilities, to deliver the goals of the organisation. HR specialists also need to understand relevant HR technical skills, with in-depth knowledge of some of them. In the CIPD Profession Map, these are leading and managing the HR function, organisation design, organisation development, resourcing and talent planning, learning and development, performance and reward, employee engagement, employee relations, and service and delivery information. To support these activities, HR specialists have to access internal and external experts. Finally, HR professionals need to understand the external and internal influences affecting their business or organisation, including political influences impacting on the direction and shape of the organisation and its performance.

In summary, taking account of its contextual circumstances, and to promote appropriate HR solutions, the HR function has to develop critical awareness of what is possible in terms of HR strategy and practices. It also has to recognise what is likely to be acceptable to managers and employees and how strategy and practice can be implemented and reviewed to promote organisational advantage. It does this in the light of the contextual constraints facing it.

1 Historically, HRM has been infinitely flexible in adjusting to the dominant macro-economic, political and other contexts within which it has operated; HRM is historically path dependent. Contemporary HRM has emerged out of the drive for competitive advantage and the search for improved performance by organisations, whether in the private, public or third sectors, and changes in the external contexts. The latest, dominant 'trend' in HRM represents a distinctive approach to managing people at work, with a strategic focus, integrated with line management and individualistic in its orientation to the managing of people. However, HRM remains a 'contested terrain' both practically and theoretically.

2 The external contexts of HRM continually change and the HR function has to respond constantly to them by developing, implementing and evaluating appropriate HR strategies, policies and practices. The insights, strategy and solutions professional area of the CIPD Profession Map identifies the substantive knowledge and behaviours required by HR professionals in order to be effective in relation to the internal and external contexts of their organisations.

3 STEEPLE is a useful analytical tool enabling HR professionals and senior managers to identify and respond to the changing external contexts acting on organisations. It covers the current and longer-term socio-cultural, technological, economic, environmental, political, legal and ethical developments affecting HR strategy and practices.

4 Major developments in the structure of the HR function are the creation of 'shared services', the 'business partner' role, 'centres of excellence', the 'vendor management' role and 'corporate HR'. Within the new HR paradigm, some HR activities are devolved to line managers. In learning and development, the focus is increasingly on 'learning' rather than on training.

5 With divisionalisation, devolved budgeting, internal markets and increased competition in product and service markets, the search for improved performance is a driving force in most organisations. Linking individual and group performance to the goals and objectives of organisations has been a critical element in the performance management cycle. This involves setting individual targets, finding ways of measuring them, appraising them, reviewing performance, rewarding performance, identifying training needs and setting new targets.

6 Delegation of HR activities to line managers results in them taking on an important role in implementing HR strategies and HR practices. To be effective in this role, line managers need to work with HR professionals and gain their support in managing their staff. Despite the difficulties of this, research shows that line managers play a critical role in motivating staff, promoting job satisfaction and improving performance.

7 Outsourcing of HR activities is another feature of contemporary HRM. It is used to save costs for organisations, draw on external professional expertise, and seek independent HR advice not available in the host organisation. Outsourcing takes various forms. HR activities typically outsourced include payroll administration, recruitment and selection, training and development, executive search, and outplacement and redundancy counselling.

8 Most HR decisions pose ethical questions, since they deal with people issues covering recruitment and selection, managing performance, equal opportunities, learning and development, employee relations, rewards and termination of employment. Also, demands for ethical investment and ethical consumption put further pressure on HR to ensure ethical decision-making in organisations. With the demise of traditional personnel management, and its 'mediatory' and 'welfare' roles between employer and employee, HR practitioners have to be aware of the ethical issues arising from employing people, rewarding them, appraising them, and managing them fairly and consistently.

9 To promote effective HR strategy, the emphasis is on integration. Vertical integration (or 'external fit') refers to the links between business strategy, the external contexts and HR policies and practices. Horizontal integration (or 'internal fit') refers to HR strategy with a high degree of compatibility amongst its various elements.

10 Internationally, a main debate has been the extent to which the Anglo-Saxon, 'new' HRM paradigm is a universal model of practice. On balance, the evidence suggests that HR practices tend to be country-specific, because of powerful institutional and historical path-dependent factors, with HRM diverging among countries rather than generally converging – although some directional convergence is noted in Europe. MNCs exhibit some convergence in HR practices among countries, but they also import HR practices from their host countries into local businesses and adapt them. Theories of capitalist diversity stress the importance of institutional complementarities in explaining differences in business and HR practices in nation states.

REVIEW QUESTIONS

1 Identify and discuss some of the main differences between the 'personnel management' tradition and 'HRM' tradition. Explain the shift towards an HRM approach to managing people at work in recent years.

2 How important is it to have ethical standards in HRM? Explain how the HR function can maintain ethical HRM standards in organisations.

3 In your organisation, what are the main external contexts that affect HR strategy and practice? How does your organisation attempt to manage these contexts? Demonstrate whether it does so effectively or not.

4 Provide examples of how any trends in international HRM impact on your organisation and its HR policies and practices.

5 Describe and analyse how the HR function in your organisation is structured, taking account of shared services, centres of excellence, the business partner role, the vendor management role and corporate HR. How could delivery of HR be improved in your organisation? Justify your response.

DISCRIMINATION ON GROUNDS OF AGE IN EUROPE

Background

In a current analysis of age discrimination in 30 European states, it is reported that public opinion has shifted dramatically since an earlier survey only a year ago. The majority of Europeans now perceive discrimination on grounds of age to be widespread, with opinions about the extent of age discrimination having turned around radically in the course of a single year. Last year, an outright majority of Europeans perceived discrimination on this ground to be rare (52%). This year the balance has shifted, with 58% now perceiving it to be widespread, compared with 37% who believe it is rare. Two per cent think that discrimination on grounds of age is non-existent in their country and a further 3% say they 'don't know'.

When respondents were asked to estimate the extent of age discrimination, they were not asked to differentiate whether it is on the grounds of old age or youth. Thus respondents would have had different ideas in mind when thinking about this question.

Regardless of this distinction, the majority view in all but six countries is that age discrimination is widespread. In fact, in 22 of the 30 countries surveyed, this opinion is held by an absolute majority. Hungarian respondents top the list, with 79% saying that age discrimination is widespread in their country. This is followed by respondents in the Czech Republic (74%), France (68%), Latvia (67%) and the Netherlands (66%).

Older respondents are more likely to say age discrimination is widespread, although it is uncertain whether respondents associate 'age discrimination' with a specific age group. But on the basis of this survey, respondents aged 40 or over are more likely to say that discrimination on ground of age is widespread. This is in direct contrast to other grounds of

discrimination, which are more likely to be seen as widespread by the youngest groups of respondents. Women (60%) are more likely to see age discrimination as being widespread than are men (55%).

Changes in perceptions of discrimination on grounds of age

Perception that age discrimination is widespread has increased throughout Europe. Since last year, the perception that age discrimination is widespread has increased from 42% to 58% (+16 points). This trend is noted in all countries surveyed, with the exception of Portugal, where only a minor increase was recorded (+2 points). Further, apart from Italy (+8 points), these shifts are above ten percentage points in all other countries surveyed. The largest increases were recorded in Cyprus (+27 points), Romania (+25 points), France and the Netherlands (both +22 points).

The economic crisis seems to lie at the core of this shift in opinion: one of the perceived consequences of the crisis is that the jobs of older Europeans are less secure.

In 14 of the 30 countries surveyed, the majority view is that age discrimination is now less widespread. This view is particularly strong in Cyprus (77%) and is next highest in Denmark (64%) and Malta (62%). Conversely, there are also three countries where at least six out of ten respondents feel the contrary: 73% of Hungarians, 65% of Czech and 60% of Slovaks think age discrimination is more widespread.

Experience of age discrimination

Age is the ground for discrimination that is most frequently experienced by respondents. Whilst public perceptions of age discrimination have shifted in the course of the year, the proportion of respondents reporting that they have been discriminated against has not changed. However, at 6%, 'age' continues to represent the most common ground of self-reported discrimination. Unlike discrimination on ground of ethnicity, there is no significant gap between experienced and witnessed discrimination on grounds of age, with 8% of respondents reporting that they had witnessed this form of discrimination. This comparatively high figure may well be due to the fact that age is a shared attribute relevant to everyone, and young and old may be susceptible to suffer discrimination under various (often differing) circumstances. Age discrimination is 'most' prominent in the Czech Republic, with 11% saying they have experienced it and 17% saying that they have witnessed it. Other countries showing higher than average levels of reported discrimination, for both measures, are Sweden and Slovakia.

Tasks

1   Why has perceived age discrimination increased in Europe during the last year?

2   What factors account for differences in perceived and experienced age discrimination amongst European states?

3   The director of HR (Europe) in the MNC where you work is both surprised and concerned about this contextual issue and its possible impact on the company. As a senior HR executive in your company, you have been asked by the director of HR to:

(a)   Identify the possible ethical issues facing the company arising from the report summarised in Case Study 1.1.

(b)   Draft a policy paper indicating how to respond to any potential age discrimination within the company in the UK division.

(c)   Outline any learning and development issues arising from the report in Case Study 1.1 to suggest how the company might implement a learning and development plan addressing age discrimination.

EXPLORE FURTHER

BACH, S. (ed). (2005) *Managing human resources: personnel management in transition*. Oxford: Blackwell.

Examines and analyses all the contemporary debates about HRM practice, as well as the impact of environmental change on the ways people are managed in the UK.

BEARDWELL, J. and CLAYDON, T. (eds). (2007) *Human resource management: a contemporary approach*. Harlow: Financial Times Prentice Hall.

In an edited volume, covers a range of topical HRM themes and debates of today, including HR strategy, gender and diversity, employee rights, and employee involvement and participation. Also examines international HRM issues, as well as the influence of multinational corporations on HR policy and practice.

MARCHINGTON, M., MARCHINGTON, L. and WILKINSON, A. (2012) *Human resource management at work*. 5th ed. London: CIPD.

Undertakes a critical review of current HRM theory and practice and is very strong on up-to-date research evidence. Is comprehensive in coverage and looks outside of the HR box in discussing major topics and includes material on HR research and change management skills.

TORRINGTON, D., HALL, L., TAYLOR, S. and ATKINSON, C. (2009) *Fundamentals of human resource management*. Harlow: Pearson Education.

Offers a comprehensive introduction to contemporary HRM issues affecting HR specialists and line managers, and covers a wide range of both theoretical topics and practical issues.

Investigating and Researching HR Issues

CHAPTER OUTLINE

- Researching HR issues
- Getting started: the research process and the skills you need
- What is research in HR?
- What kind of a researcher are you?
- Requirements for student projects
- Writing your research proposal
- Working with your supervisor
- Managing the research project
- Working as a practitioner-researcher
- Summary
- Review and reflect
- Explore further

LEARNING OUTCOMES

This chapter should help you to:

- define what is meant by research in HR and how it contributes to effective policy and practice

- identify the different components of an effective research project and the skills needed

- compare different approaches to HR research and the opportunities presented by an investigation of a business issue

- discuss the implications of being a 'practitioner-researcher'.

RESEARCHING HR ISSUES

This book is aimed at people who are undertaking an HR research project as part of a qualification-related course. You may be a part-time student who is investigating a business issue in the role of a 'practitioner-researcher' or a full-time student who will be researching into an HR issue either inside or outside of a particular organisation or group of organisations. You may be studying in your own country or abroad.

The ability to undertake good-quality research which leads to relevant practical outcomes and contributes to the knowledge-base of the HR profession is an important skill. Qualified professionals should be able to research relevant topics and write reports that can persuade key stakeholders in the organisation to change or adopt a particular policy and practice. Most people who make use of this book are likely to be: final-year undergraduate students of management or HRM; students undertaking professional HR courses such as the CIPD Intermediate or Advanced level programmes or students undertaking a taught master's course (usually an MSc or MA in HRM or a related subject).

Making a start with a big piece of work like a research project is a daunting prospect and you may be tempted to put off the moment of making a start. This book is intended to help you make a start and then to see the project through to a successful and rewarding conclusion. The book aims to be practical, accessible and relevant. It should provide you with ideas and resources to apply to your research. I hope that you will use it as a resource to develop knowledge, understanding and the practical skills you need to make best use of the research process you are undertaking and to communicate what you have learned in a convincing and credible way. The book is not a substitute for regular attendance at research methods classes nor does it replace the need to communicate with your supervisor or project tutor.

Research projects are rarely completed quickly and they compete for attention with many other important and urgent matters. Different chapters of the book will be relevant at different stages of your project from initial project idea and research proposal to submission of the final report or dissertation.

When research is done well it can provide a 'win-win' opportunity for you and the organisation or organisations that have participated in some way. Your organisation(s) can learn from the findings and decide whether to implement your recommendations. You can gain valuable personal and professional development in a wide range of areas. Each chapter in this book ends with a self-test so that you can check your understanding and there is an opportunity to review and reflect on your achievements so far. This can inform any continuing professional development (CPD) record that you will maintain if you are a member of a professional organisation, such as the CIPD. Ideas about useful reading are also included at the end of each chapter to enable you to go further or deeper as appropriate.

GETTING STARTED: THE RESEARCH PROCESS AND THE SKILLS YOU NEED

ACTIVITY 1.1

A NICE PROBLEM TO SOLVE

Imagine that a good friend contacts you and invites you to join them for a 'once in a life time' holiday somewhere very special. You are very keen to follow this up but you need to know what would be involved in terms of your time and money and the implications of such a trip for your work and other responsibilities. How will you set about finding out more about the country your friend is keen to visit and the different options that might be appropriate for you?

FEEDBACK NOTES

In order to make decisions about whether to accompany your friend and, if so, how to organise the trip, there are a number of questions that you must find the answers to. These might include:

- What are different parts of the holiday destination country like?
- What climate might you expect at different times of the year? What would be the implications for shopping in advance for clothes and equipment?
- What modes of travel are possible? How much time would be spent on getting there, getting around and getting back?
- What facilities does the country or different accommodation options have to offer?
- What is the opinion about the proposed destination by other travellers who have visited?
- What are the cost implications?
- What health insurance and immunisation requirements are there?
- How safe is the country considered to be?

To answer these questions there are a range of sources of information that you might draw on. These include:

- Internet information sites
- travel brochures/publicity materials
- opinions of others (either given to you face-to-face or through social network media)
- recommendations of experienced travellers
- price comparison sites.

With a situation like this, the more sources of information you can draw on, and the more variety of types of information you can gather (opinions as well as sales brochures; statistics as well as recommendations), the more confident you are likely to feel in your ultimate decision. Merely booking a holiday because it is cheap, it was suggested by an acquaintance you do not know *that* well and it was the first option you stumbled across are less likely to result in a happy time. To enhance the fact-finding process you must first be clear what it is you are really looking for. Then it is necessary to find out what is already known about the destination and the travel process. Next you search for further information, obtaining as many different types of data as possible. Finally, you make sense of all the information and make your decision.

THE RESEARCH PROCESS

Activity 1.1 is, at a basic level, a small and personal research activity. It involves the systematic enquiry into an issue to increase knowledge and underpin effective decision-making. The activities it would involve are, however, indicative of the components of any research process (see Figure 1.1).

Figure 1.1 Components of the research process

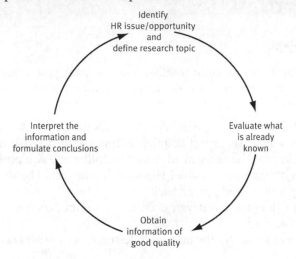

Often research is represented as a series of discrete and linear stages, and this book is structured in a similar sort of way. However, the reality of organisational research is that each stage is often interrelated with the others and experiences in later stages often lead to reconsideration of earlier ones (Saunders et al 2012).

For research undertaken to meet the requirements of the CIPD Advanced level qualifications, the general model in Figure 1.1 is elaborated on by the chief examiner, who emphasises the requirement for CIPD students to:

- diagnose and investigate a live issue of significance to a work organisation
- locate their work within a body of contemporary knowledge
- collect and analyse data
- derive supportable conclusions
- make practical and actionable recommendations
- reflect on implications for professional practice.

Each of these stages is considered in more detail in subsequent chapters of the book, but an indication of the skills you need to carry out these different elements is provided now.

THE EFFECTIVE RESEARCHER

Four interrelated skills underpin any effective research project (see Figure 1.2). You will need:

- **Intellectual and thinking skills:** knowing a lot about your topic is important, but other skills will enable you to undertake a more successful project. When you undertake research you have to act as an independent learner and this involves you being able to ask questions, probe deeply into issues and develop and justify your own thinking about the issues involved.
- **Personal effectiveness skills:** HR professionals are already aware of the importance of good interpersonal effectiveness in people management; the skills you have developed can be put to good effect in your research project, particularly your skills of time and stress management.
- **Organisational skills:** a research project is very like any other work-based endeavour: it has to be project-managed. Knowing how to break down components of a large piece of work, estimating the time requirements for different task areas, undertaking more than one task in parallel when appropriate and keeping track of progress are key skills that you can make use of and develop further.
- **Communication skills:** much of your research project involves you working on your own, but high-level communication skills are also necessary. In particular, you will need to orally articulate your ideas to your colleagues and tutors, listen actively (to get advice and also when gathering your data), share your findings within the organisation through effective presentations and produce a lengthy and well-written research report or dissertation.

Figure 1.2 The skills of an effective researcher

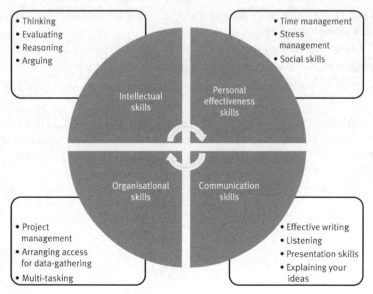

INITIAL FEELINGS ABOUT RESEARCH

It is possible that you are very excited about getting started with your research project. However, most students have mixed feelings at best, or strong doubts at worst, about their ability to complete a research project alongside all the other pragmatic and practical issues and problems facing them in their 'out of study' life.

Table 1.1 Common objections to doing research

Research is:

- just a way of proving what you already know
- best left to academics or to experts
- just a way of justifying what the CEO wants to do anyway
- too difficult
- too time-consuming
- removed from reality
- unable to change anything
- too scientific and statistical
- boring.

(Blaxter et al 2006, Jankowicz 2005)

Table 1.2 shows some recollections by students about their feelings when they were just starting out on a work-based research project required for their CIPD course.

Table 1.2 Feelings about getting started with a research project

I felt overwhelmed; I had never done anything like it before; I was anxious about choosing a 'good' topic. (Lee)
I felt nervous and concerned about how to get going. (Jane)
I was enthusiastic, but found it very daunting; where would I start? (Mike)
I felt daunted; I knew it would be a lot of work; where on earth would I begin? (Lisa)

If these sentiments reflect how you are feeling, read on (Table 1.3) to find out how much more positive the same students were once their projects had been completed.

Table 1.3 Personal benefits from undertaking a research project

I discovered that I can be highly motivated and disciplined. I found that once I feel 'passionate' about a topic I can 'throw myself into it'. (Lee)
How to deal with procrastination! Once I got going I enjoyed the work and found it interesting. I learned different ways to stop putting it off and to deal with the time pressures. (Jane)
I discovered what I was capable of! Self-determination, dogged enthusiasm and perseverance to achieve a significant challenge. (Mike)
I felt relieved and proud to learn that I can be more disciplined in my approach to time management than I ever thought possible (I normally leave things to the last minute!). (Lisa)

It would be foolish to say that doing research in HR is easy; challenges are likely for even the most confident and experienced practitioners and researchers. Personal qualities such as self-motivation, self-confidence and self-centredness will be important for your success (Biggam 2011):

- **Self-motivation:** you will need to maintain your interest and enthusiasm over quite a long period of time. Choose a topic that you are genuinely interested in and try to tackle all the different stages in the process with a positive attitude and curiosity for what you can learn.
- **Self-confidence:** self-doubt is an occupational hazard of all researchers at some point in the research process, so remember that your ideas are just as valuable as those of an established researcher or a chief executive. If you are able to learn from the advice of your tutor and student colleagues, there is no reason why your work should not be more than creditable when the time for assessment comes around.
- **Self-centredness:** the need to undertake your research over a sustained period means that, from time to time, you will have to turn down requests from family members and friends. Wise judgement is required in these circumstances, but it is important to make clear to everyone from the beginning that your project is a priority and you will appreciate their understanding and patience for its duration. Of course, after it is all over you can repay their patience many times over…

BENEFITS FROM RESEARCH

 ACTIVITY 1.2

IDENTIFYING BENEFITS FROM RESEARCH

Imagine that you still have to decide what to do for your project. The chief executive of the organisation for which you work has been to a government-backed seminar on employee engagement, and your manager thinks that 'something to increase engagement' would be a good project for you to undertake.

If you feel it would be helpful to find out more about engagement before tackling this activity, you might:

- listen to (or read the transcript of) the CIPD podcast on employee engagement, where four HR leaders from different types of organisation discuss what employee engagement means for their organisations and the issues raised for engagement when organisations are going through tough times: http://www.cipd.co.uk/podcasts/_articles/_employeeengagement37.htm?view=transcript

- skim-read some of the CIPD resources about employee engagement: http://www.cipd.co.uk/hr-topics/employee-engagement.aspx
- access the MacLeod Report to the UK Government, *Engaging for Success: Enhancing performance through employee*

engagement: http://webarchive.nationalarchives.gov.uk/+/http://www.bis.gov.uk/files/file52215.pdf

DISCUSSION QUESTIONS

1 Identify three benefits of tackling a project like this from your own perspective.

2 Identify three benefits from the perspective of your employer.

3 What problems might you foresee if you were to take on this project?

FEEDBACK NOTES

1   There are a number of benefits that may have occurred to you. Undertaking this sort of high-profile project might be good for your career prospects. Engagement is a very 'hot topic' in HRM and may well sound like an area you could get personally interested in. There should be a good level of support for you from both managers and employees as both sets of stakeholders may feel they have something to gain. You know the organisation and can have access to a considerable amount of information. Most of the work could be undertaken in work time rather than at home at weekends.

2   Your organisation also stands to benefit from such a project. Interest in employee engagement by senior managers and HR managers is high. Engagement seems to be right at the top of management's HR agenda. This may also be an opportunity for the HR department to enhance the credibility of its strategic contribution.

3   In spite of some benefits there are also some problems that would probably occur to you in this sort of situation. Practical issues such as your own time constraints may be of concern as well as the extent to which this would be a project that is interesting to you personally. Other questions you might pose include:

- Over what timescale would the employer expect you to work on this project?
- Is it possible to satisfy both your employer and the requirements for your qualification?
- Given that you are (probably) not a senior manager, how would you go about identifying urgent action for senior people in the organisation?
- Is the organisation *really* interested in this project?

Perhaps these concerns might be summed up with four questions:

1   What exactly would this project involve?

2   Is it feasible as a topic for a student project?

3   How would it add value to HR practice in the organisation?

4   How might it add value to the HR community beyond your specific organisation?

The purpose of this chapter is to explore these general questions so that you are in a better position to understand the contribution of research to real organisational situations and consider the role of the practitioner-researcher. This should help you to work out how to use this book to plan and execute your own research project.

WHAT IS RESEARCH IN HR?

There are many different ideas about what 'research' actually is (see, for example, Yin 2009 Silverman 2009). A useful and simple definition to start with is: **finding out things in a systematic way to increase knowledge**. Research is a key function of higher education and informs much of what goes on in work organisations. As a result, universities and colleges as well as professional bodies are increasingly requiring elements of research-based or enquiry-based learning at all levels of study.

HRM involves practical application of up-to-date understanding in the context of 'real world' organisations. Reliable knowledge built on accurate information is needed. To undertake effective HRM, it is important that good-quality information underpins decisions and informs the actions of those involved in the employment relationship, such as trade unions, individual employees, outsourced service providers and professional organisations (Bamber et al 2004, Therborn 2006). The definition of research in HR in this book is: **the systematic enquiry into HR issues to increase knowledge and underpin effective action**.

HR RESEARCH – THE VALUE OF APPLIED RESEARCH

Many writers about research methods distinguish between 'pure' and 'applied' research (see, for example, Van de Ven 2007, Starkey and Madan 2001), although the distinction is not always clear-cut and is best seen as a continuum relating to the purpose and context in which the investigation occurs. The main focus of pure research (sometimes referred to as 'mode 1 research') is on gaining knowledge to describe and explain phenomena, develop and test generalisable theories and make predictions (van Aken 2005, Burgoyne and James 2006). Applied research (sometimes referred to as 'mode 2'), by contrast, is more concerned with developing knowledge that can be used to solve problems, predict effects and develop actions and interventions that are applicable in particular organisational contexts. Although applied research is not always accorded high academic prestige, it may require greater skill across a broader range of areas than pure research demands.

Figure 1.3 Pure and applied research

Applied research	Pure research
Problem-solving	Gaining new knowledge
Predicting effects	Establishing causes
Concern for action	Assessing relationships between variables
Time/cost constraints	'As long as it needs'
'Client' orientated	'Academic' orientation

(Robson 2011, Easterby-Smith et al 2003, Saunders et al 2012)

Most HR research that is undertaken as part of a taught course of study is at the 'applied research' end of the continuum, involving a relatively small-scale investigation in one organisation or using information from a relatively small sample of people or organisations. This book works from the position that, in HR at least, applied research is at least as valuable as pure research. HR research that is carried out in a rigorous way can lead to more effective practice than decisions based mainly on intuition, common sense or personal preferences. Common sense tends to take many features of organisational situations for granted. A systematic process of research, however, makes it possible to challenge 'taken for granted' assumptions and so generate new ways of understanding situations that can form the basis for innovative approaches to solving complex problems. A key capability for effective HR practitioners is the analysis of HR situations and the use of systematic investigative techniques to underpin decision-making and problem-solving.

The basis of this book is that HR research is about advancing knowledge in a way that is relevant to changing organisational priorities, solution of HR problems and the continuous development of organisations involved in the research process itself.

 ACTIVITY 1.3

WEB-BASED ACTIVITY

Visit the website of an HR magazine such as *People Management* (http://www.peoplemanagement.co.uk), *Personnel Today* (http://www.personneltoday.com), *HR Zone* (http://www.hrzone.co.uk) or *Training Zone* (http://www.trainingzone.co.uk)
Run a search using the word 'research'. If you can, limit the dates of the search to the most recent one or two calendar months.

FEEDBACK NOTES

An activity such as this demonstrates how important research is to the development of HR practice. Research evidence is used to justify why certain HR practices are beneficial and is also used to evaluate the success (or otherwise) of HR policies and practices. Research contributes to the development of HR at strategic, policy and operational levels.

WHAT KIND OF A RESEARCHER ARE YOU?

Models of the research process and figures showing skill requirements can lead to an assumption that there is 'one right way' to undertake research. This is not the case and every individual HR practitioner or student is likely to undertake research in their own unique way. Indeed, research in the HR and management arena is characterised by diversity and it is important, at an early stage in your project planning process, to clarify for yourself a response to the question: 'what kind of a researcher am I?' This will help you to think more clearly about potential topics that you might investigate and how you might go about it (Brown 2006, Fox et al 2007).

INSIDER OR OUTSIDER?

Are you an insider or an outsider? There are two possible types of insider. One type is the person who will be involved in researching their own area of work in their own place of employment. The second type of insider is the researcher who is keen to find out what is going on *inside* the people that they are researching; their meanings and understandings. Two types of outsider are also possible. Outsiders are those who will be involved in researching in their own organisation but in a different place or part of it, or those who will undertake research into situations and/or organisations where they truly are an outsider. Your position as an insider or an outsider will have implications for your research. Outsiders may find it easier to establish facts and to discuss 'universals' rather than particulars. Insiders, by contrast, may be led to research that contains more 'narrative' than numbers. Examples of the different ways that a topic might be taken forward by people who are insiders or outsiders are shown in Table 1.4. The examples in this table use the illustration of talent management, but the same principles would apply to most HR projects.

Table 1.4 Insiders and outsiders? Examples of different options for research projects

Insider/outsider	Example of research project topic
Insider – who is undertaking research into their own organisation	An evaluation of talent management at XYZ Ltd
Insider – who wants to know about what is *inside* the people that they are researching; their meanings and understandings	An assessment of perceptions and attitudes towards a talent management programme at XYZ Ltd
Outsiders – who will be researching in a different part of their own organisation	An investigation into the implementation of talent management in the information systems division
Outsiders – who will research into situations and/or organisations where they have little or no connection	Research into the application of talent management programmes in retail organisations in the UK

'DETECTIVE', 'DOCTOR' OR 'EXPLORER'?

In addition to the distinction between research as an insider or as an outsider, most HR researchers have different 'mental pictures' of the purpose of their research. Brown (2006) characterises three different ideal types, which are depicted in Table 1.5. Many researchers find that they identify with more than one type. Which of these are you *most* like?

Table 1.5 Researcher similes

Researcher as detective	Researcher as doctor	Researcher as explorer
You have a clear idea about the research **problem**; for example: 'talent management programmes favour younger workers over older employees'. The researcher as detective gathers relevant information to get the clues needed to solve the problem and then marshals the evidence to prove that the solution that they have reached is the correct one.	The researcher as doctor recognises the need to work from the symptoms they are presented with to diagnose the **cause** of the situation before any appropriate 'treatment' can be prescribed. The researcher as doctor looks for the reasons behind the research issue;for example: 'what factors lead employees to be negative about talent management programmes?'	The researcher as explorer loves to enter 'unknown territory' and keep a record about what they find; for example: 'what happens in an organisation that has been acquired and is required to implement the talent management programme of the new parent company?'

(Brown 2006)

Descriptive research

If you see yourself mainly as a detective or perhaps as an explorer, it is likely that you will be interested in carrying out **descriptive** research where you set out to provide an accurate profile of situations, people or events. A descriptive research project focuses on 'what, when, where and who'. Having investigated and described the issue, you can then go further and analyse the data to ask 'why?'

and 'so what?' Both qualitative and quantitative data are useful in descriptive studies.

Explanatory research

If you see your role as a researcher to be like that of a doctor or perhaps as a detective, it is likely that you will undertake **explanatory research** by setting out to explain a situation or problem, usually in the form of causal relationships. Your focus will be on 'why' and 'how', seeking to explain organisational problems and, through assessment of the causes, to recommend changes for improvement. Both qualitative and quantitative data may be useful for achieving these research purposes.

Exploratory research

If you see your role as a researcher as more like that of an explorer, **exploratory** research will appeal to you. The purpose of exploratory research is to seek new insights and find out what is happening. There is an attempt to ask questions and assess phenomena in a new light. A more qualitative approach often (but not always) underpins this sort of research and the focus is on obtaining new insights into new or current situations and issues.

 ACTIVITY 1.4

HOW REAL IS REALITY TV?

Reality TV (as distinct from documentaries or other non-fictional TV programmes such as sports coverage and news) is a form of television programming that has become prevalent in almost every TV network since the beginning of the twenty-first century. Examples from UK channels include talent searches such as: *The Apprentice* and documentary-type programmes such as *The Only Way is Essex* and *Masterchef.* Reality TV shows claim to show ordinary people in unscripted and real situations. Identify and think about three different reality TV shows that you know about. If you do not watch reality TV shows yourself,

you can find out about them from friends or from broadcasters' websites. You might also enjoy reading commentary on *The Apprentice* in John McGurk's (CIPD Adviser for Learning and Talent Development) blog at http://www.cipd.co.uk/blogs/members/j.mcgurk/default.aspx

DISCUSSION QUESTIONS

1 How real is reality TV?

2 In what ways is reality TV *real* and in what ways is reality TV *not real*?

3 To what extent is 'heartbreak' real?

4 In what sense are dreams real?

FEEDBACK NOTES

Discussion about reality TV can evoke strong reactions. Some people watch reality TV programmes with enthusiasm and commitment; they want to decide for themselves about the qualities shown by those involved and may also identify strongly for or against one or more of the participants. Other people might describe reality TV as 'tedious', 'worthless' and 'manipulative'. The extent to which the programme that is broadcast is contrived or the effect of the editing process on what we watch might, however, be seen to make reality TV less real than its name would imply. The discussion about the 'reality' of reality TV makes us wonder how we can *know* about *reality* and this is an important issue for everyone who aims to carry out research in the *real* world.

When discussing the extent to which heartbreak is real, your opinion might be different depending on your current emotional circumstances and relationships. For others their view would not depend on their context or circumstances – they would argue that heartbreak is a feeling rather than a real thing. Others might say that they know what is real when they come across it and are able to distinguish between what *seems* real (dreams and/or heartbreak) and what actually is real as evidenced by the behaviours that they experience. Even those of us who prefer to rely on the evidence of our senses to identify what is real find ourselves challenged by the digital and technological opportunities of the twenty-first century to 're-master' or alter what we see and hear. This can lead us to wonder whether reliance on the evidence provided by our senses or on our experience is a sufficient basis from which to know about the real world (Saunders et al 2012).

WHAT IS YOUR REAL-WORLD VIEW?

Work in HR, and this includes research work in HR, takes place in the real world and is about real world issues (Robson 2011). Most of the time most of us do not trouble ourselves with thinking much about the nature of the real world; we just get on with our lives and our jobs. Before you start with your research, however, you will need to think about your own take on the nature of the real world.

When addressing the question 'what is real?' there are three prominent options (Brown 2006, Fox et al 2007). One answer is that reality is **'out there'** and this corresponds to what is termed an **objective** world-view. If your view is that reality is **'in here'** (that is, a feature of your perceptions and feelings), you may feel more comfortable in what might be called an individually **constructed** world-view. You might think that reality is **'in here'** but influenced by **'out there'**. This would be represented by what is often called a **socially constructed** world-view.

The extent to which you subscribe to an objective, socially constructed or individually constructed world-view may well be influenced by your own personal and professional background. Economists, for example, tend to operate within an objective world-view; social and care workers tend to be most comfortable with a socially constructed world-view. HR researchers are difficult to generalise about: some adopt a socially constructed world-view and others work from an objective world-view. Your assumptions about these issues, therefore, may well be different from other HR practitioners and researchers that you come into contact with. The nature of your thinking in response to these issues, however, is likely to be important for the way that you tackle your project.

If you are most comfortable with an objective world-view, it is likely that you will want to establish objective facts that can be generalised independently of the beliefs, perceptions, culture and language of different individuals and groups. This perspective is often associated with what is termed a **positivist** approach to research, which is outlined in Chapter 2. If you are more comfortable with a socially constructed world-view, it is likely that you will value information from observation or interviews mostly gathered in the form of words and meanings, pictures and other artefacts and value qualitative rather than quantitative data. This world-view is often associated with the **interpretivist** approach, which is also introduced in Chapter 2.

Research into the psychological contract

CASE ILLUSTRATION 1.1

Alex was a part-time student in a retail organisation where performance and the achievement of targets were key features of organisational culture. Anecdotal evidence led her to be concerned about the way sickness absence was managed in her organisation, the extent to which management responses to sickness absence affected levels of employee engagement in her organisation and whether managers' understanding of the 'preventative' effects of their actions with regard to sickness absence was perceived by employees as 'punitive' and the effect this had on engagement. For her research project, Alex decided to measure employees' and managers' perceptions of the absence management process and indicators of engagement, and to compare these with indicators of preventative and punitive approaches to absence which she found in the literature.

From her reading of the literature, Alex identified questionnaire items related with measures of engagement and absence management. These items included such things as: different features of managing absence (which she obtained from CIPD surveys on absence management); factors that maximise attendance at work; perceptions of absence review processes; and engagement measures (which came from her company's regular staff satisfaction survey). Alex

set out to gather and analyse the data from a range of different people who worked in a sample of the retail outlets to make some generalised conclusions about the effects of the organisation's approach to managing sickness absence.

Kingsley was also interested in taking forward research into employee engagement. However, he took a different approach. He focused on finding out about the beliefs, values, expectations and aspirations of employees through a series of in-depth interviews. Kingsley wanted to find out about the different feelings of engagement people might have even if they worked in jobs at the same 'level' and in the same organisation. Through conducting interviews, therefore, Kingsley set out to gather information that was grounded in the experiences and perspectives of those involved to provide an in-depth understanding of the issues from the different participants' perspectives.

Discussion Questions

1   What world-view underpinned the approaches to their research adopted by Alex and Kingsley?

2   To what extent (and why) is it possible to decide which approach is 'superior'?

FEEDBACK NOTES

The approach adopted by Alex was indicative of the objective world-view. She sought to measure features of absence management and engagement as indicated through generalised patterns of questionnaire responses. Kingsley's approach was indicative of the constructed world-view and he was interested in the way in which employee engagement is differently felt by different people on the basis of their unique experiences and contexts.

The different research world-views described here are distinct, but you may also have highlighted that there are overlaps between them. No experience (of employee engagement) is wholly individually and uniquely experienced; some aspects will be shared between individuals and groups. Also, 'socially derived' views (about executive pay, for example) can become so universally accepted that they can be researched as an objective fact.

You may feel that both objectivist and constructivist perspectives are useful ways forward, and research that works from more than one world-view is quite common (although not required or compulsory) within HR. The important thing is to be clear about your world-view – to yourself and to those who will read your work – so that this can be taken into account in making sense of your research and the conclusions that you draw. You may well be reflecting at this point that you can see the benefit of both objectivist and constructivist world-views, and you may be thinking about incorporating both approaches into your research. Within research in HR there is a strong tradition of what is sometimes called a 'mixed methods' approach, characterised by elements of both world-views within a project. Such approaches are discussed in Chapter 2. However, bringing insights from both world-views together can have implications for your research project that can be very time-consuming and difficult to express within a word limit of 7,000 words (which is often applied for CIPD management or business research reports).

ACTIVITY 1.5

WHAT KIND OF A RESEARCHER ARE YOU?

Think about yourself: your situation, your world-view, your preferences and your interests. Write your comments to the questions on the left in the spaces provided on the right.

About you	Response
Are you likely to undertake research in your own organisation or one where you might be considered an outsider?	

About you	Response
Are you interested in general facts and universal trends or are you more interested in getting *inside* the meanings behind particular issues and experiences?	
To what extent is your preferred research role similar to that of a doctor/ explorer/detective (or a combination)?	
Which world-view do you feel most comfortable with: 'objectivist world-view' or 'constructivist world-view'?	

Your responses to these questions might be useful to share with your tutor or supervisor as you discuss potential research topics and the way you might take your research project forward.

Figure 1.4 Factors affecting the employment relationship

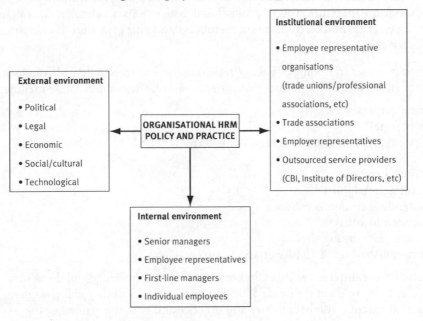

THE AUDIENCES FOR HR RESEARCH

ACTIVITY 1.6

AUDIENCES FOR HR RESEARCH

1 Use Figure 1.4 as a prompt and write down a list of different groups of people who may be interested in the implications of research into HR issues in your organisation (or one you are familiar with).

2 For each group of people that you identify, try to work out how they might find out about relevant research that has been undertaken.

FEEDBACK NOTES

Your list of likely 'audiences' for HR research might include: individual practitioners; individual managers; members of trade unions; people in central government departments; members of your local authority; specialist organisations/pressure groups; professional associations; academics; consultants; employer/trade bodies; trade union members; students; providers of outsourced HR services.

When it comes to finding out about research, there is an equally wide range of publications and opportunities that different groups might use. These include:

- newspapers
- webpages
- specific reports (may be internal or external)
- books
- trade journals
- professional journals
- attending conferences/seminars
- academic journals
- social networking sites
- unpublished research (dissertations, projects, etc).

Each of these different vehicles for communicating knowledge will do so in a different way to meet the needs of its audience. As a result they will engage to different extents with both theory and practice and with the general or the specific.

Figure 1.5 Orientation of different research outputs

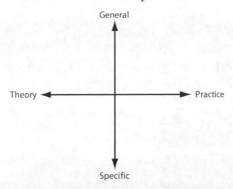

ACTIVITY 1.7

ASSESSING DIFFERENT RESEARCH
PUBLICATIONS

Study one copy of the following types of HR
publication:

- academic peer-reviewed journal (for
  example, *Human Resource Management
  Journal, Human Resource Development
  International* or *International Journal of
  Human Resource Management*)

- professional journal (for example, *People
  Management* or *Personnel Today*)
- practitioner report (for example, IDS Report
  or a CIPD Research Insight report (http://
  www.cipd.co.uk/hr-resources/research/)

Skim-read the publications and try to 'plot'
each of the features of the research articles/
reports guided by the two axes shown in Figure
1.5.

FEEDBACK NOTES

It is likely that different articles from each of the first two types of publication
may need to be plotted differently. Some studies, even within one publication, are
very concerned with one specific situation and others are more general. What is
easier to characterise is the different levels of engagement with theories, models
and concepts. Papers in a peer-reviewed academic journal such as *HRMJ* will be
significantly concerned with evaluating theories as well as with practically
focused investigations. Practitioner reports, by contrast, are more concerned with
describing practice than with explicitly locating it within any conceptual
framework. Feature articles in practitioner journals vary somewhat, although
theory is rarely a major feature.

REQUIREMENTS FOR STUDENT PROJECTS

If you are working towards a professional or educational qualification, the
principal readers of your work will be interested in its academic features as much
as the practical outcomes for the organisation(s) in which your research project is
situated. Therefore it is important that your work corresponds to the
characteristics shown in Figure 1.6.

Figure 1.6 Characteristics of a research project in HR

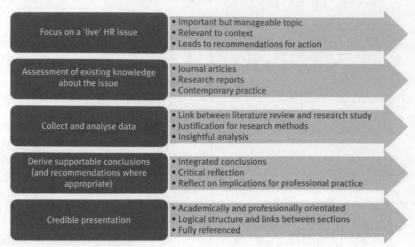

Focus on a 'live' HR issue	• Important but manageable topic • Relevant to context • Leads to recommendations for action
Assessment of existing knowledge about the issue	• Journal articles • Research reports • Contemporary practice
Collect and analyse data	• Link between literature review and research study • Justification for research methods • Insightful analysis
Derive supportable conclusions (and recommendations where appropriate)	• Integrated conclusions • Critical reflection • Reflect on implications for professional practice
Credible presentation	• Academically and professionally orientated • Logical structure and links between sections • Fully referenced

FOCUS ON A 'LIVE' HR ISSUE

Choosing a topic can be a challenging decision for first-time researchers and this issue is addressed in Chapter 2. A good project will be interesting for you to undertake and will provide the opportunity for added value to those who will read about your results (HR practitioners, student colleagues and academic tutors). Choose something that will be manageable (not too big – your time is short) but something that is challenging enough to merit an academic qualification and will be interesting to those who will find out about your work.

ASSESSMENT OF EXISTING KNOWLEDGE ABOUT THE ISSUE

Most published HR research, particularly reports that are produced for a practitioner audience, do not engage explicitly with theories, models and frameworks. Research written for an academic audience found in academic journals, by contrast, is **explicit** about theory. If your research forms part of a qualification-bearing course, an explicit use of theory is expected. You must take a constructively critical approach to the current state of knowledge in your topic area and work out how your project fits into the wider context. It is worth finding out now about the expectations of your tutors about the balance between theory and practice for your research report or dissertation.

COLLECT AND ANALYSE DATA

All projects undertaken as part of an HR programme of study require the collection and analysis of data. This may be secondary data (which has already been generated for some other purpose) as well as primary data (which you will gather to answer your research questions). If you are undertaking a CIPD course, you must collect and analyse primary data as part of your research. In many cases your data will come from one organisation, but in some circumstances data will be gathered across a range of individuals or organisations. Some HR research involves a new analysis of secondary data sources.

DERIVE SUPPORTABLE CONCLUSIONS

Once you have gathered your data and analysed it to make sense of what you have found, you will need to draw some overall and integrated conclusions. This will require you to reflect in a critical way about the limitations of your data as well as the insights you have achieved. Most HR research projects fall into the category of applied research and so you will also be able to reflect on the implications of your research findings for professional practice.

CREDIBLE PRESENTATION

Your research report or dissertation may be the longest document you have ever written and you will expend a lot of time and energy in producing it. The final product must be persuasive to those who read it; academic and professional credibility are important. The way the report is presented, the quality of your written communication, careful proof-reading, helpful graphics and charts, and the quality of referencing and citation you exhibit will all make a difference to both the persuasiveness of your report *and* to the mark your work achieves.

WRITING YOUR RESEARCH PROPOSAL

Whether you are undertaking a dissertation, business research report or other form of investigative inquiry, it is likely that your study centre will require you to write a research proposal. This is your first opportunity to write down what you plan to do. What is expected of your research proposal will depend on the qualification you are undertaking and the requirements of your study centre. You may find that a short document (one or two sides of A4 paper) is expected and the feedback you receive will be 'formative' (that is, not associated with a mark towards your final qualification). Alternatively, your centre may require a more detailed proposal of 2,000–3,000 words for which a mark will be recorded, which will count towards your final qualification.

Whatever the expected length of the research proposal, most students find this a daunting document to produce. But there are good reasons to overcome any natural tendency to put off the moment of writing. Your research project is an independent piece of work. As you undertake it you will benefit from the advice of your tutor as well as others in your study cohort and work organisation. However, the project is your responsibility and so the research proposal means you can:

- put down your initial ideas in writing
- share your ideas with your tutor/study centre
- get feedback about the strengths and possible difficulties of your idea.

Your tutor will provide you with a suggested format (and indicative word limit) for your proposal. Table 1.6 provides an indication of issues you will need to address.

Table 1.6 Research proposal contents

Topic area; aims and objectives	Provide an overview of the problem or issue you plan to address. Explain why this topic was chosen (what was the catalyst or trigger of the project? what is the value of the project?). Explain what you hope to achieve through the research. You should formulate an initial aim or 'big question' and more-specific objectives or questions (see Chapter 2 for help with this).
Literature review plans or progress	This part of the proposal shows how your research is positioned in the existing literature and where your study fits within existing knowledge about the topic. Requirements of study centres vary. Some require you to indicate the main areas for your literature search and key sources of information you are already aware of. Other centres require an initial review of the most important literature sources and an assessment of where your research would contribute to filling a gap in knowledge.
Research design and methods	This section identifies the way in which you are going to investigate the issue or problem as well as your world-view as a researcher. Your proposal should set out what type of data you intend to collect, your sampling strategy, the research methods you plan to use and your proposed approach to data analysis.
Ethical issues	Indicate here what particular ethical issues or problems you will need to address: in particular, obtaining informed consent of any organisations in which you plan to gather data as well access to individual participants. You will also need to explain the approach you will take to issues of confidentiality and anonymity for your research participants.
Suggested timetable	Present a clear and realistic timetable for the completion of your research and the production of your report. Indicate when important tasks will be carried out. Set achievable targets and time-planning contingencies and build in time for continuous review of different stages by you and your tutor.

WORKING WITH YOUR SUPERVISOR

A dissertation or a business research report is something for which you take personal responsibility. You will find it helpful to discuss your ideas and your progress with colleagues at work and with study 'buddies'. However, the key source of advice, guidance and encouragement will be your project tutor or research supervisor. Different study centres make different supervisory arrangements, and it is important to find out about the practices in your university. Figure 1.7 depicts the main areas that your supervisor will be able to discuss with you.

Figure 1.7 Feedback and discussion with your supervisor

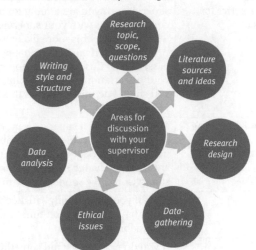

Figure 1.7 shows what a crucial contribution your supervisor can make. Establishing a good working relationship can help you to manage the research process in an effective way. The supervisory relationship is different from other tutorial arrangements as, in most cases, supervisors will work with their students on a one-to-one basis. Different supervisors will have their own backgrounds, experiences and preferred ways of working, just as you will also have your own preferences. If you want to work effectively with your supervisor, consider the list of hints and tips shown in Table 1.7.

Table 1.7 Constructive working with your supervisor

Establish the format, basis and frequency of meetings.	You may agree to meet face-to-face and have a few long meetings or shorter, more frequent meetings. You may prefer to communicate by Skype, telephone, email, and so on, if these media are more appropriate.
Identify times when either of you will not be contactable.	Check out when your supervisor may be away; let them know about your planned absences (holidays, etc). Don't send work to your supervisor just before their planned leave – they won't look at it until they get back.
Identify the key areas you feel you will need support with and discuss these at the beginning of the research process.	Discuss with your supervisor your strengths and skills that are relevant to the research process and the areas that you feel less confident with. Agree an action plan to develop in these areas and seek feedback as appropriate.
Establish project milestones and deadlines by which you will submit draft work for comment.	Your supervisor will be able to advise you about realistic targets. Don't be too ambitious but, once you have established your milestones, make sure you stick to them.

Be honest about your aspirations and priorities for the research project.	Discuss what you hope to achieve with your supervisor. If you are aiming for a distinction, commit to this with your supervisor and discuss what will make this more likely to be achieved. Alternatively, if you will be happy with a 'solid' pass, discuss this. If you are hoping to follow up your dissertation with producing a journal article, you should definitely discuss this in advance with your supervisor.
If you cannot attend a meeting or meet a deadline, make sure you let your tutor know in advance.	Nothing annoys a supervisor more than waiting around for a student who does not arrive or does not submit work at the agreed date. If you anticipate a change in your circumstances, let your supervisor know sooner rather than later.
Don't prevaricate.	Even if you are not fully satisfied with your draft work, try to submit it on time and then learn from the feedback you get.
Don't bluff.	If you do not understand something or have not actually done something, talking about it means you are more likely to get advice on how you can move forward.
Allow time for your supervisor to read your draft work carefully.	Although you will undertake a lot of work at weekends, do not expect your supervisor to do this as well. If they are to read your work carefully, they will need a sensible period of time (they have many other tasks to fulfil in addition to working with you).
Don't ask your supervisor what mark they think your project/ dissertation will achieve.	Even if your supervisor will be one of the markers of your report or dissertation, the assessment process is different and separate from the supervision process.

MANAGING THE RESEARCH PROJECT

A research project is like any other project that you undertake: it has a natural progression, following a series of different stages. To undertake any project successfully you will need to undertake the following steps. Remember that this process will not necessarily follow in such a smooth sequence and you will need to continuously evaluate and monitor progress. However, these stages – which are illustrated in Figure 1.8 and also show the logic of the chapter construction of this book – do act as a reasonable 'road map' and none of them should be left out:

Figure 1.8 Stages in your research project

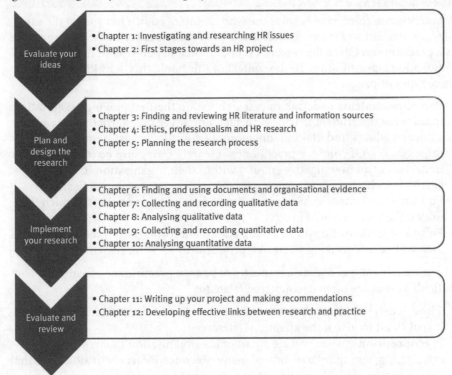

Evaluate your ideas
- Chapter 1: Investigating and researching HR issues
- Chapter 2: First stages towards an HR project

Plan and design the research
- Chapter 3: Finding and reviewing HR literature and information sources
- Chapter 4: Ethics, professionalism and HR research
- Chapter 5: Planning the research process

Implement your research
- Chapter 6: Finding and using documents and organisational evidence
- Chapter 7: Collecting and recording qualitative data
- Chapter 8: Analysing qualitative data
- Chapter 9: Collecting and recording quantitative data
- Chapter 10: Analysing quantitative data

Evaluate and review
- Chapter 11: Writing up your project and making recommendations
- Chapter 12: Developing effective links between research and practice

- **Evaluate your ideas** – at this stage you make a research proposal and refine your thinking at an early stage on the basis of feedback you receive. Issues such as the length of time available, any cost implications and achieving necessary permissions to undertake the research need to be considered at this stage.
- **Plan and design the research** – this is where you will think in detail about key activities and tasks within each of your main milestones. Careful planning about access to data and ethics, literature searching and literature review, and plans relating to data-gathering and analysis is required. Research projects without careful planning and design are less likely to be successful.
- **Implement your research** – this stage will involve processes of data-gathering, review and analysis. This stage will involve you finding and using documentary and organisational evidence, collecting and recording your data and then analysing information to make sense of it.
- **Evaluate and review** – this is an important stage of any project, and with research it is important that you undertake a careful review of your analysis and formulate meaningful conclusions. At the same time it is important to reflect on learning points to enable you to develop your practice as both a researcher and an HR professional as your career develops.

It is likely that most research will be undertaken within a specific organisational context and will be focused on the solution of a particular HR problem or issue. In this sense an action orientation is more likely and the implications of this for the practitioner-researcher are now explored.

WORKING AS A PRACTITIONER-RESEARCHER

A practitioner-researcher is someone who is employed in a job and, at the same time, carries out a research project that is of some relevance to their current role as a practitioner. Often the research is undertaken in addition to their normal duties and responsibilities. In the context of this book, this definition embraces three types of people:

- Part-time students undertaking research within their employing organisation: in this case the student may be a 'regular' employee or, alternatively, may be someone who is undertaking some form of consultancy assignment in the organisation. Of course, a practitioner-researcher may also be someone who is undertaking an investigative enquiry within their organisation (or that of a client) for which there is no link with the achievement of a qualification.
- Full-time students who have a part-time job in an organisation in which they undertake their research project.
- Full-time students for whom a work placement forms part of their course and they will be undertaking a research project within the placement organisation.

There are advantages and disadvantages of being a practitioner-researcher. The difficulties that are often encountered relate to:

- **Time:** when the project has to be undertaken in addition to normal workloads, it is difficult to give it the attention it deserves.
- **Preconceptions:** when you are a part of the organisation that you are researching, you may have formed many preconceptions about situations that someone from outside would not be influenced by.
- **Status issues:** often practitioner-researchers are not in senior positions within the organisation. This can make it difficult for their project to be taken seriously. Alternatively, they may have high status within the organisation. This can make it difficult for subjects of the research to express themselves freely.
- **Being critical:** although undertaking a research project involves adopting a critically evaluative approach to both theory and practice, in some organisations taking a critical approach is not encouraged.
- **Being instrumental:** a further danger, from the perspective of the organisation, is that where projects are linked with gaining a qualification, research can become more of a vehicle to achieve the student's purposes than being motivated by the resolution of a problem or issue.

There are also significant advantages to being a practitioner-researcher:

- **Insider opportunities:** if you know the organisation and are a part of it, you have access to a range of knowledge and experience that someone from outside would find difficult to achieve.
- **Practitioner opportunities:** as an experienced practitioner within the organisation it is more likely that actions that you recommend can and will be implemented.
- **Synergy between theory and practice:** as a researcher who engages with theory and also knows the context of the organisation, it is more likely that you will be

able to design and carry out useful studies that contribute to enhancements in both knowledge and practice.

In summary, undertaking research projects in organisational situations provides a number of advantages, but there are also dangers. A key issue for students is avoiding the temptation to merely repeat established organisational 'mantras' and making every effort to ensure that their project leads to new insights. To achieve this, practitioner-researchers must endeavour to:

- explicitly consider the wider context of the problem or issue that is being researched, both within the organisation and with regard to practice and developments outside of the organisation
- critically engage with theories, models and concepts at all stages of the research process
- encourage, where possible, the dissemination of the findings of studies so that they can inform the development of practice and understanding in other organisations and contexts.

Some more ideas about how this can be achieved are shown in Table 1.8.

Table 1.8 Maximising the value of organisational research

- Where possible, negotiate a time-allowance to carry out the research.
- Be prepared to 'sell' the idea of the research within the organisation.
- Try to establish a difference of procedure between activities connected with your research and your normal day-to-day practitioner activities. Be clear to yourself and to others about when you are acting as a researcher and when you are acting as a practitioner.
- Be explicit in your thinking about methods and sources of information. This will allow you to reflect proactively about the strengths and limitations of your research and so improve on it. It will also enable others to make an appropriate assessment of your work.
- Ensure that your research procedures are systematic and can be justified by more than convenience. If you cut corners (and you probably will), you must be explicit about the impact of the shortcuts on your findings and how you have interpreted your information.

SUMMARY

- HR research involves systematically enquiring into HR issues to increase knowledge and underpin effective action.
- Most HR enquiry can be characterised as 'applied research', being concerned with solving problems, considering effects and developing actions and interventions.
- Effective research processes involve: formulating a research topic; evaluating what is already known; obtaining information of good quality; interpreting the information and formulating conclusions.
- Effective HR researchers require a range of skills, including: intellectual and thinking skills; personal effectiveness skills; organisational skills; and

communication skills. Personal qualities such as self-motivation, self-centredness and self-confidence are also required.

- Different research world-views (for example social constructivist and objectivist) can be seen as distinct ways of making sense of the world, but there are overlaps between them.
- Projects undertaken to fulfil the requirements of an academic qualification are expected to make appropriate use of theories, models and concepts as well as primary and secondary data.
- Preparing a research proposal allows you to put down your initial ideas in writing, share them with your tutor and get feedback about the strengths and possible difficulties of your idea.
- Establishing and maintaining a good working relationship with your project supervisor will enable you to benefit from feedback and discussion of your ideas throughout the life-cycle of your project.
- There are advantages and disadvantages to being a practitioner-researcher, but organisational research, properly undertaken, can lead to new insights into HR issues, problems and situations.

 Self-test questions

REVIEW AND REFLECT

1 HR research is:

a) gathering data to show the benefits of HR initiatives

b) the systematic enquiry into HR issues to increase knowledge and underpin effective action

c) describing trends in particular employment issues

d) the development of generalised theories about the relationships between different variables

2 Put the following stages of the research process into the most appropriate order:

a) Obtain information of good quality.

b) Interpret the information and form conclusions.

c) Evaluate what is already known.

d) Define a research topic.

3 Which of the following statements best describe HR research?

a) HR research should ignore theory and concentrate on practical issues.

b) HR research should challenge 'taken for granted' assumptions and generate new ways of understanding situations.

c) HR research should not get bogged down in trying to solve complex problems.

d) HR research should focus exclusively on investigating issues at a strategic level.

4 Put the following CIPD requirements for business research projects into the correct order:

a) Diagnose and investigate a live issue of significance to a work organisation.

b) Reflect on implications for professional practice.

c) Collect and analyse data.

d) Derive supportable conclusions.

e) Locate the work within a body of contemporary knowledge.

f) Make practical and actionable recommendations.

5 The literature search for an academic HR project should rely principally on which types of information?

a) newspaper and Internet news coverage

b) professional journals and trade journals

c) textbooks and management factsheets

d) academic journals and professional research reports

6 Which of the following would not normally be included in a research proposal?

a) ethical issues

b) research design and methods

c) conclusions and recommendations

d) suggested timetable

7 Which assumptions about the nature of reality correspond to which research world-views?

a) Reality is 'out there' corresponds with a constructivist world-view.

b) Reality is 'in here' corresponds with an objectivist world-view.

c) Reality is 'in here' but affected by 'out there' corresponds with an interpretivist world-view.

d) Reality is 'in here' corresponds with a constructivist world-view.

 ## Review questions

REVIEW AND REFLECT

Carefully study the information your centre provides about the requirements for your research project or dissertation. Look closely at the assessment criteria that are provided. Study the indicative structure that may be described. Make sure that you can answer all the questions below. If you cannot, make sure you find out the answers from whoever is responsible for projects in your study centre:

1 What is the submission deadline for the final report?

2 What is the indicative word limit?

3 Over what timescale should the project be undertaken?

4 What level of engagement with theories, concepts, frameworks of best practice, and so on, is expected?

5 How important is it to gather primary data?

6 Does the research have to be based in an organisation?

7 Are recommendations for action a requirement for the project?

8 What support is available to students when undertaking their project and how can that support be accessed?

Questions for reflection

REVIEW AND REFLECT

These questions are designed for two purposes.

1 Project planning

Answering these questions should help you to identify actions and priorities that will be important in undertaking your project. The answers you make to these questions may influence:

- which chapters of this book you need to study particularly closely
- which sources of further reading will be relevant to you
- the extent to which you need to get further advice on features of the research process.

2 Demonstrating reflective practice

If you are a member of a professional body like the CIPD, you will need to undertake continuous professional development (CPD). There are many benefits to a process of reflection about your professional development and a commitment to developing your skills and knowledge. Taking this approach to CPD as part of your research process can help you to be more productive and efficient by reflecting on your learning and highlighting gaps in your knowledge and experience. This will enable you to build confidence and credibility, track your learning, see your progress and demonstrate your achievements.

Taking stock

1   What influence might your professional, organisational or personal background have on the way you approach your research? Do you see your role as a researcher as being like a detective, a doctor or an explorer? Will you be working as an outsider or as an insider? What are the implications of your responses to these questions for your choice of topic and the extent to which your research may set out to achieve a descriptive, explanatory or exploratory purpose?

2   How feasible is it for you to undertake research in one organisation? For how long do you expect to be a part of the organisation in which your research may be based? What other options may be open to you?

3   How clear are you about a topic for your project? Who do you need to discuss your ideas with to decide about the feasibility of the project? (Chapter 2 is particularly relevant to these questions.)

4   What resources or expertise and advice are available to you from your project supervisor? How can you make best use of these resources?

Strengths and weaknesses

5   How confident are you about the process of undertaking a literature search to enable you to critically evaluate what is already known about your topic? What are the skills you will need to search and critically review theories, models and concepts within the literature? (Chapter 4 is particularly relevant to these issues.)

6   How aware are you of sources of secondary data that would be relevant to your project? What skills will you need to obtain and analyse the secondary data you have in mind? (Chapter 7 is particularly relevant to these issues.)

7   What options might you consider to obtain primary data? What are the skill implications of the data-generation options that you are considering?

8 What skills and competences have you already developed that you can use in the process of undertaking your project?

Being a practitioner-researcher

9 What are the status or political issues within your organisation that may affect the process of undertaking your project? How might you be able to manage these effectively?

10 What are the timescales for your project that are required by: a)

your study centre; b) your organisation? What are the implications of this for the process of doing your project?

11 What opportunities can you identify to sell your project ideas to: a) your manager and colleagues; b) others in the organisation?

Finally

12 Describe how you will feel when you have completed your project. Hold on to that feeling!

EXPLORE FURTHER

It is very important to carefully read any handbooks or guidance notes relating to project work provided by your study centre. Most students skim through these at the beginning of their project process and only read them carefully at the very end of the process, when it is almost too late.

One of the best ways to learn about research methods is to read and critique good-quality peer-reviewed research-based articles. You can tell if a journal is peer-reviewed by glancing at its notes for contributors, which will indicate that potential contributions will go through a 'blind peer review' process.

Useful Reading

Biggam, J. (2011) *Succeeding with your master's dissertation*. Maidenhead: Open University Press.

Brown, R.B. (2006) *Doing your dissertation in business and management: the reality of researching and writing*. London: Sage.

Coghlan, D. and Brannick, T. (2009) *Doing action research in your own organisation*. London: Sage.

Collis, J. and Hussey, R. (2009) *Business research: a practical guide for undergraduate and postgraduate students*. Basingstoke: Palgrave.

Fox, M., Martin, P. and Green, G. (2007) *Doing practitioner research*. London: Sage.

Gill, J., Johnson, P. and Clark, M. (2010) *Research methods for managers*. London: Sage.

Hart, C. (2010) *Doing your master's dissertation*. London: Sage.

Robson, C. (2011) *Real world research: a resource for social scientists and practitioner-researchers*. Oxford: Wiley.

Saunders, M., Lewis, P. and Thornhill, A. (2012) *Research methods for business students*. Harlow: Pearson Education.

Yin, R.K. (2009) *Case study research: design and methods*. Thousand Oaks, CA: Sage Publications.